EXPERIENCING the Joy
LIFEdevelopment Discipleship Library.
www.lifedevelopment.info
ask@lifedevelopment.info

First published in 2010. Reprinted 2012.

British Library Cataloguing in Publication Data.
A catalogue record for this book is available from the British Library.

Pujic, Miroslav and Asaftei, Sarah K.
ISBN 978-1-904685-94-4

1. Christianity and Culture. 2. Popular Culture – Religious aspects – Christianity.
3. Postmodernism – Religious aspects – Christianity. 4. Bible. 5. Theology.

Unless otherwise indicated, all scriptures are taken from the Holy Bible, New Living
Translation® (Tyndale)

Unless otherwise indicated, all illustrations by Tompaul Wheeler.
Prayers written by Holly Messenger.
Design by Mirjana Rankovic.
Cover photo by Dragana Selakovic-Duval.
Printed by Euro Dream, Serbia.

ABOUT THE EDITORS
& WRITERS

Miroslav Pujić is director of the Ministry to Postmoderns at the Trans-European Division of the Seventh-day Adventist Church. He believes in discipleship through authentic relationships. His theology education began at Newbold College, England, and continued with a Master's degree in Missiology from Fuller Theological Seminary, USA. He then obtained a Doctor of Ministry at Andrews University, USA, specialising in the impact of postmodernism on society and its effect on evangelism.

Pujić authored THE MISSIONARY: 3rd Millennium AD and has written numerous articles. He created the LIFEdevelopment discipleship pathway concept and accompanying resources. He enjoys talking to people and loves spending time with his wife, Esti, and their two grown children, Dejan and Melita.

Sarah K. Asaftei Sarah K. Asaftei is passionate about sharing Jesus with today's generation. She graduated from Southern Adventist University, USA, with a degree in English and Religious Studies. She also earned a Master's degree at Andrews University, USA, in International Development, specialising in curriculum design for adult learning.

Asaftei has published numerous articles and stories, including writing resources for LIFEdevelopment discipleship material and media resources. Her favourite activity is sharing quality time with her husband, Pastor Marius Asaftei.

The contributing authors are a diverse and varied group, selected on the basis of their study, expertise and experience. Each writer falls into one or more of these qualifying categories:

- people who have engaged in scholarly enterprise and research;

- people who have sought to integrate the whole of their belief system into twenty-first century living;

- people who have, through leadership, learned to reflect on the graceful application of doctrine in addition to its veracity.

CONTENTS

READY, SET, TALK!

Suddenly you get cut off. The phone line goes dead. Silence. You scramble to redial and wait to reconnect, but to no avail. You experience frustration, fear, tension, urgency. What now? *How do I get back in touch?*

We've all experienced breakdown in communication – from a simple dropout of our phone service to broken relationships because of crossed wires or total misunderstandings. The need to reopen dialogue, repair or reconcile a relationship can sometimes seem daunting and not worth the hassle and yet at times it is pivotal to our core existence and matters of the heart.

God is trying to reconnect with you. Somewhere along the line a communication breakdown has occurred and, although the situation can at times seem complicated, he is doing everything in his power to continue where you left off and resume the conversation. In the Bible, a collection of ancient writings about people's experiences with God, he invited everyone to sit and chat with him – and he extends the same invitation to you.[1]

Getting to know God can happen in all sorts of ways – from discussions with friends about your experiences, to mediation, prayer and studying the Bible. The Bible is full of the varying personal experiences of people who lived long ago and how God tried to reach out to them;

what lengths he went to to find them, pursue them, win them back, rescue them and, ultimately, restore that communication that was lost somewhere along the way. Throughout all the centuries nothing has changed. He is still reaching out.

Sixteen authors have reflected on and shared their anecdotes about this same God; a God who has played a central role in their own experiences, history and continuing life story – stories of trials, uncertainty, pain, enlightenment, discovery and joy.

If there has ever been a time when you were curious about the Bible and its real meaning, then now is a good time to go exploring. Consider this book to be your guide – a menu. Open it up, flip through it, see what catches your eye, and begin there.

Maybe, for the first time, the Bible will make sense to you. Maybe you'll discover that within the greater Story, *you* have a story.

REFERENCES
1. See Isaiah 1:18

ABOUT
ESSENTIALS

1. KNOWING GOD

God, this is new to me. Sometimes I'm not even sure I believe in you, and I certainly don't understand who you are and where you live. I'd like to figure that out more, though, and I'd like to learn how I could know you better. So if that's possible for me, will you help me out?

re: tell

It kept her up at night, nagged her dreams, whispered as she wandered; a disconnection, a dangling thread. The night the power went out and forgotten stars spilled across a velvet sky, she blinked.

The stifling afternoon she stood at an old classmate's grave, the flowers wilting by the time they landed on the upturned earth. She wondered, 'If we're only atoms and molecules that join and part, bond and break, why does it hurt to lose someone you didn't even know as well as you'd like? What is opportunity when it all adds up to nothing, and if there's a higher power, when will he get back from his afternoon tea?'

re: think

Have you ever googled 'God'? He gets twice as many results as Barack Obama at the height of his popularity. There's even a page called *god.com* where people can learn about him. We are a species obsessed with a higher power. Even those who believe that God is dead are driven to debate with their believing friends, rather than letting him rest in peace. So what if he really does exist, and our obsession is about a real Being? What's he like? How can we really know him, a person we cannot see, taste or touch?

God chose to manifest himself to the human race in the form of Jesus Christ, the Son of God, who lived a life of service and love for thirty-three years in Israel. During his last days on Earth, he talked to his father about the men and women he called friends and he asked his father to give them eternal life. Here's how he described it: 'This is the way to have eternal life – to know you, the only true God, and Jesus Christ, the one you sent to earth.'[2] He knew that his existence made it possible for mankind to know God as intimately as we know our friends.

There are three ways in which the human species gathers knowledge: reason, experience and revelation. None of these stands alone. We must always be checking our experience against the information of reason, and we must always be checking our reason against the revelation of God and against our experience of the physical world.

It would take more than the scope of this chapter to expound the many means we have available for knowing God. That's what the rest of the book is for. I want to take this time to tell you some of the amazing stories of people who *have* come to know God – with their whole being, including their reason, experience and the revelation of God to them – and the value they see in having a relationship with him.

moses

Moses probably looked nothing like Charlton Heston in the famous Hollywood movie. He was probably more exotic. He was, after all, a prince of Egypt. He was educated, trained in martial law and had high morals. And he had a temper. He saw a slave being unjustly punished and he took action, killing the taskmaster and burying him in the sand. That landed him in exile, herding sheep in the desert. So much for being a prince in the most powerful empire of the day.

But God was about to introduce himself to Moses and he did so on a mountainside by setting a bush on fire and not letting it be burned down. To Moses, God was fire and passion. That encounter inspired Moses to go back to Egypt, under God's guidance, to free the Israelite slaves. Then, when the Israelites needed to know how to live, God gave Moses the Ten Commandments, and Moses begged God to show him the face of the divine.

Here's what God did for Moses: 'he passed in front of Moses, proclaiming [about himself], The LORD, the LORD, the compassionate and gracious God, slow to anger, abounding in love and faithfulness'.[3] The *essence* of God is not what makes him appealing. It's his *character* which makes him attractive – something we also appreciate about humans.

solomon

Solomon was a prince, born to parents who believed in God, yet who were guilty of murder and adultery. He was smart, took things in his stride and watched as each of his older brothers forfeited his right to the crown through selfishness and foolishness. When his father David, on his deathbed, passed the kingdom on to him, Solomon knew he had a big task before him. Not long after he took the crown, Solomon met God in a dream and asked for a 'discerning heart'[4] to rule the people graciously. To young Solomon, God was wisdom.

But after a lifetime of ruling, building a temple (which was part of one of the wonders of the world), and courting some of the world's most powerful and beautiful women, Solomon's take on life was somewhat cynical: 'When I surveyed all that my hands had done and what I had toiled to achieve, everything was meaningless, a chasing after the wind; nothing was gained under the sun.'[5]

He'd seen it all, had enjoyed the best the world could offer and had found it all empty. To the elderly Solomon, God brought meaning to life. 'So I decided there is nothing better than to enjoy food and drink and to find satisfaction in work. Then I realised that these pleasures are from the hand of God. For who can eat or enjoy anything apart from him?'[6]

13

jezebel

As Queen of Israel and Princess of Sidon, Jezebel had a deadly reputation. When she came to Israel as King Ahab's wife, she decided to clean house, starting with all the ministers of God. Once she thought they were all dead, she set up a priesthood to her cherished inanimate goddess, Asherah.

But God kept getting in the way. He sent his man, Elijah, to predict a drought and famine. Was it any surprise when there was no rain? After his kingdom withered and turned to a dust bowl, Ahab decided to take things into his own hands and went off looking for Elijah.

The result was a showdown on a mountaintop. Four hundred and fifty of Jezebel's best priests against God's man. The test: bring fire down from heaven. And Jezebel's men failed miserably. They paid for it with their lives. When she heard the news, Jezebel sent Elijah a message, 'May the gods strike me and even kill me if by this time tomorrow I have not killed you just as you killed them.'[7]

This was not a woman to be toyed with, even by a God who sent all-consuming fire from heaven. To Jezebel, God was a nuisance. In fact, when her threatened twenty-four hours had passed, Elijah was still alive and well, nowhere to be found. God had other life plans for Elijah, and Jezebel wasn't powerful enough to change God's plans.

hosea

Probably a merchant, Hosea was an average fellow when he met God. He wrote a book about the conversations he had with God, so we get the story in his own words. Somewhere along the way, God asked Hosea to marry a prostitute. And he forewarned him that she would continue as a prostitute, no matter how much Hosea pleaded with her to stay at home and love him. Worse still, God told Hosea to keep on loving her, looking for ways to win her heart and affections.

To Hosea, God was crazy. But this was God's way of showing Hosea how much he loved people and understood their fickle love for him. He said, 'I will make you my wife forever, showing you righteousness and justice, unfailing love and compassion. I will be faithful to you and make you mine, and you will finally know me as the Lord.'[8] Hosea didn't go into much personal detail about his relationship with God, but we can discern from his book that it was close enough to sustain him through a painful and disappointing marriage.

jonah

Jonah had a love-hate relationship with God. He was given a message to tell the King and the people of Nineveh that God wasn't happy with the injustice and immorality in their city. God wanted him to teach them a better way to live. But Jonah was nobody's message boy. He took off on a cruise to Tarshish instead.

When a storm threatened to sink the ship he was on, he figured God was after him, so he jumped ship. What was God supposed to do? This was his messenger, and here he was trying to drown himself! So God thought fast and brought along a really big fish to swallow Jonah and give him a slimy ride to dry land. After being barfed up on the beach, Jonah cleaned himself up and headed off reluctantly to Nineveh to preach doom and destruction.

His only problem was that the people took God's message to heart: they changed their ways. And God honoured their sincerity. He didn't destroy their city. Jonah was livid! To Jonah, God was too forgiving. He felt that God had made a fool of him by sending him on a mission without the 'told-you-so' ending. He'd entirely missed God's point in sending him.

rich young ruler

Not everyone has had a great experience with his or her glimpses of God. There was a young lawyer, a political leader born into wealth, who had it all – money, girls, clothes, power. But he wanted more. He'd been to the top, yet felt that something was lacking. He went to find Jesus and asked him how to find God. Jesus told him to sell everything – lose all the glamour –and spend the next few years wandering the countryside with a bunch of fishermen.

To this wealthy young lawyer, God was too simple. He wanted something that would fit into his complicated life and give meaning to the emptiness that surrounded him. But when Jesus asked him to get rid of the emptiness, he couldn't do it. He was not willing to pay the price of change in his life.

mary

Mary Magdalene was invisible behind the achievements and talents of her older sister, Martha. But then she met Jesus, a man she could not judge according to his income. And she was fascinated. She sat adoring at his feet, as his teachings turned everything she and her brother and sister had believed on its head. She rejoiced when her dead, beloved brother came to life at the word of Jesus.

> To Mary, God was love. Such tangible love that she spent a true fortune to show her gratitude in one simple act of humble love.

To Mary, God was love. Such tangible love that she spent a true fortune to show her gratitude in one simple act of humble love. She washed his feet with the most expensive perfume of the time, wiping them with her hair and kissing the feet of Jesus.

john

An English scholar at Oxford, John Wycliffe had the mind and ability of greatness. God introduced himself to John through his academic pursuits, and John saw a great need for such a God in the culture surrounding him. He was privileged to come to know God, because he could read Latin and Greek, but the people in the surrounding villages had limited means of truly experiencing God for themselves, having no access to an education like his. To John, God was interested in the people.

For the first time in 1,000 years, John translated the Bible from Latin and Greek manuscripts into the common language. It was the first time the written Word of God could be read in English. Now if a man or woman could read English, he or she could have the opportunity to meet God in the same way as John had done. John found meaning for his life in writing God's words in English.[9]

joseph

Joseph Bates was a salty American sailor, who moved up from young cabin boy to ship's captain. He met God through reading a Bible, packed into his suitcase by his wife. He joined a revival movement in New England and kept studying his Bible as God's word to him.

For Joseph, God lived through the truths he found in the Bible. Joseph found that the Sabbath of the Bible was Saturday, the seventh day of the week. Amid a culture of sincere Christians who thought he was misguided and ridiculous, Joseph lived his life with integrity and passion for his God.[10]

martin

Martin Luther King Jr was a preacher on a mission. He had met God, but he had also seen oppression. He knew life wasn't fair, but he longed for something more and he found the strength to pursue his ideals through faith in his God. To Martin Luther King Jr, God was freedom and unity.

He said: 'With this faith, we will be able to hew out of the mountain of despair a stone of hope. With this faith, we will be able to transform the jangling discords of our nation into a beautiful symphony of brotherhood. With this faith, we will be able to work together, to pray together, to struggle together, to go to jail together, to stand up for freedom together, knowing that we will be free one day.'[11]

you

You've probably met many different people who have told you all kinds of stories about what God is to them. Some of those stories might have piqued your interest. Some might have sent you running the other way. God's done many apparently crazy things to get different people's attention. He set a bush on fire. He gave people wisdom and meaning. He sent fire down from heaven and he sent big fish as lifeboats. But he also comes quietly into the lives of people through things they've read and experienced in their daily lives.

But God is more than stories. He's more than the energy in Einstein's famous equation. He's a person to be experienced. Let him speak to *you*, introduce himself to *you, personally*. He says of himself, 'Look! I stand at the door and knock. If you hear my voice and open the door, I will come in, and we will share a meal together as friends.'[12] And there's another thing. God is everywhere – omnipresent – so you don't have to go anywhere to find him. He's big enough to find you.

re: consider

Would you like to explore your own story with God? Where would you start?

REFERENCES
2. John 17:3.
3. Exodus 34:6, NIV.
4. 1 Kings 3:9, NIV.
5. Ecclesiastes 2:11.
6. Ecclesiastes 2:24, 25.
7. 1 Kings 19:2.
8. Hosea 2:19, 20.
9. See: *www.wycliffe.org/* and White, Ellen G. *The Great Controversy.* Pacific Press, pp. 79-96.
10. Bates, Joseph. *The Autobiography of Elder Joseph Bates.* Battle Creek Steam Press, 1868.
11. King Jr, Martin Luther. 'I Have a Dream.' 28 Aug. 1963.
12. Revelation 3:20.

2. GOD'S WORDS TO ME

God, I know relationships are about communicating with each other and I'm curious about what a relationship with you would be like. Please let me listen to and understand your promises, your instruction and your stories.

re: tell

Visit the small town of Hodgenville, Kentucky, and you'll soon learn it has a big claim: 'Abraham Lincoln was born here.' Indeed, the wooded land once the property of his family is now owned by the US government, a part of the National Park Service.

As he was one of the most famous persons ever to be born in a log cabin, Lincoln's birthplace inspires countless visitors. But if you're hoping to soak up the atmosphere and ambience that shaped the president, well, you may find a few surprises. Such as the large structure resembling a Greek temple, with fifty-six steps leading up to it (one for each year of Lincoln's life), that now stands on the site of Lincoln's birthplace.

Dedicated in 1911, it was intended to preserve the Lincoln family cabin in a humidity-controlled environment. The only problem is, the cabin within has no actual connection with Lincoln. Sideshow entrepreneurs carried it from town to town in the late 1800s, and it was long believed to include at least a few Lincoln logs, but further research found that it dated to around the time of his death.

So if you'd like to learn more about one of history's most eloquent orators, shrewdest politicians and paradoxical personalities, the best place to begin may not be with artefacts, but with his immortal words.

re: think

At this moment you are reading. Have you ever thought of what actually happens when you read?

One person thought about it and said: 'The eye follows black letters on a white paper from left to right, again and again. And beings, nature or thoughts that another man has thought, just now or thousands of years ago, step forward in our imagination. It is a miracle greater than when a grain from the tombs of the Pharaohs is made to sprout. And it happens every moment.'[13]

Reading is a powerful experience. Words on paper can create a reality different from our own. While you are reading, you 'live' in the world of the text. It lets you grasp another person's inner mind in a way that doesn't often happen in face-to-face communication, maybe even with people you know well.

There are books about good books,[14] books on how to read books,[15] and on the history of reading books.[16] We all read for different reasons – information, learning, experience. But is that all? In June 1857 the French author Flaubert wrote in a letter: 'We read to live.' Personally, I like this idea. And for me, reading to live means starting with the Holy Bible.

why the bible?

From 1456 (when Johannes Gutenberg completed the first printed Bible in Latin) until today, countless Bibles have been printed and distributed. The Bible or some part of it now exists in 2,370 languages! This means it is accessible to more than 90% of the world's population.

So why are all these people reading the Bible? It's simple, really. Bible readers have discovered the power of scripture to maintain a spiritual reality which provides rest, strength and security. A non-Christian observer once noted: 'As long as you hold on to the [Bible] text you find rest. The text is firm, unchangeable, rests in its innocence and purity, and allows for examination and study. I understand the power Christian people find in the Bible. The book becomes their unshakeable rock. The god that is outside the book is uncertain and unreachable.'[17]

I've found that reading the Bible not only awakens a longing for God but also satisfies that longing. It is both the menu and the food. It does something to you. It leads you into the world and mind of God. If you wonder about God but feel that he is absent or silent, then try reading a Bible or talking to someone who knows God. I feel that it brings me more in touch with him.

what is the bible?

It is a collection of sixty-six books, all written before AD100. The Hebrew collection (thirty-nine books, also called the Old Testament) was defined no later than around AD100 (following the Jewish author Josephus). The Greek collection (twenty-seven books, also called the New Testament) was established around AD200 (as evidenced by *Canon Muratori*), but a few New Testament books were discussed until around AD400, when they were included in the collection. The oldest parts of the Bible were written more than 1,500 years prior to that. The process of collecting these sacred books went on for nearly 2,000 years.

Each book in the Bible is very different from the others. So it's good to choose an easy translation, as well as an appropriate book of the Bible with which to start. Some are harder to tackle than others, but you're free to choose.

If you are a beginner, you may want to start reading the love poetry in the Song of Songs, the philosophy in Ecclesiastes or the wise sayings in Proverbs. You might even have a go at the treatise on human suffering in the book of Job. Whether or not you are exactly religious, you will find something to connect with in these books.

If you're looking for God, the prayers and hymns of the Psalms may be a good start, or the story of Jesus according to the gospel of John. Elsewhere in the Bible you will find historical books starting from the creation of the world, legal material from ancient Israel, books on religious instruction in prophecy and wisdom, four versions of the life of Jesus, stories about the foundation of the Christian Church, letters of instruction to new congregations, and the apocalyptic vision of the book of Revelation.

When you read the Bible, your approach may be focused along five avenues:[18]

Basic beliefs (theology)

Information (history)

Being together (community, worship)

Life guidelines (moral and practical instruction)

Expressions of your relationship with God (prayer)

Through its variety of forms, the Bible challenges you to read it as the Word of God for you. Try it and don't give up too quickly! Your own experience is important, and the experience of your friends is important, too, so reading the Bible in a group with others who meet regularly is a good way to begin. What you like and understand may help others, while they in turn may help you with the questions the Bible raises for you.

'if you have, you will be given'

The most important preparation when you begin to read the Bible is to be aware of what it claims *to be* and *to do* for you.

It sounds a bit strange, but you can't really understand what you read without some pre-understanding. In fact, scholars of textual interpretation know that the more appropriate and developed your pre-understanding is, the more likely it is that your study will be a fruitful one.[19] As a Bible reader, you need some understanding of the context of the Bible in order to understand its message. So why not read the Bible on its own terms?

Any good author seeks to build in certain instructions that help the reader discover how the text should be read. Being fair to a book begins with seeking to understand what it wants to say. You wouldn't read tonight's TV programme schedule as if it were poetry or a love letter, would you?

So give the Bible a chance to be what it claims to be! By opening yourself to the Bible you give it a chance to be understood. When you understand it, you will be able to decide what to believe.

Your primary need as a reader is a reasonable biblical view of the Bible. A good starting place for the beginner is Paul's second letter to Timothy, chapter 3, verses 15-17. This is an important passage that concerns the nature and function of the Bible.

The intended reader of this passage is Timothy, a young leader of the church in Ephesus, and Paul's two letters to this young man give instructions regarding good community leadership. In the second letter, Paul writes from a Roman prison, urging Timothy to visit before the winter (4:21) and bring his cloak and his books (4:13). We don't know if Timothy got there before Paul died, but this letter is sometimes considered to be the 'last will and testament' of the apostle Paul.

'You have been taught the holy Scriptures from childhood, and they have given you the wisdom to receive the salvation that comes by trusting in Christ Jesus. All Scripture is inspired by God and is useful to teach us what is true and to make us realise what is wrong in our lives. It corrects us when we are wrong and teaches us to do what is right. God uses it to prepare and equip his people to do every good work.'[20]

The 'sacred writings' in Paul's day were the Old Testament writings, the first thirty-nine books of the Bible also sacred to Jewish believers. We know he wrote this letter before the books as a whole had been collected into one volume. But it indicates certain basic elements of his view of the Bible.

inspired writing and reading

'All scripture is inspired by God and is useful to teach . . .'[21] This translation fits the context of Paul's intention to defeat false teachings. It means that, not only are some *parts* of scripture (not just any 'scripture' claiming sacred status) useful for building up life and faith in God, but the *whole* of the (recognised) scripture is 'inspired by God', and *therefore* it is useful for teaching.

The Greek word *theopneustos* (inspired by God) was commonly understood among Jews and early Christians in those days to mean that the Bible originated with God, not humankind.

The same idea is very strongly expressed in Peter's second letter, chapter 1, verses 20-21: 'Above all, you must realise that no prophecy in Scripture ever came from the prophet's own understanding, or from human initiative. No, those prophets were moved by the Holy Spirit, and they spoke from God.'

This indicates that the texts of the Bible were inspired by God but expressed in human writings (the Greek word for 'prophecy' means both 'forth-telling' and 'fore-telling' and may refer to an inspired saying and/or a prediction). So there is a blending of both human and divine in the Bible. You may read it at the human level and it will make some sense to you. But only when you read it as coming from both human and divine will you be reading it on its own terms. Only then can you claim to be reading it in its fullness.

> Bible readers have discovered the power of scripture to maintain a spiritual reality which provides rest, strength and security.

Paul's letter to Timothy also places an emphasis on the *function* of the Bible. Because it is God-inspired, it is (consequently) *useful* for teaching, reproof, correction and training. Its authority as God's inspired word makes it a useful and effective book to read for life.

The Bible also teaches that God reveals his 'secret wisdom' by his Spirit, who 'searches out everything and shows us God's deep secrets'.

It says that 'no one can know God's thoughts except God's own Spirit'.[22] In fact, the Bible teaches that God's Spirit and his word have a specific *revelatory* function: the Spirit is the bearer of the divine Word and *reveals* God's secret wisdom through the Word.

Not only are the Old Testament writings 'inspired by God', but also the speeches and writings of the early Christian leaders. Paul speaks of this in his first letter to the church in Corinth.[23] He states: 'We speak words given to us by the Spirit, using the Spirit's words to explain spiritual truths' (verse 13). In order to receive and understand the words of God's Spirit, Paul also claims: 'We have received God's Spirit (not the world's spirit), so we can know the wonderful things God has freely given us' (verse 12).

Besides the sacred writings of the Old Testament, which were being recognised and defined during the first century of the common era, the Christians passed on a tradition, sometimes called *paratheke* or 'deposit of received teaching'.[24] Studies show that it was based on the story of Christ and his teachings, to which were added various practical applications in the course of the development of the early Christian church.[25] This is how the writings of the New Testament also came to be considered sacred and as given by the Spirit of God.

This view of the Bible implies that it is the Word of God by inspiration. It also implies that the process of inspiration is not limited to writing alone but also includes reading – the intimate communication between the author's text and the reader. In other words, not only were the Bible authors inspired, but readers need inspiration from the same source as the authors in order to understand God's Word. The Bible becomes God's Word for you personally through the influence of God's Holy Spirit on your mind.

The Bible indicates that God is its ultimate source.[26] The Christian writers of the twenty-seven books of the New Testament constantly appealed to the Old Testament writings to confirm the truth of what they said. But they also assumed that their own writings had an authoritative character from God himself.[27]

This is not easy to grasp all at once. But be patient. Let the process begin. Seek and you will find. God has put into the Bible the capacity to explain itself, and the more I read, the more things become clear. This growth and expansion of your mind is going to be a thrilling experience and will educate you factually, morally and aesthetically. You will discover that the Bible is a wonderful source of truth, goodness and beauty. Isn't that what you are looking for?

instructive – salvation, faith, life

'The sacred writings . . . are able to instruct you for salvation through faith in Christ Jesus.'[28] One central function of the Bible is its ability to instruct you regarding the salvation that comes through faith in Christ Jesus. This is the primary *spiritual* function of the Bible. So, while we recognise that truth exists that is not found in the Bible, the Bible claims to be unique in providing the full truth needed for finding God and walking with God through Jesus Christ.

This implies both a promise and a condition. When we read the Bible in search of Christ, the Spirit of God will provide a spiritual understanding of the text. Our spiritual communion with God becomes the central topic of the Bible. We read to live in him.

how shall I read?

The Bible states that it:

- is given by God and is his inspired word that reveals his secret wisdom;
- makes you wise for salvation by faith in Jesus Christ;
- teaches, trains and equips for living a good life.

If you feel that the Bible is like a foreign country, then reading it for yourself is the best way to journey there.

First, make sure that you are the traveller. While there are many good guides, no second-hand knowledge about the Bible can replace your own personal experience of reading it.

Secondly, reading the Bible is different from any other reading experience. It demands more time to pause and examine yourself and where you are in your life.

Thirdly, read the Bible in order to meet God and hear what he has to say to you. In that way, the reading becomes a part of your life – you read to live. The Bible shows you where God was found by other human beings, how they were changed by meeting him and how they tried to find ways to live with others in relationship to the God they had discovered. Reading invites you to imitate their experience.

Fourthly, the real meaning of the Bible is something you find when you relate it to your own life. When you make such a connection between word and life, you remember what you read and let it shape you. So your Bible reading not only informs, but it transforms. Be prepared for surprises on your journey!

The authority of the Bible is based on its own claims and can only be tested and proved by reading it. As you engage in this experience, you'll discover the spiritual power and authority of God's Word for you.

The church father Aurelius Augustinus (AD354-430), who was converted to Christianity by reading the Bible, said in his *Confessions*:

'Indeed the authority of Scripture seemed more to be revered and more worthy of devoted faith in that it was at once a book that all could read and read easily, and yet preserved the majesty of its mystery in the deepest part of its meaning: for it offers itself to all in the plainest words and the simplest expressions, yet demands the closest attention of the most serious minds.'

Countless men and women have had the same experience. It is in your hands to decide to become one of them.

re: consider

What is God saying to you now that you have started reading the Bible?

REFERENCES

13. Lagercrantz, Olof Gustaf Hugo. *Om konsten att läsa och skriva*. [Stockholm]: Wahlström & Widstrand, 1985, p. 7. (Author translation).

14. See Rennison, Nick. *Bloomsbury Good Reading Guide*. A & C Black, 2006.

15. See Adler, Mortimer J., and Charles Van Doren. *How to Read a Book: The Classic Guide to Intelligent Reading*. MJF Books, 1972.

16. See Manguel, Alberto. *History of Reading*. A.A. Knopf Canada, 1997.

17. Lagercrantz, p. 55 (author translation).

18. Mueller, Steve. *The Seeker's Guide to Reading the Bible: a Catholic View*. Loyola P, 1999, p. 8.

19. See Wiklander, Bertil. *Prophecy as Literature: A Text-Linguistic and Rhetorical Approach to Isaiah 2-4*. CWK Gleerup, 1984, p. 27.

20. 2 Timothy 3:15-17.

21. 2 Timothy 3:16.

22. 1 Corinthians 2:9-12.

23. 1 Corinthians 2:6-16.

24. See 1 Timothy 6:20 and 2 Timothy 1:12-14 and other expressions in 2 Thessalonians 2:15; 3:6; 1 Corinthians 11:2, 23 and 15:3.

25. See Gerhardsson, Birger. *Memory and Manuscript: Oral Tradition and Written Transmission in Rabbinic Judaism and Early Christianity; with, Tradition and transmission in early Christianity*. William B. Eerdmans Pub., Dove Booksellers, 1998, p. 290.

26. Exodus 4:30 and 7:1-2; Deuteronomy 31:19, 22; 2 Samuel 23:2; 1 Kings 22:14; Isaiah 8:1; Jeremiah 1:9 and 36:1-2; Ezekiel 2:7; Hosea 1:2; Amos 1:3, 6, 9 and Habakkuk 2:2.

27. John 10:25 and 12:49; Hebrews 3:7 and 4:7-8; 1 Corinthians 2:13; 1 Thessalonians 2:13.

28. 2 Timothy 3:15, NRSV.

3. MY ORIGINS

God, you know the times in my life when I've wondered where I come from? I've questioned whether my life exists as a result of a world that just evolved. As I sit with you today, will you help me find some answers, so that I'll know where I belong in this universe?

re: tell

In the beginning, the first god, Buri, was licked free of the primordial ice by the cow Auðumbla. The great frost giant, Ymir, had also been formed from the ice. Buri knew his wife Bestla and fathered Odin, Vili and Ve, who slew Ymir. The blood of Ymir drowned nearly the entire race of frost giants.

Thus Buri's sons shaped Midgard: the world. The blood of Ymir became rivers and lakes and oceans; its body became the land; its bones, the mountains; its teeth became the stones we see around us. From its brains, Odin formed the clouds of the sky.

That's one story, the ancient Nordic one, of how the world began. The Bible version is a little different. . . .

re: think

Millions of people are hooked on discovering their family history. They surf the Internet or leaf through mouldy pages of old records in pursuit of information about their ancestors. It's not that surprising, because each of us craves a sense of belonging, an understanding of what makes us who we are. If we can answer the question 'Where do I come from?' then we can appreciate our past, understand our present and anticipate our future. The Bible is interested in that question, too. It tackles questions of the utmost importance like: 'Where do I come from?', 'Why am I here?', 'Where am I going?' and it tells stories in order to provide answers. We usually consider stories to be entertainment, a relaxing read on the beach, or filling in time while we wait for the dentist. But the stories in the Bible have a much higher purpose. They are used to help us *experience* and *feel* our way around issues that really matter to us. These stories paint pictures that we can relate to, experience and re-tell, inviting us to respond and express our opinion.

In answer to our questions, the Bible replies, 'Let me tell you a story,' or several stories. These accounts plumb the depths of human fear, tragedy, love, faith, hatred, betrayal – the whole gamut of human experience. But don't be fooled by their simplicity. These stories can be remembered after one reading, but they initiate a lifetime of reflection, because they are among the best and most controversial ever written.

The Bible wastes no time in dealing with the ultimate questions. On the first line of the first page of the first book – Genesis – it dives straight in: 'In the beginning God created the heavens and the earth.'[29] It tells that particular story of creation in order to explore the crucial questions of human existence.

It tells of how God created the world in one week. Now to us that sounds odd. But let's start by engaging our hearts and imaginations, not just our heads, because this is the aim of Genesis. In brief, Genesis 1 says that in the beginning God created everything. At the outset Planet Earth was in chaos, with no purpose or design. But then, over a period of six days, God designed, separated, created and organised. Next God set aside the seventh day as a distinctive period of time – the Sabbath.

It helps if we set it out in this diagram:

CHAOS

DAY 1	DAY NIGHT	**DAY 4**	SUN MOON/STARS
DAY 2	WATERS SKY	**DAY 5**	FISH BIRDS
DAY 3	LAND VEGETATION	**DAY 6**	LAND CREATURES HUMANS

DAY 7: SABBATH REST

This shows the sequence of what God created on each day. See the pattern? The days are grouped in three pairs:

- days 1 and 4: the day and night are ruled by the sun and moon respectively
- days 2 and 5: the fish live in the waters and the birds fly in the sky
- days 3 and 6: land creatures and humans both live on the land and eat the vegetation.

Each day has a 'partner', producing an overall balance. In addition, the beginning and the end are also a pair. The chaos in the beginning is balanced by the order and rest revealed on the seventh day. This final day brings a climax to this account.

It's important to experience this story with our imagination rather than analysing it with our heads. So, as we engage with it, what do we see? Among many other things, it tells me that God is in control; he creates effortlessly which is demonstrated in the repeated 'and God said....', followed by an immediate response. This stark contrast to the struggles and battles of other ancient creation myths can give confidence in the power of God, who has control over matter. It also counters the modern secular assumption that all life on Earth is the end result of the survival of the fittest and nothing more.

God is also the Lord of time and space, a fact demonstrated by his creating, naming and separating the basic elements of time and space: day and night; the heavens above; the earth and seas beneath. If he is Lord of time, then history is his arena; he is encountered not only 'back then' but also 'right now'. Therefore we can expect to encounter God in our own time and personal experience.

If he is truly the Lord of space, then he is never beyond our reach; he is the God who was there and the God who is *here*. It makes a big difference to our work, relationships, marriage and so on, if God is with us in our experiences, not just in our thoughts.

God is not simply an all-powerful creature who reigns over the universe; he is also intimate, tender and emotionally involved with his creation. We see this in the next story, in Genesis chapter 2: 'Then the Lord God formed the man from the dust of the ground. He breathed the breath of life into the man's nostrils, and the man became a living person' (verse 7). He forms human beings like a potter shapes clay, invests his creative energies in them and gives life through his breath – like the kiss of life.

Some people deal with God as an object of debate, defined by creeds or 'fundamental beliefs'. Even in general conversation God is referred to using philosophical, theological or abstract terms. But the Bible presents him as a character, a personality, not an abstract notion. As a God we relate to and with whom we have a personal relationship. Rather than discussing his attributes, or defining his essence, Genesis invites us to know and experience him. After all, we were created in his image.

Might this mean that we were created with the ability to have a relationship with God? If that is how he created us, then clearly God wants to have a relationship with us, too. He is a personal God with emotions, who craves to know us and wants to be part of our lives. It is one thing to talk *about* God. Quite another to speak *to* him. That's why it might be a good idea to set aside some time each day to speak to, and listen to, God.

Spirituality is also important in this story. Our lives, without this spiritual dimension, are incomplete.

We need look no further than the fact that God created us in his image to confirm that we were created as spiritual beings. Even more, God set apart the seventh day and made it different. This special day indicates that time itself has a spiritual dimension. Time isn't merely a matter of seconds, minutes, hours, days, months or years. These just form the framework within which God acts and is known and experienced.

We live in a scientific age when many people expect an account of our origins to present matters scientifically. The Genesis story clearly does not. But that is no accident, nor a reason for dismissing it, unless you believe that the only truth is scientific truth – a position that a growing number of scientists are abandoning. The Genesis story reaches parts that science cannot touch. Rather than asking *How?* or *When?*, this story is more concerned with *Who?*, *Why?* and *So what?* It wants to engage our hearts, emotions and wills. It wants to provide a spiritual context for us in which to live our lives to the full.

> The Bible wastes no time in dealing with the ultimate questions.

The questions concerning *When?* – the timescale of creation, or *How?* – the precise mechanism, can be put to one side for now. Let's begin by dealing with issues of prime importance – the fact that this world had a meaningful beginning. If there was no meaningful beginning, there can be no meaningful end. And without a meaningful beginning or end, *there can be no meaningful present*.

Genesis counters this bleak pessimism by assuring us that we are more than a cosmic accident. The creation story gives us a context for the past, hope for the future, and meaning for the present. Because this story engages our imagination, it asks us to imagine how to respond to it. To wake up in the morning, earn our living, love those closest to us, deal with difficult people – *knowing* that our lives have meaning. Well, that makes all the difference.

re: consider

How will knowing the creation story affect your sense of purpose and life during this next week?

REFERENCE
29. Genesis 1:1.

4. THREE IN ONE

God, you know everything about me, and I know so little about you. I'd like to learn more about how you exist in my present reality and in all of eternity. Will you please show me?

re: tell

Take a look at those speed demons zipping around the racetrack, mile after mile after mile, and you might think, 'Wake me when somebody crashes!' Hardcore race fans beg to differ – or would if they could hear you. They've got headsets on, tuned into their favourite drivers – and their favourite drivers' pit crew.

'Clear right!' a voice tells the driver, assuring him that no cars are now to his right or left, so he can make his move as needed. A few miles later the driver updates the crew on how the car is handling – loose or tight; what part of the turn is affected. The spotter watches from a high point, informing about who's leading, what accidents have occurred, the car the driver has just passed, and anything the driver is too busy driving to notice.

When the driver pauses for a pit stop, up to seven team members jump into action – jacking up the car, changing the front tyres, changing the rear tyres, filling the fuel tank, catching any fuel that's spilled, and attaching extra windshield shades to prevent late-day glare. All working together for the one purpose – that their driver wins!

re: think

Are you curious about God? Do you wonder if God is just a vague, mysterious something out there? Or is there something more solid, a relational Being? Christians view God as a concrete entity, based on experiential evidence. John, one of Jesus' followers, said it like this:

> 'We proclaim to you the one who existed from the beginning, whom we have heard and seen. We saw him with our own eyes and touched him with our own hands. He is the Word of life. This one who is life itself was revealed to us, and we have seen him. And now we testify and proclaim to you that he is the one who is eternal life. He was with the Father, and then he was revealed to us. We proclaim to you what we ourselves have actually seen and heard so that you may have fellowship with us. And our fellowship is with the Father and with his Son, Jesus Christ.' 1 John 1:1-3.

The word *trinity* (meaning three persons in one) isn't exactly common in today's vocabulary. Maybe you've heard it in the names of cathedrals or churches. The trinity concept is a distinctively Christian way of understanding God, and I doubt that the Christian faith would make sense without it.

At the same time, the idea of God as a trinity is quite a mystery.[30] Superficially, it seems to contradict common sense, making this biblical teaching require deep and extensive study.

Although the actual word *trinity* is absent from the Bible and no statement is found that clearly defines the concept, it is nevertheless there.

The understanding of God as three-persons-yet-one-entity was present early in the church. Jesus and his first followers taught from the Hebrew scripture (called the Old Testament), where God's oneness is fundamental. This scripture teaches that there is only one God and besides him there is no other god.[31] At the same time, the Hebrew Bible pictures God as one who works out his purpose through his Messiah (the Hebrew word for Christ) and through his Spirit.[32]

Emphasis on the oneness of God is also found in the Greek Bible (called the New Testament).[33] In a final commission to his followers, Jesus mentions something called baptism 'in the name of the Father and the Son and the Holy Spirit'.[34] Not only does Paul refer to a three-in-one God in his letters,[35] but he writes in 1 Corinthians 12:4-6:

'There are different kinds of spiritual gifts, but the same *Spirit* is the source of them all. There are different kinds of service, but we serve the same *Lord*. God works in different ways, but it is the same *God* who does the work in all of us.' (Italics supplied.)

Recognising that 'Lord' (Greek, *kyrios*) is a common title for Christ (verse 3), this scripture assumes a threefold aspect of God while underlining his unity in the different gifts, services and workings in the church. The unified distinctiveness of the three-in-one God is also seen in Ephesians 2:18: 'Through him [Christ] we both share the same Spirit and have equal access to the Father.' (MGE.)

Father, Son and Spirit are one in their purpose of bringing reconciliation and salvation to people. The ultimate goal of having access to the Father is achieved 'through . . . [Christ] by the . . . Spirit'. In the same biblical letter we read:

> Although the actual word *trinity* is absent from the Bible and no statement is found that clearly defines the concept, it is nevertheless there.

'There is one body and *one Spirit,* just as you have been called to one glorious hope for the future. There is *one Lord,* one faith, one baptism, and *one God and Father,* who is over all and in all and living through all.'[36] Here we see the three individuals in the Trinity: 'God the Father', 'the Lord' (Jesus Christ), and 'the Spirit'. Three distinct entities related to each other. The Father is God of all, above all, through all and in all. The Bible assumes a special relationship between the three, but it does not exactly define their relationship except for a common purpose in creating the world and rescuing humanity.

At this point, it appears that the Bible assumes the concept of *trinity* but does not explicitly dwell on it. The oneness of God is clearly mentioned; the connection of the three – Father, Son and Holy Spirit – is also found repeatedly; and the unity between Father and Son, between Father and Spirit, and between Son and Spirit, is mentioned in various ways.

So the trinity functions as a conceptual tool holding all these elements together. It helps us think of God in a unified way, while being true to the biblical revelation. It suggests that within the one essence of God we can distinguish three individuals who are neither three parts nor three modes of God, but all are equally and eternally God. What matters in the trinity is the *relationship* between the three: they are one.

We are looking at a kind of oneness which is not so much preoccupied with nature or substance. All three are divine in nature. Their oneness is about being unified in spirit, in purpose, in will, and the way they work with complete unity in creating the world and saving humanity. The trinity is unified while revealing themselves individually. They work with three different but interactive roles – the Father, the Son and the Holy Spirit.

objections

Some people question the compatibility of three in one; others claim that the trinity implies three Gods. But in my study of the Bible, I find that neither of these views does justice. See what you think about it.

First, the trinity is not a question of mathematics. It is more a way of describing God in human language, even though God is beyond our comprehension. The phenomenon of several elements joined into one, while retaining their individuality, is not really uncommon. We talk of one page with different statements on it. We talk of two individuals joined into one new family by marriage. We talk about members of one body, whether in the church, families, football teams or nations.

The combination of collectivity (one) and individuality (several) is not unusual. God's nature is one, and he reveals himself to us in three persons.

Second, *trinity* doesn't mean three Gods. This would contradict the biblical oneness of God. The Bible says there is only one God, that this God is one in nature, will and purpose,[37] but that he reveals himself to us as the Father, Son and Holy Spirit. The Bible puts major emphasis on their mutual relationship.

This biblical God is an interactive being who seeks relationship with you and me, and the essence of the trinity is the relational quality of love – a unifying power of community between single and unique individuals.

God created us as individuals with unique and individual power to be, think and act, but he also wants to relate and communicate with us. You never know – you might find that this divinity wants you to 'seek after God and perhaps feel [your] way toward him and find him – though he is not far from any one of us.'[38]

biblical evidence[39]

This understanding of God-as-trinity is not expressly stated in the Bible. Rather, it is an important underlying feature, and without it some biblical statements are meaningless. You could say: 'The deity of the Father is simply assumed . . . that of the Son is affirmed and argued, while that of the Holy Spirit must be inferred from various indirect statements found in Scripture.'[40]

Your understanding of God's trinity might make more sense by placing it in the context of a *progressive* revelation of God in the Bible. The sixty-six biblical books weren't written by one person at one time, but by several authors over a span of about 1,500 years. None of the books is a systematic explanation of divine teaching, but they were all written for different specific and practical needs of religious instruction. Not every detail was covered in each book. The biblical understanding of God shows a development towards the fullness of God found in Jesus Christ.

The oldest part of the Bible emphasises God's unity: God is one.[41] But the mystery of God's three-part nature is slowly revealed over time.

The Old Testament speaks everywhere of the Father as Almighty God and Creator. God's Spirit is distinguished separately and works towards the same purpose as God does.[42] God's Son is also present and active.

For example, in Isaiah 48:16 the Lord's Servant, who is the promised Messiah (that is, 'the Anointed One' or 'Christ') says:

'From the beginning I have not spoken in secret, from the time it [creation] came to be I have been there. And now the Lord God has sent me and his spirit.' (NRSV.)

Three individuals are mentioned here – the coming Messiah speaks of the Lord God who sent him, and of the Spirit with whom he is sent. This brings us close to the concept of trinity: God's unity is combined with a distinction between the three persons mentioned. The close relationship between the three is the underlying foundation.[43]

The evidence of God's trinity becomes overwhelming later in the Bible, in the New Testament. The divinity and distinct personality of God the Father, of course, was never in dispute.[44] Jesus and God the Father are two distinct persons, underlined in the many passages where Jesus refers to God as 'my Father'.[45] At the same time, there is also a closeness between Father, Son[46] and Holy Spirit: Jesus talked to his followers about 'the Holy Spirit, whom the Father will send in my name'.[47] Many different relations – all involving unity between the three – are described in the Bible.[48]

Early Christians recognised Jesus' divinity clearly. They referred to him as 'God', often calling him 'Lord' or 'Lord of all', 'Lord of glory', 'Jesus our Lord', 'our Lord and God' or 'Lord of Lords'.[49] Christ is celebrated as eternal, uncreated and underived, holy, unchanging, ever-present.[50] Like God the Father, Jesus is engaged in such divine works as Creation, providence, the forgiveness of sins, resurrection and judgement, and the final dissolution and renewal of all things.[51] So God and Son are equal but clearly distinguishable.

And what about the Holy Spirit? As you read the New Testament, it constantly teaches that the Spirit is a person. The Spirit does what only a person can do: he speaks, teaches, testifies, commands, intercedes, reveals, searches, sends, guides, leads and directs, declares things to come and bears witness with our human spirit.[52] The Holy Spirit can be lied to, insulted, blasphemed and grieved.[53] The Bible writers obviously thought of the Holy Spirit as a person.

It is also striking that, while the original Greek word for Spirit (pneuma) is grammatically neuter, and pronouns connected to pneuma are normally in the neuter gender, the Spirit (pneuma) in the New Testament is referred to by pronouns in the masculine gender.[54] This may best be understood in the sense that the Spirit is not merely God's power or a personification of it, but he also has an individual personality. The Holy Spirit is described as a person distinguishable from both the Father and the Son.

The New Testament's references to the Holy Spirit indicate to us that he is equal with God. He is all-knowing[55] and the works he does are God's own works. It is the Spirit who spoke to older generations through the messages of inspired men and women;[56] he bears witness to the truth that is in Christ,[57] strengthens the faithful believers,[58] convinces the world of divine judgement,[59] regenerates or gives new life,[60] sanctifies[61] and grants the community of believers the gifts of ministry.[62] In Acts 5:3-4, lying to the Holy Spirit is the same as lying to God.

The writers of the books of the New Testament put the Holy Spirit on equal footing with the Father and the Son. Not only are Father and Son mentioned side by side as jointly worthy of worship and honour,[63] but the Holy Spirit appears with both of them as a personal source of divine blessing. All three are mentioned together as co-sources of the blessings of salvation.[64]

The interrelationship among them is quite explicit:

'The grace of the Lord Jesus Christ, and the love of God, and the communion of the Holy Spirit be with you all.'[65]

'Go . . . make disciples of all nations, baptising them in the name (singular) of the Father and of the Son and of the Holy Spirit.[66]

This saying of Jesus confirms the unity of the Father, Son and Holy Spirit by keeping them together as one single name, yet maintaining their distinctiveness by repeating the definite article 'the' in front of each of them. In fact, at Jesus' own baptism all three persons of the Godhead were present and coordinated under the divine will.[67]

Although some things remain a mystery, and the topic of God's trinity could be studied in much more detail, there is strong biblical evidence to support it. In John 4:24, Jesus again identifies God with the Spirit: 'God is spirit, so those who worship him must worship in spirit and truth.'

The Trinity functions in the divine work of bringing man back to God. It comes alive in the testimony about Jesus by Christian believers.[68] When you follow Jesus towards God the Father, the Holy Spirit promises to 'teach you all things, and will remind you of everything I [Jesus] have said.'[69] It is an experience that can fill you with certainty and meaning.

what does it mean to me?

The essence of God in the Bible is love: God is love.[70] Since love is a relational concept, the relationship between the Father, the Son and the Holy Spirit is a loving relationship. This aspect of God remains a divine mystery which we may understand intuitively but may not be able to define in detail. The Bible reminds us that 'now we see in a mirror, dimly, but then we will see face to face.'[71]

Because of his love for us, God revealed and gave himself in Jesus Christ to save us from death, evil and hopelessness.[72] This act of giving himself up for others is described as the essence of humility. There Christ, 'who, though he was in the form of God, did not regard equality with God as something to be exploited, but emptied himself, taking the form of a slave, being born in human likeness. And being found in human form, he humbled himself and became obedient to the point of death – even death on a cross.'[73]

Jesus talked about the Holy Spirit's arrival: 'When the [Holy Spirit] comes, whom I will send to you from the Father, the Spirit of truth who comes from the Father, he will testify on my behalf.'[74] But, again, God's love is the unifying element: 'God's love has been poured into our hearts through the Holy Spirit that has been given to us.'[75]

In Holy Scripture, the Trinity tells us who God is, what he wants and how he is behaving in order to bring his divine essence (love) into our life. While we think of God as one God, we are enriched by relating to him as Father, Son and Holy Spirit, knowing that the unity between the three persons of God is a divine model of relational unity. In God we find the unity that is to be manifested among ourselves – the unity of relational love.

So the trinity can help us understand how to relate to God. It shows a God who isn't only love but who is actively engaged in sharing love with us. The Trinity affirms that 'God is with us' – not remote or uninterested. It proves that he uses every possible avenue to reach the human heart in order to fill you with his divine essence. The trinity challenges us to trust him and relate to him.

As the trinity reveals God's love, it remains for you to determine how God the Father, the Son and the Holy Spirit will matter to you. It's a step of faith that only you can take. But as you contemplate this, the Holy Spirit is working in your life. And the story of Jesus is a model of what you may become. And God the Father is eagerly waiting to embrace you as his child.

re: consider

As you think about God, which aspect of his identity do you feel closest to – the Father, the Son or the Spirit? Why?

REFERENCES

30. See this term in the article: Dederen, Raoul. 'The Mystery of the Trinity: God as Father, Son, and Holy Spirit.' *Adventist Review* 1993: 8-11.
31. Deuteronomy 4:35 and 6:4; Isaiah 45:5; Zechariah 14:9.
32. See Isaiah 11:1-5 and 42:1 and 48:16.
33. Mark 12:29-34; 1 Corinthians 8:4-6; Ephesians 4:4-6; 1 Timothy 2:5.
34. Matthew 28:19.
35. See 2 Corinthians 13:14.
36. Ephesians 4:4-6 (italics supplied).

37. Deuteronomy 6:4; Romans 3:29-30; 1 Corinthians 8:4; James 2:19.
38. Acts 17:27.
39. This section is based on Dederen's article. See also: Paulsen, Jan. *When the Spirit descends.* Review and Herald Pub., 2001.; Rice, Richard. *Reign of God: An Introduction to Christian Theology from a Seventh-Day Adventist Perspective.* Andrews UP, 1985, pp. 88-92.; *Seventh-day Adventists believe – a biblical exposition of 27 fundamental doctrines.* Ministerial Association, General Conference of Seventh-day Adventists, 2005, pp. 23-33.; Clouzet, Ron EM. 'Why the Personhood of the Holy Spirit Matters.' *Perspective Digest* 12 Feb. 2007: 4-19.
40. Erickson, Millard J. *Christian theology.* Baker Book House, 1998, p. 873.
41. Deuteronomy 4:35 and 6:4, Isaiah 45:5, Zechariah 14:9.
42. Genesis 1:1 and 41:38, Exodus 31:3 ; 1 Samuel 10:10 ; Isaiah 61:1.
43. See a similar saying in Isaiah 42:1.
44. 1 Corinthians 8:4, 6; 15:24.
45. Matthew 7:21.
46. John 17:20-26.
47. John 14:26, NRSV.
48. See *Seventh-day Adventists believe – a biblical exposition of 27 fundamental doctrines.* Ministerial Association, General Conference of Seventh-day Adventists, 2005, pp. 23-33.
49. Acts 11:16; Acts 10:36; 1 Corinthians 2:8; 1 Corinthians 9:1; Revelation 4:11; Revelation 17:14; John 1:1.
50. Hebrews 7:26; Hebrews 1:12; Matthew 28:20.
51. John 1:3, 10; John 3:35/Colossians 1:17; Matthew 9:1-8; Matthew 25:31-46; Philippians 3:21.
52. Acts 8:29; Luke 12:12; John 15:26; Acts 16:6-7; Romans 8:26; Luke 2:26; 1 Corinthians 2:10-11; Acts 13:2; Acts 8:29/11:12/John 16:13; John 16:13; Romans 8:15, 16.
53. Acts 5:3-4; Hebrews 10:29; Matthew 12:31-32; Ephesians 4:30.
54. John 14:26; 15:26; 16:13.
55. 1 Corinthians 2:10-11.
56. Acts 28:25.
57. John 15:26.
58. 1 Corinthians 6:19.
59. John 16:8-11.
60. John 3:8.
61. 2 Thessalonians 2:13; 1 Peter 1:2.
62. 1 Corinthians 12:4-11.
63. See 1 Corinthians 1:3; 2 Thessalonians 1:12; Ephesians 5:5; 2 Peter 1:1.
64. See 1 Thessalonians 1:2-5; 2 Thessalonians 2:13-14; 1 Corinthians 12:4-5; Ephesians 2:18; 3:2-6.
65. 2 Corinthians 13:13 NRSV.
66. Matthew 28:19, NIV, emphasis supplied.
67. See Matthew 3:16-17.
68. Matthew 10:17-20, 32-33.
69. John 14:26, NIV.

70. 1 John 4:16.
71. 1 Corinthians 13:12, NRSV.
72. John 3:16.
73. Philippians 2:6-8, NRSV.
74. John 15:26, NRSV.
75. Romans 5:5, NRSV.

ABOUT
SIN AND EVIL

5. HOW EVIL GOT STARTED

God, you know what I feel about suffering. I look around and see so much pain and cruelty and wretchedness, and it makes me wonder where you are. Why you don't put a stop to it. How can you allow so much evil to take place in this world, when you are a God of love? Help me to understand the way you relate to suffering.

re: tell

Around sixty-five years ago Elie Wiesel was a 15-year-old prisoner in the Nazi death camp at Buna. A cache of arms belonging to a Dutchman had been discovered at the camp. The man was promptly shipped to Auschwitz. But he had a young servant boy, a pipel as they were called, a child with a refined and beautiful face, unheard of in the camps. He had the face of a sad angel. The little servant, like his Dutch master, was cruelly tortured, but would not reveal any information. So the SS sentenced the child to death, along with two other prisoners who had been discovered with arms. Wiesel tells the story:

'One day when we came back from work, we saw three gallows rearing up in the assembly place, three black crows. Roll call. SS all around us; machine guns trained: the traditional ceremony. Three victims in chains – and one of them, the little servant, the sad-eyed angel. The SS seemed more preoccupied, more disturbed than usual. To hang a young boy in front of thousands of spectators was no light matter. The head of the camp read the verdict. All eyes were on the child. He was lividly pale, almost calm, biting his lips. The gallows threw its shadow over him. This time the Lagercapo refused to act as executioner. Three SS replaced him. The three victims mounted together onto the chairs. The three necks were placed at the same moment within the nooses. "Long live liberty!" cried the two adults. But the child was silent. "Where is God? Where is he?" someone behind me asked. Total silence throughout the camp. On the horizon, the sun was setting. "Bare your heads!" yelled the head of the camp. His voice was raucous. We were weeping. "Cover your heads!" Then the march past began. The two adults were no longer alive. Their tongues hung swollen, blue-tinged, but the third rope was still moving; being so light, the child was still alive. . . . For more than half an hour he stayed there, struggling between life and death, dying in slow agony under our eyes. And we had to look him full in the face. He was still alive when I passed in front of him. His tongue was still red, his eyes were not yet glazed. Behind me, I heard the same man asking: "Where is God now?" And I heard a voice within me answer him: "Where is he? Here he is – he is hanging here on this gallows." That night the soup tasted of corpses.'[76]

re: think

What is evil? Its origin? The constant conflict between good and bad? Why would a good God allow evil to exist?

Gene Roddenberry, creator of science-fiction TV drama *Star Trek*, made the point starkly: 'We must question the story logic of having an all-knowing, all-powerful God, who creates faulty humans, and then blames them for his own mistakes.'

As a script for the universe, the reality of evil points against the goodness of God, as so many have recognised. In fact, the very existence of evil is the number one objection to God. For example:

- 'If God is all good, then he is not all powerful. If God is all powerful, then he is not all good.' (Norman Mailer)
- 'The world in which we live can be understood as a result of muddle and accident; but if it is the outcome of deliberate pur-

pose, the purpose must have been that of a fiend. For my part, I find accident a less painful and more plausible hypothesis.' (Bertrand Russell)

- 'It's not that I don't accept God – it's the world created by him I don't and cannot accept.' (Dostoevsky)
- 'The fact of suffering undoubtedly constitutes the single greatest challenge to the Christian faith.' (John Stott)
- 'The only excuse for God is that he doesn't exist.' (Friedrich Nietzsche)
- 'The problem of evil. . . . Why does God permit it? Or, if God is omnipotent, in which case permission and creation are the same, why did God create it?' (Sir William Temple)
- 'The gods can either take away evil from the world and will not, or, being willing to do so, cannot; or they neither can nor will, or lastly, they are both able and willing. If they have the will to remove evil and cannot, then they are not omnipotent. If they can, but will not, then they are not benevolent. If they are neither able nor willing, then they are neither omnipotent nor benevolent. Lastly, if they are both able and willing to annihilate evil, how does it exist?' (Epicurus)

> **Either God could end evil and does not, or is not powerful and cannot – right?**

So either God is not all-powerful – because he does not remove evil even though he can. Or God is not all-knowing – since he cannot know or admit that evil exists. Or God is not all-good – since he either created or allows evil to exist.

'If God is, whence come evil things? If he is not, whence come good?' (Boethius, sixth century)

Either God could end evil and does not, or is not powerful and cannot – right? But if God is truly good, and evil does exist, then what? There must be another answer and it must include deeper reasons than just either/or.

Imagine a scenario: You are confronted by someone who calls you all the names under the sun. Liar, cheat, extortioner, blackmailer, attacker, thief, rapist, even murderer. How do you respond?

You defend yourself. You reject the charges. You complain that they are completely and utterly wrong. But your accuser continues to maintain your 'crimes'. You continue to protest your innocence. And you're into a childish playground game of, 'Are too!''Am not!'

The beginning of this situation is described in the last book of the Bible – Revelation. It reveals that 'there was war in heaven.'[77] Interesting! Most people imagine heaven as a place of perfect peace and tranquillity. So how could there be war in the place of perfection? What went wrong? What was the fight about and how is it being resolved?

The cause of the conflict? Lucifer – and his choices. As the highest created being in God's universe (Lucifer means *light-bringer*), he had freedom to choose whatever he wanted. Lucifer wanted power and control and position. Ultimately he challenged the character of God and the legitimacy of divine government. The story is told briefly in Ezekiel under the representation of the King of Tyre:

> 'In your great pride you claim, "I am a god!" . . . You were the model of perfection, full of wisdom and exquisite in beauty. You were in Eden, the garden of God. . . . You had access to the holy mountain of God and walked among the stones of fire. You were blameless in all you did from the day you were created until the day evil was found in you. . . . Your heart was filled with pride because of all your beauty. Your wisdom was corrupted by your love of splendour.' (Ezekiel 28:2, 13-15, 17.)

In other words, Lucifer decided he could be greater than God and do a better job!

Isaiah adds some further details that explain the self-centred motivation of this challenge to God: 'How you are fallen from heaven, O shining star [Lucifer], son of the morning! You have been thrown down to the earth, you who destroyed the nations of the world. For you said to yourself, "I will ascend to heaven and set my throne above God's stars. I will preside on the mountain of the gods far away in the north. I will climb to the highest heavens and be like the Most High." '[78]

god defamed

The highest ambition of the devil is to be like God, but by using tools that God would never use! His greatest device in his rebellion against God is defamation. He even had the gall to demand worship from God himself, when God came as Christ to this world: 'Next the devil took him [Jesus] to the peak of a very high mountain and showed him all the kingdoms of the world and their glory. "I will give it all to you," he said, "if you will kneel down and worship me." '[79]

The devil charges God with his own nature – evil, selfish, vindictive, cruel, severe. He claims God is not to be trusted and he wages an ongoing spiritual war of lies and deception, vilifying and misrepresenting the truth about God. The devil claims to know best – and calls God a liar.

Lucifer ended up not only deceiving others, but deluding himself as well. Right from the beginning, he, Satan (another name for the devil), has been lying about the kind of being that God is.

So how did God respond to this challenge? By demanding obedience? By asserting right based on divine power? By eliminating the source of this perversion? By killing Lucifer? No.

Ultimately, having had the opportunity to demonstrate his character and methods, Lucifer was ejected from heaven. Jesus recalls the scene: 'I saw Satan fall from heaven like lightning.'[80] Yet Satan, also called the Accuser, continues his attack on God and his truth, and we are part of it. Which is why we have become 'a spectacle to the whole universe, to angels as well as to men',[81] a demonstration of God's response to this accusation.

Why is there evil and suffering? Because the devil chose to be the opposite of God and rules his territory with deception. And humans have bought into the devil's way. We each experience the consequences, not under the punitive hostility of God, but because choosing wrong instead of right has its own natural results.

Restoring trust takes time. The ongoing battle of lies, deception, innuendo, gossip and misrepresentation all require much time to refute. And God can't refute the charges against his character by just saying,

'Hey, folks, it's not true!' To prove the charges false, God has to show his true nature over time, to reveal to everyone that the devil's accusations are wrong.

While God wants trustworthy friends, the devil enslaves those who submit to his demands. 'God seeks comrades and claims love, the devil seeks slaves and claims obedience,' writes Rabindranath Tagore.

Imagine that you purchase some new equipment. You put all the parts on the floor ready for assembly. And then you pick up the instructions, which say: 'Place knurled wheel (5) over sprocket (b) until it engages threaded spline (f2) and the grommet (see fig. 31) achieves a convoluted spiral.' You shake your head in confusion at such meaningless 'help'.

So you call in a friend who's an expert. 'Oh, yes,' he says, 'that's easy.' And he picks up the pieces and there before your very eyes the many bits are put together until assembly is complete. 'And this is how it works,' he says.

A real demonstration – and once you've seen it, you say, 'Yes, of course!' That is why we're still here in a world of evil – not because God can't or won't end it, but because of the higher cause of demonstration. Without this proof, the charges against God would never be answered. Words aren't enough – we all have to see the inevitable results.

The questions are: Who can be trusted? Who's telling the truth? Who is right and who is wrong? The great controversy is between Christ and Satan, and the situation in which we find ourselves provides the evidence from which we must make our decision. Is God a cold-hearted tyrant or divine dictator as the devil suggests? Or is the truth on God's side, and this ongoing battle a process to reveal the devil's lies?

I believe that the heart of a good God aches to heal this world of evil, to wipe away every tear from every eye, to be with his people and be their God, face to face.[82] But because he is God and he wants everyone to understand him and love him without compulsion, he waits. 'He is patient with you, not wanting anyone to perish, but everyone to come to repentance.'[83] That is something to be happy about!

Why do evil and suffering exist? Because the devil chose to act in opposition to God. How can we say that God is uncaring, that he willingly allows sin and suffering? So often we or the devil cause evil, and then we all blame God!

> The highest ambition of the devil is to be like God, but by using tools that God would never use!

Think for a moment. What is the alternative? Can God intervene in every situation: to stop the car crashing, to prevent the earthquake, to defuse the terrorist's bomb? The result would be a world in which evil is never seen for what it truly is, because its full diabolical consequences are never shown.

Only as the conflict is resolved through the unmasking of the real face of evil, only as God is demonstrated to be the compassionate being he says he is, only as we agree that he was right all along – only then can God bring this rebellion to a close.

Why did Jesus come? He came so that we could know and understand the truth. All the lies have blinded us to God's plan so that we can't see clearly. And we almost prefer the lies. Isn't it true that 'A lie travels round the world while truth is still putting his boots on'? God couldn't leave the world in this state of misunderstanding. He wants to make sure that we understand the difference, that we don't confuse truth and error, so that we can make an informed choice.

The Bible speaks of walking in the truth, abiding in the truth and of the truth setting us free.[84] In that sense, seeing *is* believing – truth revealed. That's why God says, 'Taste and see that the Lord is good.'[85] Check it out – and find out for yourself how this truth operates in reality. Experiment with God and examine what he says and does.

re: consider

What do you see as your part in this cosmic battle between good and evil? Do you want a fresh start?

REFERENCES

76. Elie Wiesel. *Night*. Bantam, 1982, pp. 75-6, quoted in *When God Was Taken Captive,*
W. Aldrich, Multnomah, 1989, pp. 39-41.
77. Revelation 12:7.
78. Isaiah 14:12-14.
79. Matthew 4:8, 9.
80. Luke 10:18.
81. 1 Corinthians 4:9, NIV.
82. See Revelation 21 and 22.
83. 2 Peter 3:9, NIV.
84. John 8:32.
85. Psalms 34:8, NASB.

6. THIS LITTLE PROBLEM

God, I've heard the word 'sin' before, but I don't know exactly what it means. Would you show me what I need to know and understand about it, so I can deal with it better than I do right now?

re: tell

Do you think babies look pure and angelic? Researchers at the University of Portsmouth found something surprising: Infants learn to 'lie' a whole lot sooner than was previously thought.

Psychologists used to think that children learned to lie at about 4 years of age. Nope, try six months! Fake crying or gurgling to get your attention! Clever distractions to hide actions you've discouraged! This is just typical behaviour for a zero-year-old. By the time they're toddlers, kids are bluffing with the best of them.

The next time a baby pauses mid-cry to see if anyone's listening, it just might be shrewder than you think.

re: think

Over twenty years ago, a disgraced TV preacher was found to be hooked on illegitimate sex, after he had assisted in defrocking others because of their immoral behaviour! In an attempt to save his multi-million-dollar ministry, he cried his heart out on television, declaring that he had sinned against the Lord. His declaration of guilt was carried by the news channels worldwide!

Sin is quite a fashionable subject. It is a far more interesting topic in novels and screenplays than virtue will ever be. Sin is exciting. By comparison, virtue feels tame and colourless. Christian talk about the danger of sin is usually unwelcome. Postmoderns, in particular, don't have much time for the concept of 'sin' in its traditional sense. For them, sin has lost its sinfulness.

Hugh Thomson Kerr, late senior editor of *Theology Today*, once said that people 'have substituted relativity for reality, psychology for prayer, an inferiority complex for sin, social control for family worship, autosuggestion for conversion, reflex action for revelation, the spirit of the wheels for the power of the Spirit.' When people make mistakes or fail to live up to their own expectations, many no longer feel guilt. They may acknowledge at the most a sense of shame or embarrassment.

But in spite of how people have devalued the term, sin is still sin. It doesn't just imply inadequacies that we'll eventually overcome or errors of judgement that are part of a life-long learning process. Sin is much more than that. A famous French writer once aptly said, 'Sin is whatever obscures the soul.'

The word stands for rebellion, disaster and death. Not for something superficial and circumstantial, but something lethal and which, unless stopped, behaves like a virus or even a cancer.

what is it?

Sin is transgression or breaking of the law of God. You can't transgress where there is no law,[86] and even scientists recognise that there are laws. The Holy Bible indicates a set of moral principles, which we usually refer to as the Ten Commandments, and every human being who has ever lived has transgressed this law.

'For everyone has sinned; we all fall short of God's glorious standard.'[87]

When God looks down from his heaven to see how we are doing, he sees that all people have been affected by sin: 'No one does good, not a single one!'[88] So there is good reason to refer to sin as a *problem*.

But, biblically speaking, sin isn't just breaking a commandment by some intentional or unintentional act. Sin also has to do with what goes on inside of us. Although we won't be held responsible for every fleeting thought that is less than pure or altruistic, God says that any wilful fantasising or conscious pondering of things we know to be wrong is just as bad as the actual deed. Hoping that someone we intensely dislike will get hit by a car is no less objectionable than actually killing that person with a shotgun. Jesus himself expressed it this way: 'I say, anyone who even looks at a woman with lust has already committed adultery with her in his heart.'[89] The 'cherishing' of a sin 'in our heart' is incompatible with a relationship with God.[90]

The medieval church may be criticised for establishing a shortlist of seven 'mortal' sins: Pride, Lust, Greed, Covetousness, Gluttony, Envy and Sloth. But the list shows a sharp awareness of sin in terms of wrong motivations and negative attitudes, rather than simply as the actual deeds of lying, stealing, murdering and adultery. The apostle James underlines God's view of the seriousness of this. 'For the person who keeps all of the laws except one is as guilty as a person who has broken all of God's laws.'[91]

Surely it is no exaggeration to refer to sin as a *problem*. On the topic of sin, the Bible does not mince words. There is sin in our actions, in our hearts, in our motives, schemings and fantasies.

'I want to do what is right,' he said, 'but I don't do it. Instead, I do what I hate.' Sounds familiar?

One of the Hebrew words translated 'sin' has the root meaning of 'missing the mark'. So sin isn't just disobeying a set of rules, in either deed or in thought, but it also includes falling short of our potential when we aim for something but fail to achieve it.

Look at some of the great individuals of the past – or the present, for that matter – and admire their talents and their possibilities. Then consider how they ruined their lives by reckless living and immoral choices. For most of us, the situation is less radical, but who dares to suggest that he or she has no sin *problem*?

Sins aren't just a few isolated acts, interspersed between the noble and the good. Sin is more like a venom that spreads and infects the entire human being. It's more powerful than we care to admit. Even the great apostle Paul had to admit that he continued to be faced with a relentless problem. He badly wanted to do what was good, but often didn't succeed. 'I want to do what is right,' he said, 'but I don't do it. Instead, I do what I hate.'[92] Sound familiar?

where did it all start?

Where did it all go wrong? Where did the sin problem originate? Even before the first human couple got off to a bad start and 'fell' into sin, rebellion against God had manifested itself in heaven. How sin could ever get started in a perfect universe is something we may never understand. It's a mystery, but we do know this much: it had to do with God's desire to give us a free will. He didn't want pre-programmed robots, but individuals who can choose to love him on their own.

At a fateful point in time a heavenly being we now refer to as Satan made a choice against God. That's where the sin *problem* began. Then this heavenly rebel introduced it on the earth, as soon as the first couple was created. Just like Lucifer, Adam and Eve were also created with free choice. They could have said 'No' to Satan's proposal, but they didn't.[93] And ever since, mankind has been affected by the consequences of their actions. Sin was instantly hereditary, and now every human being is born imperfect, with the inborn tendency to pursue precisely those things that lead us away from God. Love for self has come before love for others.

True, some sinners were historical monsters and others were great role models in spite of their imperfections. Hitler and Stalin were undoubtedly greater sinners than Mother Teresa or Martin Luther King. But not even Mother Teresa or Pope John Paul II were without sin.

All people have sinned. The sin problem is larger than life. It is superhuman. Therefore the solution to the problem must also be superhuman, if it is going to be adequate.

fixing the problem

People today tend to feel that if they have a problem, they must fix it themselves. Putting the blame and the responsibility somewhere else, they insist, is a ridiculous cop-out. It feels awkward to seek a solution beyond ourselves for our failings and inadequacies. It means looking for a truth that seems to have evaporated as modernity shifted into postmodernity.

But the Bible doesn't allow for this minimalising approach to sin. Instead, it maintains that sin is a superhuman problem. If there was ever a truth that has been experientially proven it is this: Sin has dimensions that are totally beyond our control. But there's another truth that overshadows this one. Just as the sin problem is larger than life, so is the solution. There is someone, called Jesus, who lived on this earth just like all of us, but who never gave in to sinful thoughts or actions. *He became the supernatural solution for the sin problem.* 'God made Christ, who never sinned, to be the offering for our sin, so that we could be made right with God through Christ.'[94]

Of course, we're left with questions: Is it fair that all humans became infected with the sin virus? Why must we suffer because of the mistakes of our first ancestors? Couldn't an all-wise and loving God devise some other way to deal with the sin problem? Why did sin develop in the way it did, with so much havoc and misery?

People around the world have been asking these questions throughout history. Questions whispered and shouted. Questions uttered as philosophical enquiries and curses of desperation. Sin remains a problem – in more ways than one. But, when we consider the solution, all doubt and cynicism eventually dissipate.

Jesus Christ is the solution. He came to 'save [all] people from their sins'.[95] For me, that is enough.

re: consider

How do you feel about taking personal responsibility for your wrong actions, but still looking to God for the ability to change into someone better?

REFERENCES
86. Romans 4:15.
87. Romans 3:23.
88. See Psalm 14:3.
89. Matthew 5:28.
90. Psalm 66:18, 19, NIV.
91. James 2:10.
92. Romans 7:15.
93. See Genesis 3.
94. 2 Corinthians 5:21.
95. Matthew 1:21.

ABOUT
FAITH, LOVE
AND SALVATION

7. RESCUE ME

God, sometimes this life is just more than one human being can handle. I know you have the power to rescue me, but I want to know more. Please show me how you do it!

re: tell

David, a rescue worker, scrambled through the missing child's house, searching for photos and recently worn items of clothing. Quickly but carefully he exited with a little girl's jacket for the hounds to sniff and a framed photograph of the girl holding her kitten.

He rushed back to the forest, gave the dog teams the girl's coat and showed the searchers her picture. But when the girl's father saw it he exclaimed, 'This isn't my kid – we don't even have a cat!'

David was stunned. Had he searched the wrong house, found the wrong child's jacket and sent the dogs on the wrong track? But then the girl's mother appeared to set things straight. 'I just bought that picture frame,' she exclaimed, 'I haven't even put one of our photos in it yet!'

Eventually, searchers found the lost little girl, shaken but unharmed, and David breathed the biggest sigh of relief of his life.

re: think

Is our reality friendly or antagonistic? It's easy to conclude that this universe isn't a friendly place. Earthquakes, floods, epidemics and other catastrophes take a high toll on human lives. Whether we go to a desert, the North Pole or fly into space – our very existence is in danger because of the environment, viruses or bacteria. It would be easy to assume that nobody cares.

Yet Christianity maintains that there is a God, a God of love. A good God who is like a gentle Father to us. But how do we know? It's hard to believe based on observation alone. The Bible says that one day this God came to us in the person of Jesus Christ to live among us as one of us, so that we might get a better grasp of who he is.

When Jesus lived on this earth he asked his disciples an interesting question, 'Who do people say that the Son of Man is?'[96] The basic question in Christianity is not what people say about Jesus' teaching. Of course, the element of teaching is significant in Christianity (as in other religions), but the most important aspect of Christianity is to find the right attitude towards the *person* of Jesus. We could say that Christianity = Jesus. The significance of Christ's teaching is based on who he is. Almost always when people have a hard time living out a biblical teaching, it is because they are not experiencing the person of Jesus Christ.

Let's have a look at who Jesus is. In Matthew 16:17 Christ says that if our knowledge is to be correct, it needs to be based on God's revelation and not only our thinking or other people's understanding.

the person of Jesus Christ

Early Christians believed that God himself came to our earth in the person of Jesus.[97] This explains why they saw and evaluated everything about their lives from the perspective of what this first-century Jew said and how he lived and died. They were willing to give up everything for him, even their lives.

So who was Jesus?

First and foremost, he was *human*. His disciples never doubted his humanity. From childhood to adulthood, he grew in height and strength[98] and in wisdom.[99] Through suffering he learned obedience,[100] he was hungry,[101] thirsty,[102] he was tired and needed sleep.[103] As a man he lived in full dependence on God,[104] was tempted[105] and needed to sustain his relationship with God in prayer.[106] In all these aspects, Jesus was very human, vulnerable and had experiences just like we do.

But Jesus was not *just* human, he was also truly *God*. He existed prior to his birth in Bethlehem.[107] The apostles stated that Jesus created everything.[108] He has the right to forgive sins.[109] Forgiveness comes from him as much as it comes from God,[110] which puts him on the same level as the Father.[111] He expected that his listeners would believe in him[112] and their faith, or lack of it, would determine their eternal destiny. He deserves the same honour as the Father.[113]

Christ's self-understanding is clearly seen from the fact that he uses statements like, 'I am . . .' the bread of life,[114] light of the world,[115] resurrection and life,[116] way, truth and life.[117] It would be very difficult to make it plainer than this. The connection between Jesus and the great 'I AM' which was the name of Yahweh in the Old Testament[118] cannot be overlooked. When Jesus said, 'Before Abraham was even born, I AM,' he made things so plain that his listeners picked up stones to kill him. They understood that he had just stated that he was God.[119]

What the Old Testament ascribes to Yahweh, the New Testament applies to Jesus.[120] The conclusion is clear: In Jesus, God himself came to this world.

The implications of this are clear. Either Jesus is who he claims to be (God himself) or he cannot be a good man, a teacher of morality. That's why Christians came to accept him as the true God, fully divine.

work of Jesus Christ

Once we are clear on who Jesus is, we can understand and appreciate what he came to do. He could not have accomplished what he did, had he not been who he claimed he was.

So what did Jesus do?

In Christ, God himself took care of our sin and its consequences. The apostle Paul said it this way: 'God was in Christ reconciling the world to himself.'[121] To accomplish this, it was necessary that:

1) Jesus' birth into this world was unique – supernatural. It was not possible to solve the problem of sin by divine proclamation, command or power. John says that 'the Word [Jesus] became flesh'.[122] God in a miraculous way entered our world and began an existence as a human being.[123] His virgin birth is seen as a part of the mystery of godliness which cannot be explained by using the usual laws of human reproduction. This event shows that God loved us and entered our situation because he wanted to serve us, not to rule over us. He wanted a relationship of love, not blind submission.

2) Jesus' mission in this world was unique. Jesus is our Saviour, not only because of who he was (God himself), but also because of the way he lived his earthly life and what he accomplished. With his words and deeds he proclaimed God's kingdom – a new quality of life under God's rule. He introduced God's offer of salvation to *all people,* even those who had been rejected, marginalised and ruled out of salvation in the minds of the religious people of that time.

His ministry rose above all human barriers. His teaching explained the principles of God's kingdom – that everybody is invited into it. His deeds illustrated God's character and attitude towards people. The Greek word for 'salvation' and 'healing' is the same. Jesus' miracles of healing were signs of salvation. Health is not just an absence of illness, but harmony of body, mind and spirit. Through Christ God wants to renew his original image in us sinners and to restore us to the way he intended us to be at creation.

3) Jesus' life in this world was unique. Because Jesus came to 'save his people from their sins',[124] he himself had to be without sin.[125] It is remarkable that even his enemies were not able to refute this fact and produce evidence to the contrary. The New Testament writers confirm this fact repeatedly.[126] Jesus was not sinless because, somehow, thanks to his nature, he was above temptation. Rather, his temptations were very real and cruel.[127] His temptations are another proof of his humanity, and his victory over them was the result of his continuous dependence on his heavenly Father.[128]

It is true that Jesus used to say to his potential disciples: 'Follow me,'[129] and that by his grace and in his power we can and should follow in his footprints. It is also true that Jesus showed that by total dependence on God it is possible to be victorious over sin and temptation. But we need to keep in mind that he is our rescuer and we are his disciples. He is first our Saviour and after that he is our example. Our lives on this earth can't equal his sinlessness, because our sinful natures will remain until he comes back to this planet again.[130] His mission was to become a sinless and perfect sacrifice as a pardon for our sinful choices and actions. That's why he did not need a saviour for himself, because he *is* the Saviour. We were each born into sin, so we cannot be free from sin in this life. This means that for our whole lives we will need Jesus as our rescuer.

> Either Jesus is who he claims to be (God himself) or he cannot be a good man, a teacher of morality.

4) Jesus' death was unique. Christ came not only to live on this earth but to die a sacrificial death.[131] In spite of the fact that he was sinless, he died the death of separation from God, the death that unrepentant sinners will die at the end of time.[132] This happened because he was 'handed over to die because of our sins',[133] 'died for our sins',[134] 'tasted death for everyone'.[135] So Christ's death was substitutionary, unique and unrepeatable.[136] The immediate cause of his death was not the fact that he was nailed to the cross (others died that way, too, yet they are not our saviours), but that he felt forsaken by God.[137] In this way Jesus became the reconciliation – proof of God's justice for the whole universe.[138] At the same time, the cross is also proof of God's inexpressible love towards us. Jesus did not die in order to convince the Father to start loving us, for the Father himself 'gave' Jesus because of his great love towards us.[139] God proved before the whole universe that death is the result of sin. Separation from God, who is the only source of life, unavoidably brings death.

In the Garden of Eden, Satan said to our first parents: 'You won't die!'[140] On the cross God supplied proof that Satan was wrong and God was right. He had said: 'You may freely eat the fruit of every tree in the garden – except the tree of the knowledge of good and evil. If you eat its fruit, you are sure to die.'[141] Those words were not a threat but a loving warning about the consequences of a broken relationship of trust and dependence on God. The cross reveals God's true character and demonstrates that we can serve God on the basis of selfless love rather than through fear of punishment or the thought of gaining a reward.[142] On the contrary, those who sent Jesus to the cross were those who did not know God's character.[143]

5) Jesus' resurrection was unique. Whenever the apostles talked about the death of Jesus, they also immediately added the fact of his resurrection. 'Christ Jesus died for us and was raised to life for us.'[144] 'Christ died for our sins, just as the Scriptures said. He was buried, and he was raised from the dead on the third day, just as the Scriptures said.'[145] The fact that Jesus had been resurrected was the essence of the apostolic faith. If he was not resurrected, our faith, our hope, our preaching would be in vain, our life would not have the right perspective.[146]

It was the resurrection of Jesus that completely changed the perspective of the first disciples regarding Jesus' life and death. The feeling of defeat and failure suddenly disappeared. The fact of the resurrection was for them the decisive proof that God was supporting Jesus and that his death on the cross was not a sign of God's rejection or curse.[147]

When Jesus is called 'the firstborn from among the dead',[148] it does not mean that he was historically the first person in time to be resurrected. All other people who had been resurrected (with the exception of Moses and those resurrected immediately after Jesus' death) were actually just revived back to life and then they died again. Jesus' resurrection is a true resurrection, because he 'lives forever', he is able to 'save completely those who come to God through him'.[149]

Jesus' resurrection proves that death will not have the last word in human existence. There is a future beyond the grave.[150] His resurrection is a guarantee of our resurrection. 'Anyone who believes in me will live, even after dying. Everyone who lives in me and believes in me will never ever die.'[151]

The centre of the Christian religion is the person of Jesus Christ. Christianity is not based on acceptance of some kind of creed or minutely defined set of fundamental beliefs. In its essence, Christianity means to have a positive relationship with the person of Jesus. To be a Christian means to say 'Yes' to Christ, a 'Yes' which is unequivocal, total and unconditional, because in Christ God said to us his unequivocal, total and unconditional 'Yes'.

In Christ we see that the problem of sin was never in God's relationship with us. Sin only changes our relationship with God. The God who went after Adam and Eve, asking, 'Adam, where are you?' comes to each one of us today and says: 'I love you, I accept you the way you are.' His love is never 'Yes, but . . .' That's why the response of a person who understands and personally experiences God's unconditional, total and unequivocal acceptance will be a total, unequivocal and complete 'Yes' to God.

If your heart sometimes longs really to know God the way he is, if he does not seem real to you because of all that you have done or in spite of it, if God still seems distant to you, focus on his Son Jesus, 'the exact representation of his [God's] nature'.[152] You can be sure that if you get to know Jesus you will know the Father. And to know him means to have eternal life.[153]

Pilate asked the right question: 'What shall I do, then, with Jesus who is called Christ?'[154] If you find the answer for yourself, just like Thomas who said, 'My Lord and my God',[155] you will truly experience joy.

re: consider

What is keeping you from getting to know God better?

REFERENCES
96. Matthew 16:13-17.
97. John 1:1-3; 14:18.
98. Luke 2:40.
99. Ibid, verse 52.
100. Hebrews 5:8.
101. Matthew 4:2.
102. John 19:28.
103. John 4:6; Matthew 8:24.
104. John 6:38.
105. Hebrews 4:15; cf. James 1:13.
106. Mark 1:35; Luke 11:1.
107. Micah 5:2; Isaiah 9:6; John 8:58; 2 Corinthians 8:9.
108. John 1:3; Colossians 1:16-17.
109. Mark 2:10.

110. Colossians 2:13; 3:13.
111. Matthew 28:19; 1 Corinthians 1:3; Revelation 20:6; 22:3; cf. John 10:30.
112. John 6:40; 14:1-3.
113. John 5:23.
114. John 6:35.
115. Ibid 8:12.
116. Ibid 11:25.
117. Ibid 14:6.
118. Exodus 3:13-14.
119. John 8:58-59.
120. See Romans 10:13 and Joel 2:32; Philippians 2:10 and Isaiah 45:23; Matthew 3:3 and Isaiah 40:3.
121. 2 Corinthians 5:19.
122. John 1:14, NIV.
123. Matthew 1:23.
124. Matthew 1:21.
125. John 8:46.
126. Luke 1:35; Mark 1:24; 2 Corinthians 5:21; Hebrews 4:15; 1 Peter 2:22; 1 John 3:5.
127. Hebrews 4:15; Matthew 4:1-11; Luke 22:39-46.
128. John 5:19, 30.
129. John 21:19.
130. Philippians 3:20-21.
131. Mark 10:45; Isaiah 53.
132. 2 Corinthians 5:21; Romans 6:23.
133. Romans 4:25.
134. 1 Corinthians 15:3.
135. Hebrews 2:9.
136. Hebrews 10:10.
137. Matthew 27:46; Romans 4:25; cf. Romans 1:24, 26, 28.
138. Romans 1:17 and 3:25; Colossians 1:20; Ephesians 1:10.
139. John 3:16 and 16:26-27.
140. Genesis 3:4.
141. Genesis 2:16, 17.
142. Job 1 and 2.
143. John 16:2-3.
144. Romans 8:34.
145. 1 Corinthians 15:3-4.
146. 1 Corinthians 15:13-20.
147. Deuteronomy 21:23.
148. Colossians 1:18, NIV.
149. Hebrews 7:24-25.
150. 1 Corinthians 15:12-20.
151. John 11:25-26.
152. Hebrews 1:3, NIV.
153. John 17:3.
154. Matthew 27:22, NIV.
155. John 20:28.

8. SOMETHING UNSEEN

God, people say all you need is a little faith, but I've had to have a lot more than some intangible faith in order to survive this life. I've also learned the hard way that faith in myself or my friends just isn't worth it, as we're always letting ourselves and each other down. I want to know how to trust you to guide my life. How can faith be tangible?

re: tell

A small boy was on a bus returning home from a church. The day was very warm, so the bus windows were open. The boy had received a Bible text written on a card, 'Have faith in God.'[156] As the wind swept through the bus, his card went flying out of the window. He started to shout, 'Stop the bus! My faith in God just went out the window!'

re: think

Genuine faith isn't going to fly out of your window. But is it still possible to believe in this kind of faith in the twenty-first century? Or is faith a leftover concept from less enlightened times, with no place in today's sophisticated society? What is it actually?

Believers generally, and Christians especially, talk about faith a great deal. But what do they mean when they say, 'Have faith,' or 'I don't have enough faith,' or 'I believe that I'm saved by faith'?

myths about faith

a) Faith is not merely an opinion or an idea

Many people say: 'I do believe there must be someone somewhere in the universe. It couldn't all have started by chance.' But that's not faith. That's an opinion, a viewpoint, a world-view.

Real biblical faith is more than just an opinion. The Bible actually says that even demons have 'faith' and yet they are scared.[157] In God's eyes this kind of faith doesn't have any value.

b) Faith is not just a conviction

A small schoolboy once said, 'Faith is believin' what you know ain't so!'

Some people think that if you're prepared to believe what you know isn't true, that is real faith! Is faith just believing something for which you have no evidence? If you had sufficient evidence, you wouldn't say, 'I believe,' you would say, 'I know.' Strange that we use the word 'believe' to express doubt!

Many people believe that if they're really convinced of something, if they 'truly believe', then it will happen. But is it true that if I'm truly convinced about something it will become reality?

That would suggest that having faith in something makes it a reality. So if I have 'faith' that there's a man on the moon, or an elephant in the next room, is it automatically true? Yet many Christians assert: if you truly believe, the elephant would be there, and if it's not there then it's just proof that your faith is *small*.

But that's not faith, that's mind manipulation! Faith isn't a magic wand to make God do what you ask of him. Faith's value depends on how trustworthy the object of your faith is, not how strongly you believe in it.

We have to distinguish between faith and superstition. Superstition is based on unproved connections between events (phenomena) or human inventions (like fear of black cats or Friday 13th). But faith is always based on solid foundations. My strong conviction about something isn't necessarily faith. It could easily be superstition.

c) Faith is not just a creed or churchmanship

Sometimes people ask: 'What faith do you belong to? Are you Christian/Jewish/Muslim/Buddhist?' Or people say they 'were persecuted for their faith!' or 'We live in a multi-faith society.'

It's true that in some religious systems a mental assent to doctrine is enough to consider someone a believer. This aspect of faith means embracing a certain creed (*credo* – Latin: *I believe*) or body of doctrines. But doctrine isn't going to save anyone.[158]

Genuine biblical faith is much more than just intellectual assent to a creed (set of doctrines) or membership in a certain church. Sure, doctrines are significant in Christianity, just as in other religions. But Christianity's main emphasis is on finding a right relationship with the *person* of Jesus Christ.

d) Faith and knowledge are not inversely proportional

As a child growing up under a communist government, I was told by my teachers that faith was for people who didn't use their brains. The smarter the person, they insisted, the less faith they needed – and if you were truly wise you didn't need faith at all. Faith was for old people who didn't know much and were afraid of death, so they needed a crutch to help them through. But life's reality proved more complex than the theories of communism. Faith survived; communism collapsed.

Yet there are still many people, and not only in former communist countries, who believe that faith and knowledge are inversely proportionate – the greater the knowledge, the smaller the faith and vice versa. They think that belief or faith equals turning off your capacity for logic, thinking and sound judgement.

But the solution isn't to stop thinking about your faith either. Rather, it's to continue searching until you find answers. Typically, people who become disillusioned with their faith are people who haven't thought enough about it. Unexamined faith gives us a false sense of security and makes us intolerant of people whose views differ from ours.

According to the Bible, faith and knowledge are directly proportional; the better you know a person, the more you are likely to trust him or her. (Of course, that assumes that they are trustworthy people. With some, the better you know them, the less you trust them. But that's a different story.)

Both the Hebrew *(emun)* and the Greek *(pistis)* words for faith express the idea of reliability and trustworthiness and imply more than just some abstract opinion, conviction or article of theology.

biblical understanding of faith

a) Faith is a capacity that everyone has

We all have a natural capacity for trust. When I board a train to London, I don't expect to end up in Manchester. When I get medication from a pharmacist, I don't perform chemical analysis at home to make sure I wasn't given rat poison.

We learn from experience that train drivers or pharmacists can usually be trusted. Sure, there are some exceptions, but not normally. This capacity for trust, based on facts, evidence and experience, is given to us by God. In our relationship with him, God only expects us to take an honest look at everything he has to offer, based on evidence and our own experience.

Trust can't be commanded. In this free universe, we can choose whether or not to believe.

Lots of people refuse what God has to offer without honestly or thoroughly investigating the evidence first. But if you don't have enough information, it isn't very prudent to reject what you don't know.

Some say they can't have faith, even though they want to. But the question is *whom* you believe, not *whether* you believe. Everyone has the capacity to believe. 'God has allotted to each a measure of faith.'[159] If God gave the capacity for belief only to some, then he couldn't expect all people to believe and be saved by faith.

If we all have the ability to believe, then we have to ask: How do I use it? Who do I trust? It isn't so much about belief in *something* as it is about believing in *somebody*. Biblical faith is always connected with a person. And the quality of faith doesn't depend on *how much* I believe, but on *how trustworthy* is the person in whom I believe.

In other words, the object of faith determines the outcome of faith. If I choose to trust an unworthy person, my faith will be disappointed. The object of faith determines the *quality* of faith, not its *quantity*. The Bible says God is 100% trustworthy. But we each have to discover that through our own journey of experience.

b) Faith is a relationship based on knowledge

'Faith is the substance of things hoped for, the evidence of things not seen.'[160] This famous definition, straight from the Bible, can easily be misleading.

Look at two words here: 'substance' in Greek is *hypostasis*. It literally means *that which stands under*.

When twentieth-century archaeologists excavated in Egypt, they found ancient written documents. Many of these documents were records of business transactions, of properties being bought and sold. The headings of these title deeds read *Hypostasis*.

Scholars understood that faith is a covenant, an agreement or business deal between God and us. But first we must come to trust him. When that happens, God has many things he wants to do with us. He wants to have an agreement (covenant) or understanding with us.

The second word 'evidence' (Greek: *elengkos*) often refers to the work of the Holy Spirit. It means to *convince* or *conviction*.

So if I have an experience with God, if I learn to trust him, then I become willing to hope even for things which I do not see now. Then I can be convinced that, one day, I'm going to receive the things promised and see them with my very own eyes. The Bible calls this day-by-day working relationship of trust between us and God *faith*.

God did various things in order to reveal himself to us, to introduce himself so that we might know him.[161] From Hosea 6:6-7 we learn that to love (*chesed* means 'covenant love') God means to know him and to know him means to love him. In biblical understanding, 'to know' someone means to have a close, intimate relationship of love, trust and friendship.[162]

c) Faith is saying 'Yes' to God

How do you develop intimate friendship, love and trust? We have already said that God gave each one of us some kind of 'starting faith'. Now it is up to us to develop it further.

What is God like? God reveals himself so we can learn to trust him. Where does that faith or trust come from? God connects to us through the Bible and Jesus.

'So faith comes from what is heard, and what is heard comes by the preaching of Christ'[163] or 'the Word of God'.[164] Centuries ago, people couldn't afford individual copies of the Bible, so they would listen while someone else read to them.

> Faith is a word the Bible uses to describe a relationship with God as a person.

The Bible's primary purpose is to reveal the truth about God. The most important thing for us is to learn how God treated people in different life situations. (Not so much what they did or how they reacted, because sometimes they acted wrongly.) From this we reframe our understanding of God and make our own decision about trusting him.

That's how the 'starting faith' that God gave everyone changes into 'saving faith'. If we don't know God as he is revealed to us in the Bible, then our relationship with him will be more superstition than faith. 'The point is: Before you trust, you have to listen. But unless Christ's Word is preached, there's nothing to listen to.'[165]

The Word of God plays an irreplaceable role in the process of building our faith. It will be necessary to make some effort to come to a proper understanding of God and his relationship towards us. Some parts of the Bible can be misunderstood. We are challenged to work earnestly for 'the faith that was given the holy people of God once and for all time.'[166]

This dynamic needs to be kept in balance. If I have saving faith, I don't have any merit in it, because faith is God's gift. On the other hand, if I don't have saving faith I'm responsible for it, because I didn't seek to increase my faith by reading and trying to understand God's Word with the initial faith that I received from him.

Faith is a word the Bible uses to describe a relationship with God as a person. The better we know him, the better the friendship gets. This relationship is based on what we learn about him from the Bible, and we need to understand it properly if the relationship is going to deepen and grow.

d) Faith is the solution to the fundamental problem of our universe

We could ask, 'If God desires all people to be saved, why doesn't he give saving faith to everyone?'

But trust, love and friendship cannot be commanded. It just doesn't work that way. So why are trust and love so critically important? God is asking us to really know him, to love him, to trust him and admire him.

The Bible tells a story about a breach of trust in the universe. Long ago, a rebellion against God started in heaven, and we're still caught in the aftermath. The Bible tells us that one of God's created beings, Lucifer, masterminded this rebellion and accused God of being a cruel, unloving, arbitrary tyrant who used his power to demand conformity.[167] Satan (a Hebrew word for the *enemy*) knew only too well that he could not succeed by using a direct attack against God. So he used lies, twisted the facts and manipulated evidence. He succeeded in breaking down the relationship of trust even in God's children. And it started a war in heaven.[168]

Sin, as Christians call this problem, is a breakdown of our trust in and love and admiration for God.

The only way to solve the sin problem is to re-establish trust and trustworthiness. God knows there is no point in denying Satan's charges. So he started a long process of self-revelation and explanation in order to prove over a long period of time that he is not what Satan would have us believe. The Bible tells us that when Jesus died on the cross the confidence and loyalty of heavenly beings was established for the rest of eternity.[169] Only here, on our planet, are people still continuing to rebel against God.

God gives us plenty of time to find out what he is like. He knows that if we get to know him, we'll love him. That's why faith is so important. Faith won't save us, only God saves – but he can only save those who trust him.

All God asks for is faith from us. Nothing more, nothing less. That means we need to define and understand the concept of faith properly.

You can have an attitude towards God of love, trust and deepest admiration if you get to know him. Faith in God makes people willing to believe what he says, accept what he offers and to do without reservation whatever he wishes us to do. Anyone with such faith will be saved, because God will save all who trust him. It's why faith is the only requirement for heaven.

re: consider

What would make you trust God more?

REFERENCES

156. Mark 11:22.
157. James 2:19.
158. Luke 13:25-27.
159. Romans 12:3, NASB.
160. Hebrews 11:1, NKJV.
161. John 17:3.
162. Genesis 4:1; Matthew 7:23.
163. Romans 10:17, RSV.
164. Ibid, KJV.
165. Romans 10:17, MGE.
166. Jude 3, NCV.
167. Ezekiel 28:13-17; Isaiah 14:12-15.
168. Revelation 12:7.
169. John 12:31-32; Revelation 12:7-11.

9. JUST FAITH

God, how can I know my relationship with you is good? It's one thing to hear that you love me, but it's quite another thing to put that knowledge into practice in my life. Please show me how to live by faith.

re: tell

A speaker once shared an experience about a family trip to Europe with his wife and 3-year-old daughter. At one point they had to drive three days, day and night, to get to Germany. The little girl had never travelled at night before. She was scared the first night in the car.

'Where are we going, Daddy?'

'To your uncle's house in Germany.'

'Have you been to his house before?'

'No.'

'Then do you know the way?'

'Maybe we can read the map.'

Short pause. 'Do you know how to read the map?'

'Yes, we will get there safely.' Another pause. 'Where are we going to eat if we get hungry?' 'We can stop at a restaurant.' 'Do you know if there are restaurants on the way?' 'Yes, there are.' 'Do you know where?' 'No, but we'll be able to find some.' The same dialogue was repeated a few times the first night and also the second night. On the third night, the little girl was quiet. When he looked in the mirror, he saw that she was awake and just looking around calmly. He wondered why she was not asking the questions anymore.

'Dear, do you know where we are going?'

'Germany, to Uncle's house.'

'Do you know how we're getting there?'

'No.'

'Then why aren't you asking anymore?'

'Because Daddy's driving.'

re: think

When asked, 'Are you saved?' some Christians will immediately and spontaneously answer, 'Yes, I am saved.' Many refer to themselves without any hesitation as 'born-again Christians'.

But many others don't like this direct question. It feels too presumptuous to them. How can they be sure they are going to be saved? How do they know they are good enough?

Personally, it took me some time before I came to the point where I dared to say: 'I am saved.' I'm far from perfect, but my Bible tells me that I am accepted by God, as long as I have faith.

Being a Christian and being sure of salvation is not primarily about having certain views and opinions on certain issues. The Bible states that what we believe is a matter of life and death – that is: a matter of *eternal* life and *eternal* death. Embarking on the path of faith means 'crossing' from death to life.[170] Salvation is a serious business. The apostle Paul admonished the members of the church in the city of Philippi (as everywhere) to 'work out [their] salvation with fear and trembling'.[171] That's pretty graphic terminology, don't you think?

The idea of 'salvation' or its equivalent is also a serious business in non-Christian belief systems. It usually demands a lot of hard work and sacrifice – maybe even a life-long process of intense prayer and meditation.

- The orthodox Buddhist follows the eight-fold path – a way of life consisting of eight steps in which he disciplines himself till all earthly desires are eliminated. Great self-control and many lifetimes are required to reach 'perfection'.

- The strict Jew observes a long list of prescribed practices in all domains of life in order to become 'acceptable to God'.

- Islam points to five pillars. Any believer in Allah and follower of the prophet who hopes to arrive in paradise must carefully observe the 'pillars' of his faith, such as the five daily prayers, giving of alms and at least one trip to the holy sites in Mecca.

Non-Christian world religions all seem to offer a system of *salvation* through *human works*. So is Christianity different?

Christianity's core teaching is summarised by the apostle Paul: 'We are made right with God by *placing our faith* in Jesus Christ. . . . For everyone has sinned; we all fall short of God's glorious standard. Yet God, with undeserved kindness, declares that we are righteous. He did this through Christ Jesus when he freed us from the penalty for our sins.'[172]

faith or (also) works?

If this is true, why do so many Christians frantically attempt to earn their salvation? Ever heard of Simeon Stylites? Prior to his death in AD459, he spent thirty-six years on the top of a 20-metre pillar, preaching to the passers-by. Granted, he was an extreme example. But it doesn't take long for anyone who studies Christian history to find lots of people who spent their entire lives in acts of mortification,[173] often in total isolation.

There have always been Christians who believed that a rigid regime of spiritual discipline would earn them brownie points with God. Roman Catholicism traditionally stressed the value of good works as a necessary condition to salvation, and many Protestants who *say* they believe in salvation though grace have often also focused on strict observance of rites and rituals. The way they practise their faith suggests that their eternal destiny depends on strict obedience to the commandments of God and careful adherence to church rules. So this can get confusing.

Salvation by faith alone was a core doctrine of the Protestant reformers. Formulated by Martin Luther, it is a controlling doctrine in that all other teachings stand or fall by it. Do the following words of Paul leave you in any doubt? 'God saved you by his grace when you believed. And you can't take credit for this; it is a gift from God. Salvation is not a reward for the good things we have done, so none of us can boast about it.'[174] Paul also said, 'Therefore, since we have been made right in God's sight by faith, we have peace with God because of what Jesus Christ our Lord has done for us.'[175]

So, if these statements are so clear, why do Christians disagree so much over faith versus works? Why do so many Christians agree verbally that they are saved by faith alone, but practise something else? One reason: there are other texts in the Bible which seem to suggest the opposite about salvation.

Directly after asserting that people who make it to heaven will get there by their faith and not because their good works have earned them entrance, the apostle Paul in his letter to the Ephesians states: 'For we are God's masterpiece. He has created us anew in Christ Jesus, so we can do the good things he planned for us long ago.'[176]

> Real faith gives direction to what we do and leads us to make conscious choices.

The apostle James says: 'What good is it, dear brothers and sisters, if you say you have faith but don't show it by your actions? Can that kind of faith save anyone?'[177] A few lines later James asserts that if someone claims to have 'saving' faith, he (James) will show his faith 'by my good deeds.'[178]

what kind of faith?

What do we make of this contradiction? Is this a case of totally opposing viewpoints? No, not really. The contradiction is only *apparent*. James doesn't claim that he is actually *saved* by what he does, in his own power, through his good works. He only stresses that genuine faith isn't a hidden secret but will manifest itself visibly in our lives.

Real faith gives direction to what we do and leads us to make conscious choices. 'Works' aren't *the condition* of our salvation, but they are *the results* of having been saved. This gets clearer when we look back at Ephesians 2. If we keep reading, Paul says we can't claim any personal credit for the 'good works' that we are 'created . . . to do' (NIV). Ultimately, it isn't what *we* may be able to do through our own willpower and perseverance. Another text underlines this even better: 'For God is working in you, giving you the desire and the power to do what pleases him.'[179]

So it all depends on what God does for us, not on what we try to do for him in return. Of course, God expects us to show our gratitude by our loyalty and adherence to the guidelines he has provided for a happy and satisfactory life. But if we had to depend on what we ourselves could do, we'd never be able to make the minimum requirements. Our good works would never cancel out our fundamental sinfulness and our constant failure to come even close to a state of perfection.

> Love is powerful enough to change even the way we act.

When all is said and done, the basis of our religion is summed up in one wellknown Bible passage: 'For God loved the world so much that he gave his one and only Son, so that everyone who believes in him will not perish but have eternal life.'[180]

Yet something still needs to be added: we must be sure we have the right understanding of what these words 'believe' and 'faith' mean. Some define 'faith' primarily in intellectual terms – to have faith, they say, means to believe in the existence of God. Of course, we must get to the place where we accept the existence of a Creator-God. Anyone who comes to God 'must believe that God exists'.[181] But that is not enough. Even the devil believes that God exists, but that doesn't save him.[182] Faith is more than mere intellectual assent. The kind of faith that brings salvation is *trusting* faith, and 'trusting the LORD means safety'.[183]

Faith isn't based on scientific evidence that we can verify with our senses. The faith that God wants us to have is different. It is 'being sure' – deep down – of 'what we hope for' and being 'certain of what we do not see'.[184] It is a relationship, a surrender, a commitment, an inner attachment to the God who is eager to save us.

This trusting faith relationship is an *active* faith. It comes as a free gift from the one who created us and wants to see us fulfilled and happy in this life and to have us near him for all eternity.

The ultimate difference depends on whether we *live* our faith in such a way that people recognise something of Jesus' character in us.

Yes, we are saved through faith, but it is a faith that expresses itself through love.[185] And love is powerful enough to change even the way we act.

re: consider

How do you see faith and action fitting together in your own life journey?

REFERENCES

170. John 5:24, NIV.
171. Philippians 2:12, NIV.
172. Romans 3:22-24 (italics supplied).
173. mor·ti·fi·ca·tion [mawr-tuh-fi-key-shuhn] – noun
1. a feeling of humiliation or shame, as through some injury to one's pride or self-respect.
2. a cause or source of such humiliation or shame.
3. the practice of asceticism by penitential discipline to overcome desire for sin and to strengthen the will. See: *http://dictionary.reference.com/browse/mortification*
174. Ephesians 2:8-9.
175. Romans 5:1.
176. Ephesians 2:10.
177. James 2:14.
178. Ibid, 2:18.
179. Philippians 2:13.
180. John 3:16.
181. Hebrews 11:6.
182. James 2:19.
183. Proverbs 29:25.
184. Hebrews 11:1, NIV.
185. Galatians 5:6.

10. STARTING OVER

God, so many times I've heard people talking about 'repentance' and being 'born again', but I really don't understand what it means. What am I supposed to 'repent' of? What does it mean to be born again? I hope you'll answer my questions as we sit and spend this time together.

re: tell

In our home it was natural to fear our father. Even mother was afraid of him. As children, my sister and I thought every family was like us, with an unpredictable alcoholic who was impossible to please and a praying Mama to protect the children. We thought God planned it that way.

We were good children; Mama always told us so. Partly because we dared not do anything. We were quiet, timid children who rarely spoke, especially when Daddy was home.

Then one day we found something new and fun. We knew it wouldn't upset anyone. Our house had a wooden door, and we discovered we could draw chalk pictures that would rub right off.

We set to work drawing and making lots of pretty pictures all over it. We were proud of our work and knew Mama would just love it. All her friends would come and maybe they would want us to do their doors, too!

But the expected praise did not come. Instead of the beauty in our work, all Mama saw was the time and effort it would take to clean. She was mad. We didn't understand but we knew all about anger! Off we ran to find a place to hide.

In our woods it wasn't hard for two small children to huddle behind a tree unseen. Soon we heard frightened voices calling out to us but still we didn't budge.

The sun set and it grew dark. The searchers became more anxious, but the longer we hid, the harder it was to come out. By now Mama had called the police.

As we clung together in the dark, we recognised another voice with horror – our Daddy. But he sounded strangely different. Fear, agony, despair – then came a prayer; tears and prayer mingled together.

Was that our Daddy on his knees? Our Daddy – promising God his life if he would safely return his girls?

We were drawn to him like a magnet. We don't remember actually walking to him. But we remember those arms holding us, as though we were precious. After that, we had a new Daddy. God had replaced him with someone who loved us.

Mama always said that God was a God of miracles, and I guess she was right. He changed our whole family with a piece of chalk.[186]

re: think

con·ver·sion [kuh n-vur-zhuhn] – noun

The term conversion implies a radical transformation of personal attitudes, emotions, values and behaviour. In this process a person's viewpoint changes from one of indifference, disbelief or antagonism to one of acceptance, faith or enthusiastic support.[187]

I cannot tell you exactly when I experienced conversion. Now Martin Luther could name the place, the date and the precise hour when he was converted. John Wesley, the founder of Methodism, also knew when his conversion had taken place.

Many Christians can pinpoint exactly this crucial event in their lives. But does the fact that I didn't have the same kind of experience mean that I am not converted? Let's look at what conversion is and what it does for us.

It's always a challenge adequately to express supernatural truth in human language. At best, our words only superficially capture what God does in us. Fortunately, metaphors help us point to certain aspects and complete the picture, especially when we talk about the beginning of the Christian life.

'Repentance', 'conversion' and 'new birth' are frequently used terms. These words suggest that there is both a divine and a human element involved when someone becomes a Christian. Repentance and conversion point to a change in ourselves, connected with our own free will. There is a decision we can make freely, a direction that we can decide to choose.

> The term conversion implies a radical transformation of personal attitudes, emotions, values and behaviour.

But at the same time, this new beginning doesn't result from our own initiative; it comes from outside of us. It happens to us if we open ourselves up to the Force that brings new life in the fullest sense.

a new direction

*re·pent*1 [ri-pent] – verb (used without object)

1. to feel sorry, self-reproachful or contrite for past conduct; regret or be conscience-stricken about a past action, attitude, etc. (often fol. by of): He repented after his thoughtless act.

2. to feel such sorrow for sin or fault as to be disposed to change one's life for the better; be penitent.

– verb (used with object)

3. to remember or regard with self-reproach or contrition: to repent one's injustice to another.

4. to feel sorry for; regret: to repent an imprudent act.

Let's look first at what it means to *repent* and to be *converted*. In today's vocabulary these are pretty unpopular concepts. If people talk about them at all, they tend to downgrade them to the realm of likes and dislikes or an external change. Some say, 'I've done nothing in my life that I need to feel sorry about!'

But we can't understand the full import of repentance and conversion unless we've adequately grasped what sin really is and how it isolates us from God, until we accept his offer to take us to a new level of life. When we begin to understand the seriousness of sin and realise its destructiveness, we begin to see the dilemma; we suddenly want to repent and get away from where we are.

This repentance isn't a superficial sense of misgiving or shallow feeling of regret. It's more than admitting that maybe we should have tried a bit harder in our efforts to overcome a few unfortunate tendencies.

The apostle Paul refers to a much deeper kind of repentance when he coined the term 'godly sorrow'. This serious, heart-felt realisation that we'll lose everything if we don't turn our lives around and make a new start is the only kind of sorrow that does any good and it 'leads to salvation'.[188]

'Godly sorrow' is seeing the truth about ourselves and realising that we are like the believers in Ephesus. Paul wrote to them (and us): 'Once you were dead because of your disobedience and your many sins. You used to live in sin, just like the rest of the world.'[189] This is pretty strong language, but then sin is pretty strong stuff. No wonder some of the words in the original Hebrew and Greek language, when translated into English as 'to repent', have the connotation of *to pant, to sigh, to groan* and *to have remorse*. This kind of godly repentance encompasses our entire being. It is the absolute prerequisite for forgiveness for our sins.

One Greek word translated as 'repentance' *(metanoia)* has a different nuance. It points to a change of mind and purpose. It indicates, as one Bible scholar once so aptly expressed it, to 'a pilgrimage from the "mind of the flesh" to the "mind of Christ"'.[190] Here is a subtlety of the Greek language that provides us with valuable insight. The change we experience results in a new 'heart'– a totally new approach to life and a fresh orientation in values and ideals – a 'renewing of [our] mind'.[191]

extreme makeover

When you embark on a life journey with Christ, you are a 'new person'.[192] But how is that apparent? It's a total life makeover, starting with the core of our being and moving outwards to affect the way we look, act, speak and dress. It imports a heavenly quality of life into our existence.

'New' can sometimes mean 'consecutive' or 'next' – as when one episode is followed by a new episode. The Greek word for this 'new' is *neos*. But when these writers spoke of the 'new' person who is 'in Christ', they chose the word *kainos*, which stresses total intrinsic newness – a newness in quality. This is 'a spiritual renewal' of our 'thoughts and attitudes'.[193]

People who have received this newness no longer live as they did before. They 'no longer live for themselves. Instead, they will live for Christ'.[194] They display a 'new nature', because they have become new creatures, 'created to be like God – truly righteous and holy'.[195]

This newness doesn't come from anything we can contribute. 'All this [newness of life] is a gift from God.'[196] New life comes from outside ourselves, from a superhuman source. It is life with the imprint of divine power. It is the abundant life that Christ came to offer in all its fullness.[197]

What more fitting metaphor could refer to this new start in life than the *new birth*? Jesus introduced the term when he spoke with Nicodemus, a powerful Jewish religious leader. Nicodemus acknowledged Jesus' divine credentials, but his mind, theologically astute as it may have been, didn't comprehend the good news which Jesus came to share. Jesus startled him with a statement that has been repeated millions of times: 'Unless you are born again, you cannot see the Kingdom of God.'[198]

Seeing how Nicodemus failed to grasp this profound statement, Jesus tried to fill in the blanks. He added,

' "I assure you, no one can enter the Kingdom of God without being born of water and the Spirit. Humans can reproduce only human life, but the Holy Spirit gives birth to spiritual life. So don't be surprised when I say, 'You must be born again.' The wind blows wherever it wants. Just as you can hear the wind but can't tell where it comes from or where it is going, so you can't explain how people are born of the Spirit." '[199]

allow for the supernatural

The Holy Spirit is like the wind, totally beyond our comprehension and control. It breathes into our life from another world. Through the Spirit we no longer live as we did before, we can now live a 'new' life that fills any previous void in our soul.

This new birth in many ways resembles our natural birth. We receive life from beyond ourselves and we need constant nurture in order to grow. It's a striking metaphor, but there's a significant difference. People often say, 'I never asked to be born into this world!' However, when it comes to this spiritual new birth, it only happens if we ask for it.

The gospel of John tells us that this birth is about water and Spirit. Water refers to the rite of baptism by immersion, a demonstration of faith when we repent, turn around and experience a new life in Christ. (See chapter 38 for more about baptism.)

But we can't forget the Spirit aspect of the new birth, because the change that takes place in us is never complete. While it is essential that we turn away from our sinful habits with 'godly sorrow' when we begin a new orientation in life, this is only just the start. There is always the risk of 'infant death' or 'life-threatening circumstances' along the way. A newborn needs the right kind of pastoral care and spiritual food to grow.

'The Lord – who is the Spirit – makes us more and more like him as we are changed into his glorious image.'[200] Notice the last phrase in particular. God is the life-giver. He creates new life. He nurtures growth. He guarantees a perfect outcome.

When we look back on the new life that we received when we turned towards him, we will gratefully say: 'It was God [not I] who made it grow!'[201]

re: consider

When you accept the new life that Jesus offers, what do you hope will change?

REFERENCES

186. Holly Smeltzer, Nova Scotia, Canada. Edited. *www.sermonillustrator.org/illustrator/ sermon3b/piece_of_chalk.htm*. 10 April 2006.

187. For a more detailed presentation of the biblical usage of this rich concept, see Orr, James, M.A., D.D. General Editor. 'Definition for 'CONVERSION'. 'International Standard Bible Encyclopaedia'. *www.Bible-history.com* - ISBE; 1915.

188. 2 Corinthians 7:8-11, NIV.

189. Ephesians 2:1, 2.

190. Chamberlain, William D. *The Meaning of Repentance*. Westminster P, 1943, p. 47.

191. Romans 12:2, KJV.

192. 2 Corinthians 5:17.

193. Ephesians 4:23.

194. 2 Corinthians 5:15.

195. Ephesians 4:24.

196. 2 Corinthians 5:18.

197. John 10:10, NIV.

198. John 3:3.

199. John 3:5-8.

200. 2 Corinthians 3:18.

201. 1 Corinthians 3:6.

11. RECONCILIATION

God, I've learned about sin and I've learned about your love which made you send Jesus to Earth to rescue mankind. But there's got to be more to the story. I want to have a deeper look. I want to understand why Jesus would have to die just because somebody ate some fruit, and how his death really means freedom for me.

re: tell

In his book *Written In Blood,* Robert Coleman tells the story of a little boy whose sister needed a blood transfusion. The doctor explained that she had the same disease the boy had recovered from two years earlier. Her only chance for recovery was a transfusion from someone who had previously conquered the disease. Since the two children had the same rare blood type, the boy was the ideal donor.

'Would you give your blood to Mary?' the doctor asked. Johnny hesitated. His lower lip started to tremble. Then he smiled and said, 'Sure, for my sister.' Soon the two children were wheeled into the hospital room – Mary, pale and thin; Johnny, robust and healthy. Neither spoke, but when their eyes met, Johnny grinned. As the nurse inserted the needle into his arm, Johnny's smile faded. He watched the blood flow through the tube. With the ordeal almost over, his voice, slightly shaky, broke the silence. 'Doctor, when do I die?'[202]

re: think

In our world we see evil, pain and death and we ask if this is how things were meant to be. In almost every culture, concepts of heaven, a golden age and paradise suggest that we are programmed to long for something more than the defective existence we experience here. C. S. Lewis wrote in his book *Mere Christianity*: 'If I find in myself a desire which no experience in this world can satisfy, the most probable explanation is that I was made for another world.'

The very existence of ideas about good and evil, right and wrong, point to origins outside of this world and this life. Where do such ideas come from?

'My argument against God was that the universe seemed so cruel and unjust. But how had I got this idea of just and unjust? A man does not call a line crooked unless he has some idea of a straight line. What was I comparing this universe with when I called it unjust? . . . Consequently atheism turns out to be too simple. If the whole universe has no meaning we should never have found out that it has no meaning: just as, if there were no light in the universe and therefore no creature with eyes, we should never know it was dark. Dark would be without meaning.' (C. S. Lewis.)

We live in a world that is messed up. We recognise the wrong in ourselves, whether we call it evil or sin or dysfunction. If we're all alone in this crazy world, there's not much else to do but cry.

But if there truly is a God, then what? This is the vital issue behind the idea of coming back to God, to being 'at one' with him once more. The question is how?

First we've got to work out what went wrong. Some people understand the story of mankind's first sin, in Genesis 3, to mean that Adam and Eve broke an arbitrary law and so were punished by God and expelled from his presence. This very legal perspective makes the solution legal, too – that God in some way should fix our legal position so we can come back to him. But a closer reading of the story reveals much more than disobedience to a law. It's a total crisis of distrust and the massive breaking of an intimate relationship.

The serpent insinuates that God cannot be trusted, that God is a liar, that God is preventing freedom and self-development and individuality. The issue is about whom to believe – God or the snake.

The damage done to the human-divine relationship becomes apparent when God goes looking for the pair in the garden. They hide from him, admitting they are now afraid of him. This is the tragic result of misplaced trust and the deliberate rejection of truth.

the sin problem

A movie poster advertised one of Sylvester Stallone's films, *Cobra*. The slogan read: *Crime is a disease. Meet the cure.* Perhaps we could use that slogan, slightly altered: *Sin is a disease. Meet Jesus – the cure.*

What is sin? One definition says, 'Sin is lawlessness'.[203] What does that word make you think of? Lawless? Westerns? Outlaws? Frontier towns? Bandits?

Why were they lawless? Because they chose to go out and break the law? Or because of their inner attitude?

Lawlessness speaks of a mental attitude, a way of thinking and living that is out of harmony with the standard of conduct that the law expresses. A Bible definition can help us here: 'Everything that does not come from faith is sin.'[204] What is faith?

Faith is trusting God, having confidence in him. So what is the opposite of faith? Distrust or not having confidence in God. Our definition may come out something like this: *sin is not trusting God.*

Sin is that antagonistic attitude, that spirit of rebellion that separates us from God – and any actions or choices that re-

> The very existence of ideas about good and evil, right and wrong, point to origins outside of this world and this life.

sult from that attitude. We've gone away from God, built a barricade and like spoilt children we refuse to come back to the only One who can really help us. So God broke through our barricade and came to us to ask us to let him take us home again.

A true understanding of God's solution starts with recognising what went wrong. Was it disobedience to an arbitrary requirement, the rupturing of relationship, a refusal to trust in the trustworthy God? Our answers depend on our concept of God and our view of his requirements.

The problem of fallen humanity isn't so much a question of legal difficulties with God, but rather our attitude of suspicion and distrust towards God. Reconciliation between man and God is the only way to change the situation.

at-one-ment

Atonement really means at-one-ment; the idea of being at *one,* in harmony. It's a made-up word, formed by joining 'at' and 'one' together, as the rather free Bible translators of the sixteenth century were fond of doing. It means to *reconcile* and keeps the old pronunciation of *one,* just like in *alone* (all-one) and *only* (one-ly).

The understanding of the word *atonement* has changed as a result of the word being used as a description of systems in which salvation is defined as a kind of legal adjustment of the sinner's standing before God. It involves some transaction that is carried out between Christ and God in which compensation is effected, punishment cancelled and anger silenced.

Today we use it most commonly in this new sense – we atone for wrongdoing by trying to provide compensation or payment. *But the word did not originally have this meaning.*

Originally, during the time of the ancient Israelites, *atonement* focused on a ceremonial sacrificial system to explain the process of restoring harmony.

But soon the Israelites completely misunderstood the process. Again and again God objected to their 'meaningless gifts',[205] because the worshippers had grown to believe that they were set right merely by fulfilling rituals. Through human prophets God rejected this kind of mechanical worship, pleading for more understanding and true rela-tionship. Even though God had given the system of ceremonial sacri-fices, he said that he had no pleasure in the blood of bulls and goats.[206] God wanted far more than sacrifice – he craved relationship, under-standing, recognition of meaning, true worship, considered thought.

Atonement – it's a beautiful word in need of rescue. It describes what Christ came to achieve – the one-ness of Creation, the reuniting of humanity with God. Then we can experience the joy of rediscovering the wonderful graciousness of our loving Father.

It is a celebration of being made right with God by his transforming power, through Jesus on the cross. We are made one with God by God himself, not through legal manoeuvrings. Our need is not primarily to be forgiven (although that is also important) but for our relationship with God to be changed – from rebellious enemies into trustworthy friends. That is the goal of the *at-one-ment*.

This is the emphasis of the gospel: bringing back harmony, agree-ment and oneness with God by God through a restored relationship. Such a view is inherently non-legal, since friendship isn't based on the observation of rules and requirements. Love cannot be required, only pleaded for.

Through the life and death of Jesus, God is revealed as he truly is, giving us an opportunity for trusting admiration and reconciliation. Harmony isn't restored by due process of law but through agreement with God. This is the answer to the devil's division and separation, hos-tility and deception.

When we are 'at one' with God, we no longer live in lawlessness (since sin has more to do with an attitude towards God than the ac-tual breaking of laws), but in harmony with his will and ways. In other words, the transformation of our attitude towards God brings with it a transformation of our actions and choices.

the cross

Satan insists that God is an autocratic tyrant who demands sacrifice and self-denial from his created beings, but Jesus' death on the cross negates that charge, because it proves that God was willing to make the sacrifice instead of demanding it from us. This is the reality of the atonement – opening the way back to God through Jesus' death so that we might love and trust him once again.

The crucifixion both attracts and repels. Recognising the wonderful love of God, we are drawn to the cross but, in its harsh reality, its cruel suffering, it rightly repels us. Here we see the results of sin and how far God will go, not just for our salvation, but to restore harmony throughout the universe. Here we see God as he really is.

Jesus' heart-rending cry from the cross, 'My God, my God, why have you forsaken me?' (Matthew 27:46, NIV) demonstrates the natural consequence of sin: fatal separation from God and bitter loss.

When just before he died Jesus said, 'It is finished' (John 19:30), he was telling the world that the work he had come to do – to reveal the Father's character – was now complete. Not simply the completion of some ritual sacrifice, but giving conclusive proof of who God is.

reconciliation

This is the reconciliation which God makes to bring us back to oneness with him:

'All this is from God, who reconciled us to himself through Christ and gave us the ministry of reconciliation.' (2 Corinthians 5:18, NIV.)

'Together as one body, Christ reconciled both groups to God by means of his death on the cross, and our hostility toward each other was put to death.' (Ephesians 2:16.)

'And through him to reconcile to himself all things, whether things on earth or things in heaven, by making peace through his blood, shed on the cross.' (Colossians 1:20, NIV.)

'For if, when we were enemies, we were reconciled to God by the death of his Son, much more, being reconciled, we shall be saved by his life. And not only so, but we also joy in God through our Lord Jesus Christ, by whom we have now received the atonement.' (Romans 5:10, 11, KJV.)

Receiving the atonement – by being reconciled to God as trusting friends instead of rebellious enemies. What is required for this true *at-one-ment* with God? Healing and change.

'I pray that they will all be one, just as you and I are one – as you are in me, Father, and I am in you.'[207] This is the at-one-ment. The ancient scripture promises that eventually all those who choose repentance will be united with God – one with him.[208]

re: consider

Do you want reconciliation with Jesus? What are some tangible evidences of your new at-one-ment with God?

REFERENCES

202. Thomas Lindberg. *www.sermonillustrations.com/a-z/a/atonement.htm*. 11 April 2006.
203. 1 John 3:4, NIV.
204. Romans 14:23, NIV.
205. Isaiah 1:13.
206. Isaiah 1:11.
207. John 17:21.
208. See Revelation 21:3.

ABOUT
HOPE

12. WHO'S IN CHARGE?

God, the Bible – your Word – can be exciting but it's also unnerving, because it's weird to think that I can and will meet an invisible God face to face. But I want to focus on the excitement of meeting my Creator and the wonder that you, the God of the universe, are making plans to visit Earth again.

re: tell

'Excuse me sir, could you please tell me how to ride the bus?' I asked a nicely dressed businessman on Fifth Avenue in New York.

'I've been standing here but they don't seem to stop for me,' I continued. 'I don't know if I'm supposed to use money or a pass or where to catch it or where to stand. . . .' My voice trailed off. With a bemused look, he kindly offered to help me by accepting my fare and using his pass to get me on the bus. It turned out we were going the same way.

The ride should have taken five minutes, but turned into thirty because of terrible traffic. So we were forced to get acquainted. He seemed fascinated by stories of my upbringing in Africa and my job, teaching art lessons to people who can't even draw a straight line.

As we got off and walked towards the Met together, he said, 'You've led a fascinating life. We write stories about people like you in my magazine.'

'Which magazine is that?'

'*People* magazine,' he replied.

I was blown away. For over ten years I'd dreamt of being written about in *People*. I knew that first I'd have to write my books and get my videos out. I had hired a publicity agent, but it's incredibly difficult to access the right people. Here was *People's* senior writer, asking for my card.

If that wasn't surprising enough, I was actually supposed to be on a plane to California. That morning I had impulsively decided to take a later flight and catch one more museum.

On this four-day business trip, I hadn't really taken time to pray and read my Bible. I was so busy doing business that I hadn't made time. But this morning I'd read a story in a magazine called *Guideposts* about a man who lost his wedding ring in a rubbish bin. He travelled to the tip to search and after scouring through bags for hours he remembered that he hadn't asked God for help. He knelt down in the rubbish heap and prayed. When he looked up, there was his ring, glistening in the sun.

I got the message. I had been doing my business without checking in with God. So I knelt down and asked God to lead me, bless my day and direct me whether to take the scheduled flight or linger in New York.

That day, he placed me on the right street corner, with buses refusing to stop, and directed me to the senior writer for *People* magazine. Then he prolonged our ride so we could chat. Since I didn't know who the man was, I was relaxed and acted naturally. And if that wasn't enough, he asked for my card, not the other way round. Wow!

I just love it when God makes it so obvious that he's in charge.[209]

re: think

At some time or another, perhaps on Monday mornings, every one of us has asked, 'What's the point of it all?' Is there anything beyond the daily grind of getting out of bed, grabbing breakfast, going to work, coming home and getting back into bed?

The Bible deals with this – when people start to read the Bible, they are often surprised by its richness and variety. It is anything but boring. We can find stories, parables, proverbs, songs, genealogies, lyrical poetry, oracles and we can also find apocalyptic prophecies. Perhaps more than any other part of the Bible, these apocalyptic passages address those Monday-morning blues.

What is 'apocalyptic' exactly? Apocalyptic language, which is highly symbolic, presents stunning visual images of bizarre animals with multiple heads or horns and it talks about time periods in intriguing ways, because ordinary language just isn't adequate for important issues.

But what does 'apocalyptic' mean in general terms? First, that this world contains both good and evil. This might not seem a great insight – most people at your bus stop would be willing to accept as much. But an apocalyptic approach says: 'Listen to the latest news bulletin and you could easily think that evil is stronger than good. But in reality good is stronger than evil, because things aren't what they seem to be and, despite appearances, God is actually in charge.'

Secondly, an apocalyptic approach says that history isn't a meaningless cycle of accidents and coincidences – a long string of Monday mornings. History had a meaningful beginning and will have a meaningful end. History is a journey of discovery with a definite destination, because God is in charge.

Is there anything beyond the daily grind of getting out of bed, grabbing breakfast, going to work, coming home?

Thirdly, an apocalyptic approach puts good and evil together on the one hand, with our journey through history on the other. At this point in history we are living under the influence of evil and it really does have the upper hand – for now. But things aren't what they seem to be. This present state of affairs won't last forever. God will act decisively, once and for all, and good will reign supreme again, because God is in charge.

Now that sounds good, perhaps too good to be true, and on one of those bad Monday mornings, as we listen to the news headlines, we might feel like saying, 'Well, it doesn't seem that way to me!' The apocalyptic perspective replies, 'Well, of course not, because things aren't what they *seem* to be'.

With that in mind, let's turn in our Bibles to the ancient book of Daniel. Daniel was a young man living in Jerusalem about 600 years before Christ. King Nebuchadnezzar of Babylon, the current world superpower, defeated Jerusalem and took Daniel and some other Israelites as prisoners of war. They were marched to Babylon and educated for careers in the Babylonian civil service. They were cut off from their culture, language and religion – everything that made their life understandable and worth living. It's in this setting that we find some of the most memorable apocalyptic prophecies in the Bible.

One night, King Nebuchadnezzar had a dream which made a profound impression upon him. Like many ancient monarchs, he employed a full staff of dream interpreters, but this time the king couldn't remember his dream, so his interpreters were clueless! Usually they would listen to the dream, look up the symbols in their dream manuals and then provide the 'official' interpretation. The king was so angry at their incompetence that he ordered their mass execution! Daniel, however, saved them all by praying for guidance and asking God to reveal the dream and its interpretation to him.

In his dream the king had seen a large metal image. It had a head of gold, chest of silver, belly and thighs of bronze, legs of iron, and feet of iron mixed with clay. Then a mysterious stone flew through the air, hit the feet of the image and ground the whole lot into powder which was blown away by the wind.

When Daniel gave the king his interpretation, he emphasised this stone of destruction. He rushed through the interpretation of the precious metals, but dwelt on the stone and the destruction of the image. So what did the dream mean?

Daniel began the interpretation by explaining that the sequence of metals represented the rise and fall of kingdoms.[210] It is interesting to note that this image became an idol or object of worship to the Babylonians. This idol represented not only political powers, but also the way human beings worship and glorify political power. In contrast to the metals, there was the stone of destruction which was quarried 'not by human hands'. In other words, the stone is not representing a human power but the kingdom of God.[211]

In its entirety the dream presents an outline showing the succession of major historical superpowers. It begins with the head of gold representing Babylon.[212] Next is the chest of silver representing the Medo-Persian Empire, followed by the belly and thighs of brass symbolising Greece and, finally, the iron legs representing Rome. Rome's eventual disintegration is portrayed by the iron and clay of the idol's feet (two elements that definitely do not mix together).

All of this is impressive in itself – an accurate prediction of human history foretold centuries in advance! But, most important of all, it presents a picture of hope at the end of these human kingdoms through the establishment of the kingdom of God.

This divine kingdom is anticipated in the Old Testament, but the New Testament gives even more detail, showing a devastating and complete annihilation of human power. It illustrates the establishing of God's kingdom when Jesus returns to this earth. Some New Testament writers, like John the Revelator, use highly imaginative language: 'The sky vanished like a scroll rolling itself up, and every mountain and island was moved from its place,'[213] and 'the heavens will be set ablaze and dissolved, and the elements will melt with fire'.[214] In these passages, as in Daniel 2, the authors are describing an event no one has ever experienced. So they paint incredible figurative pictures in order to catch our attention.

It's important to understand the significance of this picture that Daniel paints of the future. Prophecy in general, and this dream in particular, doesn't claim that every detail of human history has been predetermined by God. All they claim is that the *end* of history is certain.

The exact route history takes, the details of human politics, our individual decisions – we determine it all. We are free to plan our lives. Choose our spouse. Pick a career. But the end *will* come, because God is in charge.

The emphasis on *this* end could explain why Daniel never identified the kingdoms that came after Babylon: he is far more interested in the stone missile. Just as the moving stone contrasts with the immobile image, so the kingdom of God contrasts with kingdoms of man.

Each of the kingdoms (represented by different metals) exercised power for a while, before succumbing to another. But God's kingdom, represented by the stone, 'will itself endure forever'.[215] Not only that, but it also 'filled the whole earth'.[216] So the kingdom of God will dominate time ('forever') and space ('the whole earth'). One of the human (metal) kingdoms filled the earth,[217] but only the kingdom of God lasts forever.

The story began with the inept wise men in the Babylonian court saying, 'May the King live forever', but it concluded by telling us that only the kingdom of God lasts forever. This contrast underlines the fact that things are not what they seem to be. Because God is in charge.

The biblical book of Genesis tells us that this world had a meaningful *beginning*. The biblical book of Daniel emphasises that the world will have a meaningful *end*. If the world had a meaningful beginning and will have a meaningful end, then one thing is clear: our lives really *do* have a meaningful *present*. Even on those bad Monday mornings.

Daniel invites us to live life to the full in the *present*. He invites us to know that we are part of a journey that started with a meaningful beginning at creation and is travelling towards the meaningful end at the second coming of Christ, when God sets up his eternal kingdom. We can have confidence in this world as it is, with its catalogue of evil and despair, knowing that things are not as bad as they seem to be.

Because God is in charge.

re: consider

Have you relinquished your ego to God? How could you go about doing that?

ABOUT HOPE

REFERENCES

209. Sandra Angelo (c) 2002. *www.sermonillustrator.org/illustrator/sermon3/first_things_first.htm*. 11 April 2006. Edited.
210. See Daniel 2:37-41, 44.
211. See Daniel 2:44.
212. Daniel 2:37-38.
213. Revelation 6:14, NRSV.
214. 2 Peter 3:12, NRSV.
215. Daniel 2:44, NIV.
216. Ibid 2:35, NIV.
217. See Daniel 2:39.

13. READING THE SIGNS

God, thank you for your Word that tells me where we are in history. This is why we call you Lord: you know all things before they happen. I want to understand better how my present reality fits into the stream of time from your perspective. Please show me your plans for me and the planet I call home – on the grand scale.

re: tell

My first year of college I didn't have a car. So when a group of high school friends from out of state had a small reunion at a beach a couple of hours away, I convinced one of my new college friends to take me on a road trip.

He drove; I navigated. Then we came to a T-junction in the road, and I got confused. Trying to recall the route from memory, I told him to turn left.

'Are you sure? It just feels as though we should go right,' he said.

'Nope. I remember, we go left here,' I insisted. About thirty miles later, landmarks still weren't looking familiar. He pulled over to ask directions and, to my dismay, he had been right. A humiliated half an hour later, we whizzed by the original intersection. There in plain sight was the sign we had missed.

We eventually got to the right beach, and fifteen years later we're still friends. But he's never let me forget the day when I missed the sign.[218]

re: think

I like signs. I read them regularly. I am informed; I am warned; I am secure.

Some don't seem to share my appreciation, like the California driver who plunged off the end of an earthquake-damaged highway because she ignored the danger signs. Or the people who are completely unfazed by the warnings on cigarette packs. Or those who refuse to check a road map and drive in the wrong direction.

Signs exist for a reason. We may not always follow what they say, but they still have a definite purpose.

So what signs is this world giving us? Do they say that time is running out? That we can't go on much longer? That we're facing a crisis?

Walking the streets, I once saw a sign proclaiming: 'We are on the cusp of change'. Movies and bestsellers focus on surviving the end of the world. It's interesting that so many people should be expecting something.

Without falling for stereotypes, but looking at the way things are going, what should we expect?

There are plenty of fanciful predictions, from giant meteors to aliens from outer space. But what about the signs identified by Jesus as he described what would precede his return?

Why did Jesus talk about signs? Was it to provide secret knowledge or special inside information – or to give comfort and confirmation? Unfortunately, too many have focused on the signs themselves, instead of what they represent.

Jesus shared the signs of his return with those who were going to be devastated at his departure. He wanted to encourage them (and us) that his leaving would not be permanent, and that he would return, so that those who follow him might be encouraged as they saw things happening in history. He wanted to give us joy instead of sorrow:

'Do not let your heart be troubled . . . I will come again, and take you home with me.' (John 14:1, 3, author's paraphrase.)

So how will it be? How will it happen? And, most importantly for you individually, How will it be *for me*?

unmissable

You can't miss it. Jesus won't come quietly or secretly so that only a few notice. It will be an earth-shattering event that no one will miss! Jesus' return will be like the lightning streaking across the sky, and every person will see him. If anyone tells you he's already arrived secretly, Jesus himself says, *'Don't believe it!'*

We won't just *see* the light from Jesus' coming, we'll *hear* him, too. 'For the Lord himself will come down from heaven with a commanding shout, with the voice of the archangel and with the trumpet call of God.'[219] It'll be loud enough to wake the dead – literally.

According to the Holy Bible, this event will be intensely personal and very real. Angels told Jesus' disciples, 'This same Jesus ... will come back in the same way you have seen him go into heaven.'[220] Jesus left as a physical person and when he returns he will be just the same.

> Just like spring says summer is coming soon, events around us tell us that Jesus is coming soon.

warnings

'Don't let anyone mislead you.'[221]

It's easy to get so involved in working out each sign so specifically that you get it wrong. Some people believed that a single event *proved* Christ would come within a certain time frame, and then were devastated when their 'definite sign' turned out to be wrong.

Jesus also warns about those who falsely claim to be Christ, and those who say that he has come secretly:

> 'For many will come in my name, claiming, "I am the Messiah." They will deceive many. . . . So if someone tells you, "Look, the Messiah is out in the desert," don't bother to go and look. Or, "Look, he is hiding here," don't believe it! For as the lightning flashes in the east and shines to the west, so it will be when the Son of Man comes.'[222]

non-signs

Sometimes the events that seem the most dramatic are not signs at all. Jesus tells us: 'And you will hear of wars and threats of wars, but don't panic. Yes, these things must take place, but the end won't follow immediately.'[223]

For Christians living during wartime it must seem that Jesus has to come soon. But if they understand war itself to be the final sign of his coming, they will be disappointed. Battles and revolutions and rebellions and famines and earthquakes – Jesus tells us these are to be expected, but they are not proof of his immediate return.[224]

real signs

one: atheism, persecution and false religion

Jesus points first to the *growth of evil* as a major sign:

> 'Sin will be rampant everywhere, and the love of many will grow cold. . . . Then you will be arrested, persecuted, and killed. . . . And many will turn away from me and betray and hate each other. And many false prophets will appear and will deceive many people.'[225]

Are these things happening now? What is the evidence? Just check the statistics related to how many people doubt the existence of God, rising crime (even among children), the collapse of marriage and family, pornography and abuse, persecution in totalitarian countries, and the growing number of people who claim to be Jesus or the Messiah on Earth.

two: telling others about Jesus

> 'And the Good News about the Kingdom will be preached throughout the whole world, so that all nations will hear it; and then the end will come.'[226]

Global evangelism fits well here. Today the good news of Jesus is being preached more than ever before. Modern means of mass communication – literature, radio, TV, DVD, Internet – help people share Jesus around the world.

three: moral state of the world

How many of this world's population really care about God or about living with integrity and morals? Today's philosophy is to look out for 'number one'. Hit the other guy before he hits you, grab what you want while you can, get to the top by any means. It's a religion of total selfishness and greed.

Jesus spoke about his modern situation by comparing it with the ancient corruption of the people living before the biblical Flood:

'When the Son of Man returns, it will be like it was in Noah's day. In those days before the flood, the people were enjoying banquets and parties and weddings right up to the time Noah entered his boat. People didn't realize what was going to happen until the flood came and swept them all away. That is the way it will be when the Son of Man comes.'[227]

four: final world shaking, visible signs

'Immediately after the anguish of those days, the sun will be darkened, the moon will give no light, the stars will fall from the sky, and the powers in the heavens will be shaken. And then at last, the sign that the Son of Man is coming will appear in the heavens, and there will be deep mourning among all the peoples of the earth. And they will see the Son of Man coming on the clouds of heaven with power and great glory.'[228]

It's an awesome description of the coming of Christ, preceded by some pretty catastrophic signs.

but when?

That's the question. We always want to know how much time we've got! We like to plan ahead, so we want to know when. We demand a definite date, because we just can't stand the wait! So, if Jesus is returning to planet Earth, when will it happen?

All through history people have tried to pinpoint the date of Jesus' return. And all have failed. Why? Because Jesus himself said: 'But of that day and hour no one knows . . . but the Father alone.'[229]

No one will be able to work it out by charts or mathematics or computers. It's something we can't know. Jesus has already told us: 'You do

111

not know on what day your Lord will come' and 'The Son of Man will come at an hour when you do not expect him.'[230]

So we just can't know the answer to 'When?' But remember that through signs God is also saying, 'Time's up!' So if we can't pinpoint the exact date, which clues give us an idea?

defining the time

Jesus told a simple illustration about the approach of his coming: 'Now learn this lesson from the fig tree: As soon as its twigs get tender and its leaves come out, you know that summer is near. Even so, when you see all these things, you know that it is near, right at the door.'[231]

So while we may not be able to say exactly when Jesus will come, there will be enough evidence to know that his coming is near. Just like spring says summer is coming soon, events around us tell us that Jesus is coming soon. We should be aware: 'If he comes suddenly, do not let him find you sleeping. What I say to you, I say to everyone: "Watch!"'[232]

So let's watch and see what happens. We can't say exactly when but, like the fig tree in Jesus' word picture, it looks as if the end time is about to blossom.

your own personal time

While you may not know exactly how much time this world has left, one thing is sure – or not sure! We never know how much time we have left! Jesus gave us this information and the signs, not so that *we* could calculate when everything will happen, *but so we could get ready*. That is the real message. Be ready! How do you know when time's up for you? You don't. So how much time can we each count on? None!

We typically want to know *when* so that we can leave things to the last moment. Your essay is due on Monday morning, so you wait until Sunday night to start it.

But it doesn't work that way with Jesus. God doesn't give us a definite date, because he wants us to be ready all the time, not just at the last minute!

now!

We have no control over the past, no guarantee of the future. All we have is now.

God says to us:

'Choose *today* whom you will serve.' (Joshua 24:15, italics supplied.)

'*Today*, when you hear his voice, don't harden your hearts.' (Hebrews 3:15, italics supplied.)

'*Now* he commands everyone everywhere to repent.' (Acts 17:30, italics supplied.)

'*Now* is the time of God's favour, *now* is the day of salvation.' (2 Corinthians 6:2, NIV, italics supplied.)

This is the reason Jesus wants us to know about his coming – so we can be ready. Not just some time in the future, but *now* – which is all the time we have.

Some of the signs I like best are the ones held up by people meeting others at the airport. In a strange country I am always delighted to find someone holding up a sign with my name on it. I'd like to believe that, after all the signs here, God will be holding up a sign with my name on it at the end of my journey. How about you?

re: consider

If Jesus is coming, how can your relationship with him help you become a better person now?

REFERENCES

218. Story by Sarah K. Asaftei.
219. 1 Thessalonians 4:16.
220. Acts 1:11, NIV.
221. Matthew 24:4.
222. Matthew 24:5, 26, 27.
223. Matthew 24:6.

224. See Matthew 24.
225. Matthew 24:12 and 9-11.
226. Matthew 24:14.
227. Matthew 24:37-39.
228. Matthew 24:29, 30.
229. Matthew 24:36, NKJV.
230. Matthew 24:42, 44, NIV.
231. Matthew 24:32, 33, NIV.
232. Mark 13:36, 37, NIV.

14. COMING BACK

God, I've been learning through the last few chapters about the time when you will end history's progression by coming again to Earth in the bodily form of Jesus Christ. Please be present with me as I read to help me understand how, when and why he will come.

re: tell

Emily Crowhurst never knew her father, Thomas Hughes. He died when she was only 2, in 1914, one of the first of the millions of victims of World War I. However, twelve days before his death, Hughes tossed a bottle into the English Channel. A note inside, intended for his wife Elizabeth, read, 'Dear Wife, I am writing this note on board this boat and dropping it into the sea just to see if it will reach you. . . . Ta ta, sweet, for the present. Your Hubby.'

In 1999 British fisherman Steve Gowan found the bottle in the River Thames. Elizabeth Hughes had long since passed away, but 86-year-old Emily lived in New Zealand. The *New Zealand Post* newspaper flew Gowan and his wife to Auckland, where they personally delivered the long-lost letter.

Moved beyond words, Crowhurst accepted the letter with gratitude. She'd spent a lifetime trying to learn more about her father and had proudly worn his military medals at memorials. 'I think he would be very proud it had been delivered,' she reflected. 'He was a very caring man.'

re: think

The people of the Seventh-day Adventist Church worldwide, despite all the hopelessness around us, dare to hope and believe that the God of Israel will fulfil his promise to return. The name of the *Seventh-day Adventist* Church points to a meaningful beginning for human history (the creation week ending with worshipping God on the seventh day) and to a meaningful end (looking towards the second coming or *advent* of Jesus). If human history has a meaningful beginning and a meaningful end, wouldn't it mean that our present existence might also be meaningful? Does that make sense, or does it make us fools? And what is our evidence for this hope in a promised future?

creation of the world

First, our faith that Jesus will come back is based on the biblical teaching of *the creation of the world*. The Bible gives only one definition of faith: 'Faith is being sure of what we hope for and certain of what we do not see.'[233] The first part, 'being sure of what we hope for', points to a hope in the future kingdom of Christ. The second part, 'certain of what we do not see', points to the past creation of the world. The essential element of Christian faith is belief in creation. It means to acknowledge that beyond this visible world exists God, the Creator. What we see, touch and taste didn't just always exist. Everything has a beginning.

One event which occurred in 2005 deserves our attention. A legendary British philosopher and atheist, Anthony Flew, who had been an icon and champion for unbelievers for decades, changed his mind and accepted the existence of God.[234] Flew stated that developments in modern science had led him to accept the action of an Intelligent Mind in the creation of the world. In 'Has Science Discovered God?' Flew states that he was influenced by developments in DNA research: 'What I think the DNA material has done is to show that intelligence must have been involved in getting these extraordinary diverse elements together.'[235] Over the decades, Flew authored twenty-eight books and edited twelve others. At least ten of his books were critiques of belief in God.

DNA and other structures in the human body contain mutually dependent parts which couldn't have appeared by any conceivable series of chance occurrences. The principle of *irreducible complexity* is present everywhere. The evolutionary theory can't explain how a fragile, complex and exquisite orchid can exist in the jungle. Why are the tail feathers of a peacock not just bright enough to attract a mate, but gorgeous? Why the excess?[236]

What if this planet hasn't always existed? What if there is a God with intelligence beyond our understanding?

We know only as much about him as he reveals to us. He exists and he speaks. And he has promised that he will come again and make everything perfect.

resurrection of Jesus

The concept of Jesus' resurrection has its critics. Scottish sceptic David Hume and Jewish pantheistic writer Benedict Spinoza claim that the universe is run by universal, unchanging laws. For them, this resurrection is a miracle that alters the unchanging laws of nature. Since it is impossible to change these unchangeable laws, Jesus must still be dead. But they didn't consider that God is the cause of all nature's laws. Miracles exist only for us, as limited human beings.

For me, few historical events have been supported by as many textual evidences and witnesses as Jesus' resurrection. Denying this event denounces the very principles used in the science of history. The resurrection of Jesus is proclaimed in the New Testament with such firm conviction, assurance, certainty and sincerity. The disciples were extremely discouraged and confused when Jesus died. But after the resurrection everything changed. Now they were witnesses of life and they constantly repeated the message:

> 'That which was from the beginning, which we have heard, which we have seen with our eyes, which we have looked at and our hands have touched – this we proclaim concerning the Word of life. The life appeared; we have seen it and testify to it, and we proclaim to you the eternal life, which was with the Father and has appeared to us.'[237]

Citizens across the Roman Empire believed in Christ and proclaimed to the world that they'd found a cure for the most devastating human problem – death. The belief of the apostles was so absolute that most of them gave their lives defending it.

> What if there is a God with intelligence beyond our understanding?

According to Paul, 'Christ has indeed been raised from the dead, the first fruits of those who have fallen asleep.' (1 Corinthians 15:20, NIV.) Because Jesus came to this planet, lived here, died on the cross and was resurrected from the dead, we have hope that he will come again, just as he promised.

promise of Christ

In addition to the event of creation, the resurrection of Jesus and prophecies throughout the Bible, the New Testament supports our hope that Jesus will return based on his own promise:

> 'Do not let your hearts be troubled. Trust in God; trust also in me. . . . I am going there to prepare a place for you. And if I go and prepare a place for you, I will come back and take you to be with me that you also may be where I am.'[238]

The apostle Peter writes:'But in keeping with his promise we are looking forward to a new heaven and a new earth, the home of righteousness.'[239] The New Testament mentions the promise of Jesus' second coming 319 times. That means every twenty-fifth verse reminds us about it!

Jesus also talked about the signs that will help us know that he is coming soon. Although we don't know the exact day he'll come back, we can recognise that it is close. We've already studied some of the signs of the end that Jesus spoke about, like wars and threats of wars, famines and illnesses, anxiety and depression related to the future, the false feeling of peace and security; *signs in nature* such as earthquakes; *signs in the field of ethics* such as materialistic ways of thinking and living; *signs in the field of religion* such as formality in Christian religion at the end of time, false religious movements, the increase in understanding of biblical prophecies, and the preaching of the gospel to the entire world.[240]

According to Jesus himself, his second coming will be: first, *cata-clysmic*. Since God wants to establish 'a new heaven and a new earth',[241] the end of this world is going to be a catastrophic, worldwide phenomenon. As the Flood destroyed the ancient world, so the second coming of Christ will cause the earth to be burned.[242]

Second, Jesus' return to Earth will be *audible* and *visible*, because all nations of the world will hear and see him.[243] Diminishing this to a mysterious and invisible event is contrary to the New Testament teaching.[244]

Third, the second coming will be *personal*. Angels announced to the upset disciples that this Jesus would come back in the same way he went to heaven.[245]

Fourth, the coming of Jesus will be *sudden*, because no one knows the moment, not even the angels or Jesus,[246] but only God the Father.

Fifth, the second coming of Christ will be *glorious and triumphant*, because Jesus will return as King of kings and Lord of lords.[247]

hope of the second coming

This hope of Jesus' return has an impact on those who are waiting for it. Each passing day gives us an opportunity to become better people while we wait. God expects his followers to show specific ethical characteristics, such as holiness, humility and love.[248] Hope makes anxiety, fear of the future, worry and anguish fade away.[249] While we wait we're invited to bear fruit, to be the salt of the earth and the light of the world.[250] This means that we change into better people, provide good flavour in our social groups around us, and share what we've learned with others.

Moreover, this hope inspires us to develop a sense of social justice and values because we cannot be insensitive to the issues of the world.[251] The time we spend waiting for Jesus to come back gives the Holy Spirit a chance to work on the minds and hearts of people so that their lives are developed into stronger, happier experiences. God's disciples work with him to help others get ready for when Jesus will return.[252]

So in this time 'of distress such as has not happened from the beginning of nations'[253] we still dare to hope, and our hope is based on

119

the creation of the world, on Christ's resurrection, biblical prophecies and the promise of Jesus himself.

Just like Joshua, the ancient desert warrior from the Bible, we are invited to fall face down to the ground and recognise that everything is dust and then to express our faith that God is able to transform our dust into life. When Jesus comes for the second time, 'he will wipe every tear from [our] eyes. There will be no more death or mourning or crying or pain, for the old order of things has passed away.'[254]

re: consider

As the idea that Jesus is coming again affects your personal journey, who can you tell about it?

REFERENCES

233. Hebrews 11:1, NIV.
234. See *www.biola.edu/philchristi*.
235. Ibid.
236. See Brandstater, Bernard. 'Intelligent Design: The Argument from Beauty.' *Journal of the Adventist Theological Society 15* (2004): p. 12.
237. 1 John 1:1, 2, NIV.
238. John 14:1, 3, NIV.
239. 2 Peter 3:13, NIV.
240. Matthew 24:6, 7; Luke 21:25; 2 Peter 3:3; 2 Timothy 3:1-4, 5; Matthew 24:24; Daniel 12:4; Matthew 24:14.
241. Revelation 21:1, NIV.
242. 2 Peter 3:10.
243. Matthew 24:30.
244. 1 Thessalonians 4:16.
245. Acts 1:11.
246. Matthew 24:36.
247. Revelation 19:16.
248. Luke 13:6-9.
249. Luke 21:28.
250. Matthew 5:13-16.
251. Philippians 4:8; 1 Corinthians 6:2, 3.
252. Matthew 24:14.
253. Daniel 12:1, NIV.
254. Revelation 21:4, NIV.

ABOUT
MANKIND

15. LIVING FOREVER

God, you gave me life, and yet each one of us dies. Help me to understand from your Word what death really means and how I can live with you forever.

re: tell

A young business owner was opening a new branch office, and a friend decided to send a floral arrangement for the grand opening. When the friend arrived at the opening, he was appalled to find that his floral tribute was a wreath which bore the inscription: 'Rest in peace.'

Angry, he complained to the florist. After apologising, the florist said, 'Look at it this way – somewhere a man was buried under a wreath today that said, "Good luck in your new location." '[255]

re: think

Filmmaker Woody Allen once said: 'I don't want to achieve immortality through my work. I want to achieve it through not dying.'

Woody isn't alone in his wish to avoid death. The search for immortality has been a constant theme in literature for centuries. Numerous myths detail the chase for a fountain of eternal youth. Contemporary society spends an enormous amount of effort and money in retaining youthful appearance. But in the end, at best we only slightly delay the inevitable.

True, life expectancy has increased in many parts of the world. The words of the ancient poet may now seem a little pessimistic: 'Seventy years are given to us! Some may even live to eighty. But even the best of these years are filled with pain and trouble!'[256] But few live to one hundred years.

We probably don't need to be reminded of our own mortality. Death is present everywhere. The news tends to be dominated by war, accidents and death. Once we pass middle age, each time we look in the mirror we are reminded of our own mortality. An elderly friend of mine jokes with his young friends, 'You're old age positive. You're just not showing symptoms yet!'

Life loses its deeper meaning if there is nothing beyond. Some people hope for a measure of immortality through their children. Others believe their achievements may make them immortal. Politicians and scientists are anxious to be listed in a 'Who's Who' or get a street named after them or be mentioned in the history books. For them, this implies some sense of living on after death.

Others dream of genetic immortality, hoping for a chance to be cloned in the future. They conveniently forget that their clone may be someone *like* them, but it won't *be* them! Philanthropists donate money to get their name on a building so future generations will remember their generosity.

But none of these strategies actually keeps us from dying.

death defined

According to Holy Scripture, death is the result of sin. Since every person who ever lived on this earth has been tainted by sin, 'death spread to everyone'.[257] So, one thing is pretty clear: *Humanity is mortal.* Only 'almighty God, the King of all kings and Lord of all lords' possesses immortality. 'He alone can never die.'[258]

Many Christians get upset when they hear this statement. They argue that this isn't true. 'Yes,' they say, 'human beings must die. But the most important element survives – the immortal soul.' They say that the body dies, but the soul – whatever that is – continues to live and goes

123

either to heaven or hell at the very moment of death. Most Christians never stop asking whether this is what the Bible says.

Certainly, there are a few biblical passages that seem to suggest some divide between material and non-material components. But when we look at all the evidence, we see that this view of man is borrowed from Greek philosophy and is not derived from the Bible.

Life is a mystery. Despite our advanced knowledge about the human body and what to do when it malfunctions, we really know very little about its fundamental processes. We can't define the secret of life. We realise there's more than atoms and molecules and physiological processes; there is also a spiritual component.

We can eat and reproduce, but we also think and remember, hate and love. But these components can't be separated from each other. Without the living part, we don't have any feelings left or any way to express them. At creation we are told, 'The Lord God formed the man from the dust of the ground. He breathed the breath of life into the man's nostrils, and the man became a living person.'[259]

mystery of death

What happens when a person dies? Honestly? We don't know. No one has ever physically come back to tell us what takes place when we breathe our last breath. Even 'near death' experiences don't shed any real light on the mystery of death, for they are just that: *near*-death experiences. The metaphor that best describes the mystery of death is probably the word *sleep*.

> When we have a relationship with God, we also have something to look forward to after this life.

Jesus used this word to describe the state of his friend Lazarus after he had died. 'Our friend Lazarus has fallen asleep.'[260] It indicates that death is a form of unconsciousness, not a state of separation between a decaying body and a conscious, disembodied soul.

When human beings die, 'they breathe their last, they return to the earth, and all their plans die with them.'[261] 'The living . . . know they will die, but the dead know nothing.'[262]

end of death

If this is the end, there's no hope. Life has no meaning, and fatalism replaces faith and trust. We've got to be the most miserable people in the world.[263] The truth, though, is that death isn't eternal nothingness. When we have a relationship with God, we also have something to look forward to after this life.

Jesus told his followers what to expect. 'The time is coming when all the dead in the graves will hear the voice of God's Son, and they will rise again. Those who have done good will rise to experience eternal life.'[264]

So even though we die now, mortal humanity has the promise of immortality. We can't achieve it by delaying old age or by erecting a statue in the village where we were born. For those who have accepted God, 'our dead and decaying bodies' will 'be changed into bodies that won't die or decay'[265] at the resurrection.

How does this work? How can we return to life after our bodies have decomposed? Within a few decades of death, none of our body's matter still exists after burial. So how can we rise again? It requires faith and taking God at his word. But couldn't the fact that Jesus rose from his grave guarantee that he is stronger than death? Might his own resurrection have secured the victory over the death of all his followers?

Of course, we're talking about miracles. There is no human explanation. And even if today someone returned from death, most people would probably try to find some alternative explanation. But if you trust God it isn't that difficult to believe. It's not any harder than the idea that we owe our present life to a divine source.

Only God has absolute immortality. The immortality that is within our reach is *conditional*. 'Anyone who believes in God's Son has eternal life.'[266] That's the Good News. It's simple, but profound. It's free, but its value is beyond comprehension.

re: consider

If death is like sleeping, and you get immortality as a gift from God at the resurrection, how does that affect the choices and actions you make right now?

REFERENCES

255. Bits & Pieces, 23 June 1994, p. 4. *www.sermonillustrations.com/a-z/d/death.htm*. 11 April 2006.
256. Psalm 90:10.
257. Romans 5:12.
258. 1 Timothy 6:15, 16.
259. Genesis 2:7.
260. John 11:11.
261. Psalm 146:4.
262. Ecclesiastes 9:5.
263. 1 Corinthians 15:19, KJV.
264. John 5:28, 29.
265. 1 Corinthians 15:53, CEV.
266. John 3:36.

ABOUT THE HOLY SPIRIT

16. NO FEAR

God, people are searching in all kinds of ways to find peace and meaning. I know that the occult can create a feeling of a supernatural presence and become mesmerising because of that supernatural power, but I want to know that the supernatural power in my life is from you alone. So I need your presence to help me understand the true way to finding spiritual peace.

re: tell

As a very small child, April was afraid of the dark. But hers was not the typical childhood fear. April's parents were involved with the occult and black magic and had thus opened their home and their hearts to a malevolent force April could not explain. Often she sensed 'presences' of both good and evil in her home. But how could she describe such things to outsiders? Who would believe her?

'Many nights I would lie awake, crying, just watching these demons sit in my room, waiting for their chance to pounce on a defenceless child,' she says. 'I knew there was a God that loved me, but I didn't understand why he didn't just waltz into my room, in all of his glory, and destroy these scary things once and for all.' At the age of 13 April moved out of her parents' home to live with her aunt and uncle. But, to her dismay, the demons followed. She was plagued with dark, frightening shadows when she lay awake and nightmares when she slept. Her doctors could find no physical or emotional reasons for her problems.

When her aunt and uncle realised what was happening, however, they had a solution. They were both ardent Christians and they explained that there was power in the name of Jesus. She was to use that name – reverently but with authority and confidence – the next time she felt under attack. April was ecstatic. She could hardly wait for the opportunity to try out this newfound source of strength.

'I remember it so clearly,' she says. 'It was a hot summer night, and I was asleep in bed. The room was pitch black, so dark it seemed almost void of air. Suddenly I was jolted awake by a familiar, terrifying presence. My fears came rushing back, and I began to sob uncontrollably.' April felt defeated. She could actually see a figure standing in the corner of her bedroom, watching her, as if he knew that he was still reigning over her.

But then she remembered – she could pray! As she did so, she felt a transformation take place. 'Jesus, Jesus,' she murmured softly, then with growing boldness. 'In the name of Jesus, I demand that you flee this room! You no longer have control over me.' All at once, she looked up and realised that the ceiling was becoming a white sheet. Weightlessly, it floated down upon her, covering her completely, cool and scented like the night air, as if angel wings were embracing her. April was filled with an amazing sense of peace. The fears that had held her captive for so many years were gone, never to return.

'Now I am a grown woman, with children of my own,' she says. 'And to this day, on those hot summer nights, I find myself taking cool sheets from the linen closet and tossing them over my children as they sleep. I pray that angels will protect them and once again I am filled with that same peace that brought me through on that night so long ago.'[267]

re: think

People have been intrigued by the occult since history began, but 'modern' spiritism dates from the 1840s in the United States of America. Several major movements originated during this time. The spiritual awakening of the 1830s and '40s, with its emphasis on the second coming of Christ, led to the birth of Seventh-day Adventism. Around the same time (1848) the Fox sisters in Hydesville, New York, began hearing mysterious rappings in their house. This is usually regarded as the beginnings of spiritism in its modern garb.

Since then, spiritism and its allied form – spiritualism – and a multitude of other occult phenomena have become popular. Horoscopes are often regarded as the most innocent manifestation of the occult world. Most horoscope readers may not take the daily predictions too seriously. My horoscope in today's newspaper told me to exercise extra care in my dealings with others during the coming week. That I might face some opposition from colleagues. That the coming week won't bring many romantic surprises.

I'm certainly not going to lose sleep over those predictions. Probably most others who share my star sign won't either. But many people still desperately want to know what is written for them in the stars. They consult occult 'professionals' in order to find out what the stars (or their palms or the tarot cards) can tell them about their future.

a source of fear

Anthropologists sometimes suggest that Christian missionaries ought to stay away from 'primitive' people groups who, they say, are happy in their beliefs. They argue that Christian missions destroy the authentic primitive experience and this results in the disappearance of those ancient cultures. There is no doubt that Christian missionaries have often shown too little regard for other cultures. But worshippers of animistic nature religions live in constant fear of the powers that threaten their health, livelihood and existence. Ominous threats of the unknown attract people to the powers of darkness all over the world. As a result, many live in constant fear.

Today's fascination with the occult isn't limited to the millions who, even after converting to Christianity or Islam, still buy their mystifying *gris-gris* at the local market. Western TV shows cleverly benefit from the occult's popularity. Wicca is regarded as a 'normal' religion. New Age practitioners blend Christian and occult elements. And many people still refuse to travel on Friday 13th!

Many occult practices, both in primitive cultures and the developed world, are based on a fundamental misconception regarding the reality of death.[268] They either believe that the soul continues to live after the body dies, or that you're reincarnated over and over. Reincarnation claims that you live and die, but your essence or soul lives on in another body (either human or animal) in the next life.

Mistaken ideas about death have led to many theories and practices that bring fear and frustration. But this isn't new – it started right after creation. God had told Adam and Eve that disobedience would result in death. But Satan suggested differently, saying, 'You will not surely die!'[269] They decided to risk disobeying God's instructions and see for themselves. Now millions share in the belief that when you die, you're not truly dead.

Many people who believe that the dead are still alive also hope for some contact. The Bible talks about someone who tried to get advice from the 'spirit' of a trusted adviser who had died. In the Old Testament, King Saul went to a medium, hoping to contact the prophet Samuel.[270] Saul not only went against the instructions he himself had issued, but against a divine principle. Saul knew God didn't approve of 'talking' to the dead. 'Why are you trying to find out the future by consulting mediums and psychics? Do not listen to their whisperings and mutterings. Can the living find out the future from the dead? Why not ask your God?'[271]

is it real?

But you ask, 'Aren't there many strange things the human mind cannot understand? Don't we have to admit that there are healers, magicians and channellers who know things and do things that are totally inexplicable?' Yes, there are occasions when we are bewildered by what *seems* to have occurred. So what can we say about these things?

Anyone who believes in the Bible admits that there are strange spiritual forces. The Bible itself is clear about the existence of an all-powerful God. It is just as clear about the existence of an evil power. The ancient book talks about 'rulers ... authorities of the unseen world ... mighty powers in this dark world, and ... evil spirits in the heavenly places'[272] and these are intelligent powers. So it shouldn't surprise us when there is occult knowledge or if some predictions come true. But if we believe that Satan exists, we also have to accept that he has plenty of experience and might accurately guess how things tend to go.

What about sickness and healing? We know God can heal sickness and can bring people back from the brink of death if he chooses. But what about those spectacular healing sessions by preachers who wilfully deny biblical truth? Does this healing come from God or not? In some cases, the so-called 'healings' are engineered by a clever miracle-manager. Occasionally there are copycat miracles, regardless of whether the healer realises it. After all, Satan knows how to execute his devious designs and often 'disguises himself as an angel of light'.[273]

Yes, there is a constant controversy, a struggle between good and evil. But the Holy Bible says that it isn't a combat between equals. Wherever the fight takes place, Jesus is the conqueror. During his life on Earth, demons trembled when Jesus' name was spoken.[274] The power of his name is as great today as it was two thousand years ago in Palestine.

So what do I do personally? Stay away from anything that seems part of the occult. Sometimes the best thing to do is restrain your curiosity. And if you don't know what to make of things you see and hear, maybe suspend judgement until you find out more.

But always remember: 'You belong to God, and you have defeated these enemies. God's Spirit is in you and is more powerful than the one that is in the world.'[275]

re: consider

What actions or activities can you avoid so that you and your home are not open to evil influences?

REFERENCES

267. Joan Wester Anderson. This story first appeared on her website: *www.joanwanderson.com*. Used with permission. Copyright 2002. *www.sermonillustrator.org/illustrator/sermon4/who_would_believe_her.htm*. 11 April 2006.

268. See chapter 14 in this book.

269. Genesis 3:4, NIV.

270. Read 1 Samuel 28 for the whole story.

271. Isaiah 8:19 (author paraphrase).

272. Ephesians 6:12.

273. 2 Corinthians 11:14.

274. Luke 10:17-20.

275. 1 John 4:4, CEV.

17. PIECES OF GOD

God, I want to know you at my very core. I want to know how your Spirit can live in me, and how I can live in you. Thank you for making it possible for me to have such an intimate connection with you.

re: tell

Three blind men gathered together to explore a strange creature called an elephant. But they each experienced different parts of the same thing.

The first blind man felt all over the leg of the elephant and said to the others, 'It is like a strong tree.' The second held the trunk, explaining, 'It is like an ever-changing vine.'

The third blind man ran his hands across the large body of the elephant and exclaimed, 'No, it is endless, like a wide mountain.'[276]

re: think

Lots of people struggle to find God. They become agnostic (believing that they cannot know God), atheistic (denying the existence of God) or simply indifferent.

While the Bible recognises that a *full* understanding of God not possible for us,[277] it also poses a solution to help us comprehend him better. We know that God created us as companions for each other and for him and we know that he loves us. And since sin has separated us from him until we get to heaven, he's made a plan to keep us connected – he's sent his Spirit to help bridge the gap.[278]

The Bible says: 'No one can know God's thoughts except God's own Spirit' and when we human beings speak about spiritual things, 'We do not use words that come from human wisdom. Instead, we speak words given to us by the Spirit, using the Spirit's words to explain spiritual truths.'[279] Being spiritual means being connected with God's Spirit and learning how to listen and converse with him.

When you don't know the Spirit of God, it's only natural to wonder how you can progress further on your spiritual journey. Let's take a closer look at what the Bible says.

spirit

We're all aware of spirits. People talk about spirits, movies exaggerate them, music refers to them. But have you ever pondered the word itself? What does it really mean, and how do you define a spirit?

Generally, a spirit is assumed to be fundamentally different from physical matter, something that exists beyond our normal senses, with a powerful influence. You can feel it and you know it, but you can't describe it.

However, when we speak about the Holy Spirit in the Bible, we're talking about the Spirit of God, a *person* or *being* whom we can't see but who has the power to change us. Jesus said of this Spirit:

'The wind blows where it chooses and you hear the sound of it, but do not know where it comes from or where it is going. So it is with everyone who is born of the Spirit.'[280]

The Bible was written essentially in Hebrew (the Old Testament) and Greek (the New Testament). The Hebrew word for 'spirit' is *ruach* and the Greek word is *pneuma*. Both words literally mean 'wind' or 'breath'. The Bible describes the Holy Spirit as being like the wind – invisible, outside of our control and yet powerful.

I'm reminded of the story of the prophet Elijah, hiding from persecution in a cave.[281] God appeared to him, manifesting his presence not

135

in the violent storm, not in the earthquake, not in the fire – but in the gentle breath of a whisper, which led to a conversation.

For biblical writers, the speech or breath of God is intimately connected with the appearance of his Spirit. Jesus breathed on his followers and told them to receive the Holy Spirit.[282] The Spirit of God emanates from him, belongs to him, and exists to accomplish what God wants.

Bible readers see God's Spirit often associated with mystery and power. It is never dependent on man's feelings. This Spirit wasn't born in a human community and cannot be invoked by 'magical' acts or words. He isn't the product of need or emotions. He's always manifested as a super-human power coming from outside of ourselves, from God himself.[283]

who is he?

God reveals himself in the Bible as one entity through the Father, Son and Holy Spirit, a unity of three co-eternal beings. The Holy Spirit is a being in this threesome or 'trinity' as it is often called. Statements in the Bible, such as 'it seemed good to the Holy Spirit and to us',[284] show that the earliest Christians accepted him as a distinct being. Christ also spoke of the Spirit distinctly: 'He will glorify me, because he will take what is mine and declare it to you.'[285] The passages in Matthew 28:19 and 2 Corinthians 13:14 reveal the Holy Spirit as a living being beside the Father and the Son.

So you could conclude that the Holy Spirit is God and 'God is Spirit'.[286, 287] The Bible also ascribes divine attributes to the Holy Spirit: life,[288] truth,[289] love and holiness.[290]

When God acts in the world, or in the lives of human beings, he does so together with or through the Holy Spirit.

'For his Spirit searches out everything and shows us God's deep secrets. . . . No one can know God's thoughts except God's own Spirit.'[291]

The Bible also describes the Holy Spirit as all-powerful,[292] everywhere present[293] and all-knowing.[294] No one can escape this divine influence.[295]

God's gift of life is also associated with the Spirit. The creation of man and resurrection from the dead are achieved by God through the Holy Spirit. 'The spirit of God has made me, and the breath of the Almighty gives me life.'[296]

The Bible presents the Holy Spirit as equal with the Father and Son in baptism,[297] blessing[298] and the giving of spiritual gifts.[299] When we talk of the Holy Spirit, we are really talking about God, the Spirit of God who leads us to belief, and instructs us about truth.

his work

The Holy Spirit reveals God. And when God acts in the world, or in the lives of human beings, he does so together with or through the Holy Spirit.

As you read your Bible, you will find that the Holy Spirit has been at work in the world from the moment of creation.[300] God's Spirit interacts closely with humanity.[301] Ancient scripture also promised that God's Spirit would rest on Jesus, the Messiah or the Christ.

'The spirit of the Lord God is upon me, because the Lord has anointed me; he has sent me to bring good news to the oppressed, to bind up the brokenhearted, to proclaim liberty to the captives and release to the prisoners.'[302]

Reading this text to a crowd hundreds of years later, Jesus said: 'Today this scripture has been fulfilled in your hearing.'[303] After his resurrection from the dead, Jesus sent his followers into the world to share their experiences of him with others, and he promised them the power of the Holy Spirit.[304]

Jesus promised that a helper would come to them, called the Holy Spirit. '[He] will teach you all things and will remind you of everything I have said to you.'[305] Jesus also assured his followers: 'You will receive power when the Holy Spirit comes on you.'[306] These promises of the Holy Spirit came true on the day of Pentecost in Jerusalem, when 3,000 people became followers of Jesus after listening to Peter preach.[307]

New Testament writings reveal that the Holy Spirit's work is especially manifested in the *gifts* of the Spirit (a power that enables the believer to witness about Jesus Christ),[308] and by the *life* of the Spirit through Christian virtues.[309] In order to accomplish this, the Holy Spirit works in the believer's life in two ways: he *enlightens* your mind[310] and *resides* in your body.[311]

God's spiritual enlightening of our minds implies that knowledge of the things of God is important. While our personal experiences matter, the revealed truth of God matters more. So we should avoid saying that what matters in the end is 'not doctrine but experience'. The Holy Spirit enlightens our minds to understand the things of God – especially when we read and study the Word of God, which is Holy Spirit inspired.

God's spiritual residence in our bodies means that, through the Holy Spirit, God is living and working in us. When we realise this, we become more careful regarding what we eat, drink, watch, read or listen to. You might even decide to strengthen your faith by various spiritual disciplines, such as abstinence (solitude, silence, fasting, frugality, chastity, secrecy, sacrifice) or engagement (study, worship, celebration, service, prayer, fellowship, confession, submission).

> 'For as you know him better, he will give you, through his great power, everything you need for living a truly good life. . . . But to obtain these gifts, you need more than faith; you must also work hard to be good, and even that is not enough. For then you must learn to know God better and discover what he wants you to do.
>
> Next, learn to put aside your own desires so that you will become patient and godly, gladly letting God have his way with you. This will make possible the next step, which is for you to enjoy other people and to like them, and finally you will grow to love them deeply. The more you go on in this way, the more you will grow strong spiritually and become fruitful and useful to our Lord Jesus Christ.'[312]

Any spiritual discipline we choose to follow must never obscure the fact that it is the Holy Spirit who works within us. We co-operate with him by seeking him and we place a priority on using our spiritual gifts for God and living a spiritual life.

A very common theme in the Bible is 'life in the Spirit', particularly referred to in the instructions given to the early Christian church.[313] Living in the Holy Spirit is living a new life from God through Jesus Christ. Closely connected with this is the association of the Spirit with water, cleansing and renewal.[314]

In the gospel of John, 'the idea of "water" merges with the expression "Spirit" to signify purification, initiation, and newness'.[315] Often the identification between Spirit and water as a sign of renewal is also connected with life-giving rain. The two rain seasons in ancient Israel started the concept of 'the early rain', which gave the first fruits (associated with Pentecost and the outpouring of the Holy Spirit upon the first Christians), and 'the latter rain' which came at the end of the year during the final harvest time.

conclusion

The Bible tells us that the *Holy Spirit* activates the power of God in our life and explains the things of God to us through the inspired reading of the Word of God. Wouldn't you agree that before we dismiss God as non-existent or indifferent, maybe we ought to test him out?[316]

In our search for God, the Holy Spirit is a key. And Jesus said that your prayer for the gift of the Holy Spirit would be answered.[317]

re: consider

How would you like to have God's Spirit work in your life? What would you like to happen? Could you ask for the Spirit?

REFERENCES

276. *www.inspirationalstories.com/0/42.html*
277. Isaiah 55:6-11.
278. John 16:13.
279. 1 Corinthians 2:11-13.
280. John 3:8, NRSV.

281. See 1 Kings 19.

282. John 20:22.

283. See Genesis 41:38; Exodus 35:31; Judges 3:10; 1 Kings 22:24; Isaiah 61:1 for examples of the Spirit filling humans.

284. Acts 15:28.

285. John 16:14, NRSV.

286. John 4:24.

287. This is exemplified in the story of Ananias and Sapphira in Acts 5. When Ananias lied to the Holy Spirit, he lied to God.

288. Romans 8:2.

289. John 16:13.

290. Romans 15:30; Ephesians 4:30.

291. 1 Corinthians 2:10-11.

292. 1 Corinthians 12:11: He distributes spiritual gifts: 'It is the one and only Spirit who distributes all these gifts. He alone decides   which gift each person should have.'

293. John 14:16. He will 'never leave you'.

294. 1 Corinthians 2:10-11, because the Spirit 'searches out everything'.

295. Psalms 139:7-10.

296. Job 33:4; Psalms 104:30; Romans 8:11.

297. Matthew 28:19.

298. 2 Corinthians 13:14.

299. 1 Corinthians 12:4-6.

300. See Genesis 1-2; Job 33:4; Psalm 104:30.

301. 2 Chronicles 24:20; Numbers 11:25; Exodus 31:3.

302. Isaiah 61:1, NRSV.

303. Luke 4:21, NRSV.

304. Luke 24:49; Acts 1:8; 2:1-40.

305. John 14:26, NIV. (Read about the significant role of the Holy Spirit in the Christian life as outlined by Jesus in John 14–17.)

306. Acts 1:8, NIV.

307. Acts 2.

308. 1 Corinthians 12:1-14:25.

309. Galatians 5:16-26.

310. 1 Corinthians 2:10; Romans 12:2; Ephesians 4:23.

311. 1 Corinthians 6:19.

312. 2 Peter 1:3-8, TLB.

313. Romans 7:6; 8:2-11; 2 Corinthians 3:6; Galatians 5:16, 25 and 6:8.

314. John 3:5-8; 4:1-26; 1 Corinthians 6:11; 12:13; Titus 3:5; 1 John 5:6-8.

315. Paulsen, Jan. When the Spirit descends. Review and Herald Pub., 2001, p. 60.

316. 1 Thessalonians 5:19-21.

317. Luke 11:9-13.

18. SPIRIT OF TRANSFORMATION

God, help me to see the power involved in establishing your family on the earth. Show me how I can participate in that family with you and with the people in my community of friends.

re: tell

Grandpa Elmer wasn't much of a grandfather – or husband or parent or even much of a man. Disabled physically (by an on-the-job accident early in life) and emotionally (thanks to his family who sent him away on his own at the age of 12), by the time he married in his early 30s he was never more than a moment from anger. His soul simmered with rage – at life, at family come and gone, and soon at the meddling God his wife and sons insisted on worshipping.

Once free of an abusive childhood, Elmer's son Gerald made his estrangement complete by blocking all thoughts of his father from his mind. It worked well for one decade, then two, a quarter of a century – until something convicted him: 'Pray for your father,' a voice urged, silent as a sunrise yet clear as a songbird. 'Now?' Gerald winced. 'After all this time?'

But Gerald prayed, and soon his father, now in his 80s, began to transform. He surprised his wife with unexpected thoughtfulness. At suppertime, he insisted someone say grace and in ways both subtle and astonishing God revealed himself to the once bitter old man. Before

Elmer died he surrendered to the God who'd created him, the Son who'd saved him, and the soothing Spirit who'd so long pursued him.

re: think

God is all about relationships. He wants people to know him personally and live with him as a part of their lives. That's why he gave us the Holy Spirit. The community of believers (the church) exists to demonstrate God's character and personality through what the Bible calls the *fruit of the Spirit*, so that other people can learn to know God and love him. Jesus said, 'Your love for one another will prove to the world that you are my disciples.'[318]

The Bible often reminds us of our need to be 'filled with the Holy Spirit'. Believers are to be a Spirit-filled community. So how does this affect you and me?

coming of the holy spirit

The book of Acts in the New Testament describes the rapid growth of the Christian church after the coming of the Holy Spirit. The story happened in Jerusalem at the Jewish feast of Pentecost, when people from many parts of the world were gathered for worship celebration.[319]

About 120 of Christ's followers were praying together when the Holy Spirit came to them. The Bible says there was a sound of rushing wind, and something like tongues of fire appeared above each person's head. It may sound suspicious to us, but the results were amazing. The disciple Peter, who had had little formal education, went out and preached the gospel to the crowds in the city. He told them:

> 'Repent, and be baptised every one of you in the name of Jesus Christ so that your sins may be forgiven; and you will receive the gift of the Holy Spirit. For the promise is for you, for your children, and for all who are far away, everyone whom the Lord our God calls to him.'[320]

And everyone, no matter what language they spoke, understood what he was saying! That day 3,000 people accepted Jesus and were baptised.

There's an important sequence of events here:

**repentance from sin + baptism in the name of Jesus Christ
= God's forgiveness of our sins**

The people listening were baptised later,[321] and when Peter said, 'You will receive the gift of the Holy Spirit,' this was a future event, too. He's talking about the repentance and baptism of his present audience as well as of their future generations and people everywhere. The Holy Spirit has already come to the community of believers and will continue to come to everyone who repents and is baptised.

This great story at the beginning of the early Christian church was not just a random historical event in Jerusalem. It *initiated* the church's witness to the world, as Jesus had said.[322]

And it has been a *model* for all Christians ever since. After Pentecost, the promise of the Holy Spirit remained, and biblical Christians choose to live their lives according to the 'fruit of the Spirit', which we'll talk about more in the next chapter.

filled with the spirit

With the help of the Holy Spirit, Peter talked to 3,000 people from different countries and they all understood his words![323] In the same way today, the Spirit enables us to share Jesus. That's how Jesus defined the purpose of the Spirit in Acts 1:8 – it equips us for God's mission to the world.[324]

Acts 2 describes this experience as being '*filled* with the Holy Spirit'.[325] The same expression is used in reference to Peter,[326] Peter and the apostles,[327] Stephen,[328] Paul,[329] Barnabas,[330] groups of believers[331] and all the believers in the church:

> Paul said: 'No one can say "Jesus is Lord" except by the Holy Spirit.'

'When they had prayed, the place in which they were gathered together was shaken; and they were all filled with the Holy Spirit and spoke the Word of God with boldness.'[332]

So being 'filled with the Spirit' has two phases: one in ancient history and one in personal life. One Christian explained it like this:

143

'Just as Jesus came at one point in history, but nevertheless does not become my Lord until I am drawn by him and respond by accepting him, so the Spirit, who came to the community of believers at Pentecost as a gift to the church (and that gift has never been withdrawn) must find access to my life in order for the gift to become real *to me*.'[333]

Being filled with the Holy Spirit means being influenced by the Spirit of God. This is the gift we receive when we come to God in Jesus Christ. Paul said: 'Do not get drunk with wine, for that is debauchery; but be filled with the Spirit.'[334] He contrasts being filled with wine and being filled with the Spirit. This demonstrates the choices we have about what influences control us. Every believer has the gift of being influenced, guided and controlled by the Spirit of God.

God has a purpose when he fills us with the Spirit: we are to proclaim the Word of God and give glory through Jesus.[335] By the Spirit we receive power to share with others about God and his salvation in Christ.

Through the Spirit, we receive power to serve and live for God. This is demonstrated through the *gifts of the Spirit* (for service) and *the fruit of the Spirit* (for daily life), and both expressions of the Spirit serve to witness to the glory of God.

baptism with the spirit

Peter basically says: *Repent, be baptised, AND you will receive the Spirit.* Based on the original language, the connecting word 'and' could be either explanatory or cause-and-effect. But when we compare it with other Bible verses, it seems clear that we receive the Holy Spirit *in the process* of repentance and baptism; so there is no time gap between baptism and the Holy Spirit coming to the person who is repenting.

The Bible teaches that the gift of the Holy Spirit is given to the believer at the point of his repentance or conversion, resulting in baptism. For example:

Peter and the apostles told the Jewish Council and the High Priest: 'And we are witnesses to these things, and so is the Holy Spirit whom God has given to those who obey him.'[336] *The gift of the Holy Spirit is for all who repent and obey God.*

'The church then had peace throughout Judea, Galilee, and Samaria, and it became stronger as the believers lived in the fear of the Lord. And with the encouragement of the Holy Spirit, it also grew in numbers.'[337] *All believers have the Holy Spirit.*

Paul said of the Christian believers: 'You are not controlled by your sinful nature. You are controlled by the Spirit if you have the Spirit of God living in you. (And remember that those who do not have the Spirit of Christ living in them do not belong to him at all.)'[338] *Having the Holy Spirit is a condition for being a Christian.*

Paul said: 'No one can say "Jesus is Lord" except by the Holy Spirit.'[339] *All Christian witness is by the Holy Spirit.*

Paul also said: 'Some of us are Jews, some are Gentiles, some are slaves, and some are free. But we have all been baptized into one body by one Spirit, and we all share the same Spirit.'[340] *The baptism with the Spirit is collective and includes every believer.*

These and other texts show that the Holy Spirit belongs to us as we repent and are baptised in the name of Jesus Christ for the forgiveness of our sins. We believe the Bible teaches that there is only one baptism with the Holy Spirit in the life of every believer, and that takes place at the moment of conversion to Jesus Christ.[341] The gift of the Holy Spirit is what unifies the church.

The distinction between the two companies (the 120 and the 3,000) is of great importance, because the standard norm for today must surely be the second group of 3,000 and not the first group:

'The fact that the experience of the 120 was in two distinct stages was due simply to historical circumstances. They could not have received the Pentecostal gift before Pentecost. But those historical circumstances have long since ceased to exist. We live after the event of Pentecost, like the 3,000. With us, therefore, as with them, the forgiveness of sins and the "gift" or "baptism" of the Spirit are received together.'[342]

It appears, therefore, that the baptism of the Holy Spirit is something which occurred on those crucial initiatory occasions in the early church, when the faith in Christ moved beyond the small group of 120 believers in Jerusalem. Both the so-called 'Samaritan Pentecost'[343] and

145

the conversion of the Roman centurion Cornelius in Caesarea[344] mark new stages in the expansion of the original group of believers.

The Bible teaches that all believers receive the Holy Spirit, who comes to fill them at the time of their conversion. Our relationship to God in the Holy Spirit is therefore a matter of receiving and having faith, living in the Spirit, using our spiritual gifts in God's service, and developing the fruit of the Spirit in giving glory to God and reflecting Christ's character.

how do I receive the spirit?

Anyone may be filled with the Holy Spirit. The Bible actually makes it a command for all Christians: 'Be filled with the Spirit.'[345] If you are keen to receive the Spirit, then here are some biblical suggestions:

Make sure you understand, first of all, that the continuous 'filling' of our lives with the Holy Spirit comes from God. 'God has poured out his love into our hearts by the Holy Spirit, whom he has given us.'[346]

Jesus said we should *seek the Spirit and pray for it.*[347] Seeking is a powerful attitude and usually helps us to find what we're looking for!

Pray to God with faith. Our prayer for the Holy Spirit is particularly powerful when we pray with the conviction that God will answer.

God promised to answer our prayer for the Spirit. But are we able to see and hear the answer? Our sensitivity to spiritual direction may not be well trained. So in order to experience God's answer to our prayer, there are some steps we might take.

1). Understanding – The Bible instructs us 'for salvation through faith in Christ Jesus.'[348] To be filled with the Holy Spirit, we need to understand salvation and faith as revealed by the Bible. We also need to understand who the Holy Spirit is and how he works.

2). Submission to God's will – We need to become humble, giving up our way and following God's way. This means different things to different people in different situations. By spiritual activities like Bible reading, prayer, worship experiences and conversations with other people, we can discover the things in our lives that separate us from

God. Once recognised, we need to verbalise them and then seek to change, co-operating with the Holy Spirit who is already at work in us.

3). Walking by faith – When you feel a longing to pray for the Holy Spirit, that is the Spirit working in you. When you seek understanding, that is the Spirit working in you. When you submit yourself to God, that is the Spirit working in you. When you have faith, that is the Spirit working in you.

Walking by faith means that the Holy Spirit is already filling us, but if we want to stay with him and grow in him, we need to be led by God under the guidance of the Holy Spirit.

Life is stressful. Sometimes it's hard to concentrate on spiritual matters. It helps to have a routine that allows you a little time each day to set everything else aside and spend some moments with God. Maybe there are certain mental images or music that help to move your mind towards spiritual themes, making your heart humble and receptive. For me, the mental image of two enemies becoming reconciled and forgiving each other is very moving. The moments when we experience such mental images don't necessarily equate to a spiritual mood, but by making our hearts soft it may prepare us for satisfying our thirst for God and his Spirit.

Being filled with the Spirit doesn't happen just once and for all. It has to be a continuous reality every day. Regular daily quiet times with God are a great way to keep this experience alive, strong and growing. Let me invite you to experience the reality that Paul describes in this prayer:

'I pray that out of his glorious riches he may strengthen you with power through his Spirit in your inner being, so that Christ may dwell in your hearts through faith. And I pray that you, being rooted and established in love, may have power, together with all the saints, to grasp how wide and long and high and deep is the love of Christ, and to know this love that surpasses knowledge – that you may be filled to the measure of all the fullness of God.'[349]

re: consider

What could you do this week to change your routine and spend some quiet relationship time with God each day?

REFERENCES

318. John 13:35.
319. Acts 2.
320. Acts 2:38-39, NRSV.
321. Ibid verse 41.
322. Luke 24:49; Acts 1:8.
323. Acts 2:4, 11.
324. See Isaiah 43:10; Psalm 46:10: Revelation 14:7.
325. Acts 2:4.
326. Acts 4:8.
327. Acts 5:32.
328. Acts 6:5 and 7:55.
329. Acts 9:17.
330. Acts 11:24.
331. Acts 13:52.
332. Acts 4:31, NRSV.
333. Paulsen, Jan. *When the Spirit descends.* Review and Herald Pub., 2001, p. 83.
334. Ephesians 5:18, NRSV.
335. Acts 4:31.
336. Acts 5:32, NRSV.
337. Acts 9:31.
338. Romans 8:9.
339. 1 Corinthians 12:3.
340. 1 Corinthians 12:13.
341. Seven passages in the Bible directly mention baptism with the Spirit. Five of these refer to a future event: four were spoken by John the Baptist and one by Jesus after his resurrection. (Matthew 3:11; Mark 1:7-8; Luke 3:16; John 1:33.) A sixth passage looks back to the events and experiences of the day of Pentecost, (Acts 1:4-5) in fulfilment of the promises spoken by John the Baptist and Jesus. Only one passage, the one in 1 Corinthians 12:13, speaks about the wider experience of all believers. The first six passages all refer to the extraordinary event when the Holy Spirit was poured out at Pentecost according to Acts 2. On this occasion, the baptism with the Holy Spirit was given first to the 120 believers, who already believed in Jesus as Lord (Acts 11:15-17), and then to the 3,000 new believers who were baptised and received the gift of the Holy Spirit at the same time. (Acts 2:1-4.)
342. Stott, John R. W. *Baptism And Fullness: The Work of the Holy Spirit Today* (Ivp Classics). IVP Books, 2007, pp. 28-29.
343. Acts 8:14-17.
344. Acts 10:44-48.
345. Ephesians 5:18.
346. Romans 5:5, NIV.
347. Luke 11:9-13.
348. 2 Timothy 3:15, NIV.
349. Ephesians 3:16-19, NIV.

19. GIFTS WITH BENEFITS

God, I'm here to learn more about how you live in me, and how that works out in my life. Please show me ways in which our connection can be unique and practical so that it makes a genuine difference in who I am and how I live and treat others.

re: tell

Mayu sat in the same spot in the same pew week after week, but that was it. She slipped out of the side door after each service, never offering prayer or special music or even preparing a dish for a fellowship meal. She preferred life on the sidelines.

On one occasion, though, the church asked several members to share stories of meaningful relationships in their lives. When Mayu stood up, she electrified the room with a hilarious and inspiring tale of love and affection. Suddenly the shadow-dweller, the sideliner, had become the star of the show; all because she'd finally been asked to do something she was born to do.

re: think

Human relationships revolve around trust. It's the same in our relationship with God – we give him our trust and he gives us the Holy Spirit as a gift.[350]

When the Spirit begins to fill our lives, God influences and directs us. He wants to relate to us in order to develop and strengthen us. A relationship with God is always about revealing him to others and bringing people back to him. God's mission is to save the world and make it happy and whole again.[351]

When the Spirit of God works in us, we begin to use our spiritual gifts to serve him and other people. It influences our personality and how we interact with people.

spiritual gifts

The Bible gives four lists of spiritual gifts. Reading them in their context helps make them clear:

1. 'There are different kinds of spiritual gifts, but the same Spirit is the source of them all. There are different kinds of service, but we serve the same Lord. God works in different ways, but it is the same God who does the work in all of us. A spiritual gift is given to each of us so we can help each other.' (I Corinthians 12:4-7.)

2. 'Now these are the gifts Christ gave to the church: the apostles, the prophets, the evangelists, and the pastors and teachers. Their responsibility is to equip God's people to do his work and build up the church, the body of Christ.' (Ephesians 4:11, 12.)

3. 'Because of the privilege and authority God has given me, I give each of you this warning: Don't think you are better than you really are. Be honest in your evaluation of yourselves, measuring yourselves by the faith God has given us. Just as our bodies have many parts and each part has a special function, so it is with Christ's body. We are many parts of one body, and we all belong to each other. In his grace, God has given us different gifts for doing certain things well. So if God has given you the ability to prophesy, speak out with as much faith as God has given you. If your gift is serving others, serve them well. If you are a teacher, teach well. If your gift is to encourage others, be encouraging. If it is giving, give generously. If God has given you leadership ability, take the responsibility seri-

ously. And if you have a gift for showing kindness to others, do it gladly.' (Romans 12:3-8.)

4. 'God has given each of you a gift from his great variety of spiritual gifts. Use them well to serve one another. Do you have the gift of speaking? Then speak as though God himself were speaking through you. Do you have the gift of helping others? Do it with all the strength and energy that God supplies. Then everything you do will bring glory to God through Jesus Christ. All glory and power to him forever and ever! Amen.' (1 Peter 4:10, 11.)

What a variety! At least twenty distinct gifts are mentioned; no one gift occurs in all four lists, and thirteen of the gifts are mentioned only once.[352] Obviously, the Bible doesn't limit the number of spiritual gifts or emphasise one over the others. A spiritual gift is defined not by a specific activity or ability, but by its function.

Looking at 1 Corinthians 12, these are the essentials:

(a) *Who has a spiritual gift?* Only those prepared to confess that Jesus is Lord are truly led by the Spirit (verse 3). This implies accepting God as the only God, receiving forgiveness of sins through Jesus, and being controlled by the Holy Spirit.

(b) *What is a spiritual gift?* Gifts vary greatly (verses 4-6). There are many different abilities, possibilities and situations through which we may serve Jesus. These are 'spiritual capacities with real-life opportunities.'[353]

'A gift and the job in which to exercise it, or a job and the gift with which to do it.'[354]

(c) *What is the purpose of a spiritual gift?* They are given 'for the common good' (verse 7, NIV). For the building up of the

> 'If we live by the Spirit, let us also be guided by the Spirit.'

people in the church and the community, so that others may find God.[355] The gifts he gave were 'to equip God's people to do his work and build up the church, the body of Christ.'[356] Spiritual gifts are not for selfish use, but to build up the unity of the community of believers and to glorify God.

How do you recognise your own spiritual gifts? It's easiest within the fellowship of a church family, where various ministries and needs arise.

Accept that God has given you at least one spiritual gift, and he wants you to know what it is and how to use it for his glory.

Pray that God will guide you to know your spiritual gift. It may take some time, and perhaps you might misjudge it, but continue to pray and test yourself until you know.

Ensure that you are willing to use the gift(s) you have in a way that honours God.

Read the Bible until you understand its teaching about spiritual gifts.

Know and understand yourself and your abilities. (Community with other people will help you know who you are.)

Always remember that spiritual gifts are received and used by individuals in the body of Christ. They're not for selfish enjoyment but for service to others, for building up the church.

fruit of the spirit

When we're filled with the Holy Spirit, our actions and habits change. The Bible calls this the 'fruit of the Spirit'.[357] This passage in Galatians 5 tells us to live by the Spirit and not to serve our selfish desires.[358] Paul sharply contrasts the selfish desires of the sinful nature with the fruit of the Holy Spirit.[359]

> 'The fruit of the Spirit is love, joy, peace, patience, kindness, generosity, faithfulness, gentleness and self-control. . . . If we live by the Spirit, let us also be guided by the Spirit.'[360]

This fruit, given by the Spirit, characterises those who belong to Jesus. Being Spirit-filled doesn't just affect our internal life, relating to standards and character. It also affects our external actions, the result of belonging to Jesus and having faith in him. The fruit of the Spirit should be apparent in all Christians.

Love comes from God who gave himself in Jesus on the cross. Love gives freely without asking for anything in return.

'Love is patient; love is kind; love is not envious or boastful or arrogant or rude. It does not insist on its own way; it is not irritable or resentful; it does not rejoice in wrongdoing, but rejoices in the truth. It bears all things, believes all things, hopes all things, endures all things. Love never ends. . . .' (1 Corinthians 13:4-8, NRSV.)

Joy is independent of outward circumstances. It is rooted in a sense of security in God, rather than fluctuating according to what happens around you.

Peace is a tranquillity that results from a right relationship with God and/or other people. It is especially connected with the blessing and presence of God.

Patience is keeping steady in the midst of provocation and injury caused by others. It is an enduring outward expression of love.

Kindness and *generosity* are a favourable disposition to those around us, and expressions of love for others. They include a sense of hospitality and welcome towards others.

Faithfulness means being trustworthy, honest and reliable in our dealings with others. It exudes integrity and dependability.

Gentleness is also humility, mildness towards others, and includes tolerance and forgiveness of injury from others.

Self-control means mastering our desires and passions, choosing to be in control of things around us rather than letting addictions or dependencies control us. It also means holding ourselves in check when our natural impulse is to act in an ungodly way.

On the one hand, these attributes are very definite: you either have them or you don't. There is nothing called 'almost love'. Love is either genuine or it isn't.

On the other hand, the way in which these qualities are displayed in our personalities can vary to a greater or lesser degree. They may be already strongly developed in the characters of some, and less so in others. This is where we have room for growth – not so much in our behaviour, but more in how completely we allow the Holy Spirit to enter our lives and thoughts. In this work the great model is Jesus Christ: 'I am the vine; you are the branches. Those who remain in me, and I in them, will produce much fruit. For apart from me you can do nothing.'[361]

This is the secret of a spiritually fruitful life. You receive the Holy Spirit when you rest in Christ and he lives in you.

1. If Christ's words remain in you, you remain in him.[362]

2. If you remain in Christ's love, you remain in him – and you remain in his love if you obey his commands.[363]

3. His command is: 'Love each other in the same way I have loved you.'[364]

It's like a circle. Wherever you enter the circle you are part of a fruitful development that leads to fullness. By Christ's love, you remain in Christ, and by remaining in Christ you receive the fruit of the Spirit. The fruit of the Spirit is love, but it is also the attitudes and actions by which you express that love. This makes you remain even more in Christ's love, so that you grow more and more. In this way, your faith in him expresses itself through love, and the Bible teaches us that this true, transforming love is 'the only thing that counts.'[365]

community

Both the gifts of the Spirit and the fruit of the Spirit function in the context of a community of people. The gifts are services that build up the community, making it grow. The fruit is our Christ-like character that encourages and participates in our neighbour's joys and sorrows. It is a way of bearing one another's burdens.[366]

God is all about relationships. He created us for relationships. Then he sent Jesus Christ to restore our broken relationship with him. And now he continuously sends the Holy Spirit to heal, cleanse and renew us so that we are capable of loving relationships with him and others. It gives to the whole world evidence of the God in whom we believe.

The church community is a place where we share these relationships, showing to the world that God is truly God and that, when his love is expressed in Christ and kept alive in us by the Holy Spirit, the kingdom of God is present.

'The church is the repository of the riches of the grace of Christ; and through the church will eventually be made manifest . . . the final and full display of the love of God.'[367]

re: consider

How do you feel about the idea that spiritual fruit grows best in a community of disciples who support each other, like a church?

REFERENCES
350. Acts 2:38-39.
351. John 3:16.
352. Stott, John R. W. *Baptism And Fullness The Work of the Holy Spirit Today* (Ivp Classics). IVP Books, 2007, p. 88.
353. Paulsen, Jan. *When the Spirit descends*. Review and Herald Pub., 2001, p. 89.
354. Stott, John R. W. *Baptism And Fullness The Work of the Holy Spirit Today* (Ivp Classics). IVP Books, 2007, p. 87.
355. See 1 Corinthians 14:24-25.
356. Ephesians 4:11-12.
357. Galatians 5, NIV.
358. Ibid verse 16.
359. Ibid verses 19-25.
360. Galatians 5:22-25, NRSV.
361. John 15:5.
362. John 15:7.
363. John 15:10.
364. John 15:12.
365. Galatians 5:6, NIV.
366. Galatians 6:2.
367. White, Ellen G. *The Acts of the Apostles*. Pacific P, 1970, p. 9.

20. SORTING OUT THE FUTURE

God, thank you for this opportunity to learn more about you. Would you please join me and teach me and guide me as I discover more about who you want me to become?

re: tell

In 1870, while visiting a small denominational college and staying at the home of its president, a bishop expressed the firm conviction that the Bible predicted that nothing new could be invented. The educator disagreed.

'Why, in fifty years I believe it may be possible for men to soar through the air like birds!' he said. The visiting dignitary was shocked.

'Flight is strictly reserved for the angels,' he replied, 'and I beg you not to repeat your suggestion lest you be guilty of blasphemy!'

That bishop was none other than Milton Wright, the father of Orville and Wilbur! Only thirty years later near Kitty Hawk, North Carolina, his sons made their first flight in a heavier-than-air machine![368]

re: think

When we talk about prophets and prophecy, it isn't easy to define *revelation, inspiration* and *illumination*. There's always that elusive quality, an element of mystery. But that doesn't mean that it isn't real or that prophets might not have a valid message for us.

Biblical evidence makes it possible to say that *revelation* is a divine act through which God reveals himself and thus enables a prophet to understand something he could not have discovered alone. *Inspiration* is also a divine act where God enables a prophet to grasp and communicate in a trustworthy manner the message which has been revealed. Finally, *illumination* is a divine act where God enables any person in a right relationship with him to understand what has been revealed.

People who believe in *encounter theology* claim that when any prophet comes into the presence of God, no information or truth is communicated to him since he is only in a state of awe, adoration and wonder. This would make the Bible merely a compilation of testimonies of faith, without binding instruction, because it contains only the personal opinions of its writers. It means that truth couldn't be applied to any statement of the Bible since Jesus alone is the truth.[369] Encounter theologists say that the purpose of the Scriptures is only to increase our faith in Jesus, but not to help us understand how to live or what is right and what is wrong.[370]

But according to the Bible, revelation and inspiration are the disclosure of propositions or truths. When God reveals himself to a prophet, he discloses mysteries which a human being would not be able to understand alone. For instance, in the book of Daniel it says: 'During the night the mystery was revealed to Daniel in a vision' and 'Surely your God is the God of gods and the Lord of kings and a revealer of mysteries . . .'[371] In the book of Amos it says: 'Surely the Sovereign Lord does nothing without revealing his plan to his servants the prophets.'[372]

The purpose of God's self-disclosure to human beings is to restore the relationship between us and God, the relationship that was lost in the beginning when Adam and Eve chose to sin rather than obey. Before that sin, God was coming to Adam and Eve in the cool of the day, and he wants to recapture that companionship with us even now.

The *revelation* of God through his word is just as complex as his *revelation* through the person of Jesus Christ. In the epistle to Timothy, Paul, speaking about the incarnation of Christ, states that 'the mystery of godliness is great: he appeared in a body.'[373]

157

'But the Bible, with its God-given truths expressed in the language of man, presents a union of the divine and the human. Such a union existed in the nature of Christ, who was the Son of God and the Son of man. Thus it is true of the Bible, as it was of Christ, 'the Word was made flesh, and dwelt among us.'[374]

Jesus' act of risking his life and becoming human was misunderstood among God's followers for centuries. Some have emphasised the human nature of Christ at the expense of his divine nature; others have emphasised his divine nature at the expense of his human nature; and a third group believed that the two natures were mysteriously blended into one person. And people have treated the inspiration of scripture in the same way. Some people emphasise the divine nature of the scripture at the expense of its human nature, while others emphasise its human aspects at the expense of the divine ones.

It seems that problems over understanding prophecy stem from the challenge of understanding the process or nature of *inspiration*. In the Bible we have only incidental references to the 'how' in the cases of Balaam,[375] Daniel, John and Paul. But they never fully explain the process or nature of it. Even the prophet Moses never explained how he received the facts of creation.

Eastern minds are much more concerned with the 'what' questions. Westerners are fascinated by the 'how' questions. So it seems that God reveals 'what' he wants, through 'whom' he wants, 'when' he wants and 'the way' he wants.

But there's still that part of us that wants to know *how*. We want to qualify prophecy and put it in a neat little philosophical box. We have a hard time with mysteries that we can't solve through scientific formulae. We want to know if *every* word of a prophet is inspired. Was his grammar and punctuation inspired, too? Yet sometimes we just have to trust the mystery.

There is nothing in the Bible to support a concept of *verbal* or *mechanical inspiration*. That's where the prophet is just a passive instrument, conveying the exact words given by God. Instead, scriptural evidence maintains that the totality of the prophet is involved in the phenomenon of revelation and inspiration: his personality, age, education, gender, occupation, time and culture all affect the writings he puts down. This view is called *organic inspiration* and it emphasises the fact that in the process of inspiration the divine mind and will are combined with the human mind and will, and the writings of the human prophet become the Word of God.[376]

One author puts it this way: 'The treasure was entrusted to earthen vessels, yet it is, none the less, from Heaven. The testimony is conveyed through the imperfect expression of human language, yet it is the testimony of God; and the obedient, believing child of God beholds in it the glory of the divine power, full of grace and truth.'[377]

So the language of Bible authors is not divine but human, and 'everything that is human is imperfect.'[378] The human authors were subject to all the weaknesses and failures of humanity. They were not free from sin, they had doubts, they were fearful and at times they yielded to temptation.[379] *Therefore, we can logically conclude that it is the thoughts and concepts in the Bible and prophetic writings that make up the truth about God, not the isolated words.*

The biblical writers do not usually explain the 'how' of revelation since they are interested more in the 'what' of revelation. They did not always fully understand what they conveyed in their oral or written message. They sometimes made mistakes, because they were human beings. Some of them were polished writers with beautiful syntax and grammar; others were less formally educated and more rough in their writing style. However, these issues are essentially trivial and never distort the continuity of their theological concepts and thoughts, which constitute the Word of God.

It is important to notice that the Bible gives no expiration date on the possibilities of prophetic revelation. It is entirely possible for the phenomenon of *revelation* to function in exactly the same way in more modern times as it did in the Bible.

What, you may ask, is the extent of inspiration? Is a prophet always inspired? It seems obvious from biblical evidence that the *revelation/ inspiration* phenomenon does not necessarily have power over the inspired person twenty-four hours a day from the moment he is called to prophetic ministry. God does not only reveal himself to *whom* he wants, *what* he wants, the *way* he wants but also *when* he wants.

Revelation does not depend on the inspired person but upon the inspirer. An inspired writer or prophet can make mistakes when he or she is not under the direct guidance of the Spirit of God. For instance, Samuel the prophet was, on one occasion, wrong about the future king of Israel.[380] He looked at one handsome young man and said: 'Surely this is the Lord's anointed.' Only after God told him to look at another young man, David, was he able to anoint the right person.[381] One more modern prophet, Ellen White, wrote about her own experience:

> 'There are times when common things must be stated, common thought must occupy the mind, common letters must be written and information given that has passed from one to another of the workers. Such words, such information are not given under the special inspiration of the Spirit of God.'[382]

How, then, can we know which things are said under the direct influence of the Holy Spirit and which things are 'common'? The application of certain principles of interpretation of the biblical text itself is the only way to determine the message of God in any prophetic writings.

rules of interpretation

Whenever you read prophetic writings, either biblical or contemporary, much confusion and misunderstanding can be avoided if you apply a few rules of hermeneutical interpretation. The word 'hermeneutics' comes from the Greek verb *hermeneo*. Jesus used this word in Luke 24:27 when 'beginning with Moses and all the Prophets, he explained *(diermeneusen)* to them' the truth about the Messiah. (NIV.) Here are some key hermeneutical rules:

Sola Scriptura (only Scripture): Seventh-day Adventists believe that the Bible alone is the *norm* of truth, the sole *foundation* and *final authority* of Christian faith.[383]

Yet the New Testament indicates that there are prophets who come after the time of the Bible. 'Here are some of the parts God has appoint-

appointed for the church: first are apostles, second are prophets...' Paul wrote.[384] Adventists believe in modern prophecy and acknowledge inspired writings after the Bible. The nineteenthcentury author Ellen White, whose many books are often referred to collectively as 'the Spirit of Prophecy', is regarded as a modern prophet.

However, any writing outside the Bible itself – no matter how inspired – is still secondary to scripture and can never be considered equal in its authority. The writings of Ellen White are not 'the final norm of truth' or the 'basis of doctrine', but they do provide 'comfort, guidance, instruction, correction' as well as 'guidance in understanding the teaching of Scripture and application of these teachings.'[385] Ellen White belongs to the group of non-canonical inspired writers like Nathan, Gad, Ahijah and Iddo.[386] The message of these prophets bore the authority of God, although they wrote nothing for the biblical canon.

> It is important to notice that the Bible gives no expiration date on the possibilities of prophetic revelation.

Tota Scriptura (totality of Scripture): This hermeneutical principle is important for accurate interpretation of sacred writings and it declares that there is a unity of thought within Scripture since there is one divine author behind the entire book. If the sacred writer is inspired by God, then his/her writings will contain a unified, harmonious and consistent message from God to human beings.[387] *Thus, one must take the total range of what the sacred writer has written on a particular subject in order to be able to determine what the position is.*

Many people read inspired writings with their own presuppositions and they take only what they want to find, clearly overlooking the totality of statements on any particular issue. *Therefore, before we reach any conclusion about a writer's authenticity, we must include all that they have said on the subject.*[388] And all writings must be compared against the biblical scripture to be proven true.

Scriptura Suis Ipsius Interpres (Scripture is its own interpreter): 'Scripture is explained by Scripture.'[389] The Bible is its own expositor.[390] The principle that the sacred writings in the Bible and the prophetic writings of Ellen White contain a harmonious, unified message from God does not assume that all texts are equally clear. *Consequently, the overall message of the sacred writings provides the final context for the meaning of any less clear word or sentence.*[391]

Spiritalia Spiritaliter Examinatur (spiritual things are spiritually discerned): Often it is hard for the unbeliever to understand some aspects of Christian faith, because 'The man without the Spirit does not accept the things that come from the Spirit of God, for they are foolishness to him, and he cannot understand them, because they are spiritually discerned.'[392] Both the sacred writings of the ancient Scripture and the more recent prophetic writings of Ellen White help to explain things about God and should be approached with a spiritual mind.

Many systems of faith force the ancient Scripture to share authority with other writings, but not the Seventh-day Adventist Church. Even as a prophet, Ellen White placed a constant and strong emphasis *on the essentiality and centrality of the Bible in the theology and practice of believers.* Most traditional churches cannot claim the Bible as their sole foundation of theology and practice. For example, if one asks a well-informed member of the Catholic Church what he believes and why he believes it, the answer would be: 'I believe what the Church tells me to believe.' In both Catholic and Orthodox religions, the ancient Scripture's authority is placed behind that of the church leaders and the church tradition.[393] In the Church of Jesus Christ of Latter-day Saints there is a dual foundation – the Bible and the Book of Mormon.[394] The authority of the Bible in many Protestant churches is considerably weakened by allowing other writings to hold equal or even higher authority than the Bible.

Seventh-day Adventists accept the *sola scriptura* principle, acknowledging the Bible as the *sole foundation* and the *final norm* for the truth. We also recognise that one of the gifts of the Holy Spirit is prophecy, which was manifested in the ministry of Ellen White.

As we continue to explore and understand more about the Holy Bible and how it applies to our lives, our understanding of sacred inspiration is key. If we get confused with the roles of different writers and prophets, then the Bible loses its authority and power in our lives. But when the Scripture is held as the final word on matters of faith, our journey as God-followers becomes more clear.

re: consider

How can you apply something from prophecy to the choices you make every day?

REFERENCES

368. Adapted from: *http://elbourne.org/sermons/index.mv?illustration+4578.*
369. See Schnucker, R. V. 'Barth, Karl.' *Evangelical Dictionary of Theology.* Baker Academic, Paternoster P, 2001, p. 126.
370. Ibid.
371. Daniel 2:19, 47, NIV.
372. Amos 3:7, NIV. See also Matthew 11:25ff; Ephesians 3:1-6.
373. 1 Timothy 3:16, NIV.
374. White, Ellen G. *The Great Controversy.* Pacific P, 1971, p.vi.
375. Read Numbers 22.
376. 1 Thessalonians 2:13.
377. White, Ellen G. *Selected Messages. Vol. 1.* Review and Herald Pub., 1958, p. 26.
378. Ibid 20.
379. 2 Samuel 11:1-27; Numbers 20:10-12; Exodus 4:10-14; Luke 22:54-62.
380. 1 Samuel 16:1-7.
381. There are other examples in the Bible when inspired biblical writers erred: Nathan (2 Samuel 7:1-17), David (2 Samuel 11, 12; Psalms 51), Peter (Acts 10; Galatians 2), Paul (Acts 21).
382. White, Ellen G. *Selected Messages. Vol. 1.* Review and Herald Pub., 1958, p. 39.
383. See Isaiah 8:20 and 66:2.
384. 1 Corinthians 12:27-29.
385. *Ministry* Magazine Aug. 1982: 21.
386. 1 Chronicles 29:29; 2 Chronicles 9:29.
387. See Douglass, Herbert. *Messenger of the Lord.* Pacific P, 1998, p. 394. Also 2 Tim, 3:16; 2 Pet. 1:20-21.
388. Ibid 394.
389. White, Ellen G. *Selected Messages. Vol. 1.* Review and Herald Pub., 1958, p. 42.
390. See Luke 24:27; 1 Corinthians 2:13.
391. Douglass, 394.
392. 1 Corinthians 2:14, NIV.
393. See Abbott, Walter M. *Documents of Vatican II.* New Win Pub, 1966, p. 114-119.
394. Hexham, I. 'Mormonism.' *Evangelical Dictionary of Theology.* 1987, p. 735.

21. THE FUTURE TODAY

God, life can get confusing – and it's always a challenge to know how to prepare for what's coming next. I'd really like to avoid facing the future alone. Would you help me to understand how you're trying to help me with the resources you've given me to live a happier life?

re: tell

Carmen stared straight ahead, her knuckles turning white at the wheel. 'I could have sworn the park was right after that last turnoff. . . . Let me see the map.'

Diana pulled the road atlas closer to her nose. 'Um, why don't you keep driving or at least pull off somewhere. I'm just sorry. I thought I'd packed my GPS unit!'

Carmen felt a burst of hope and smiled, 'My GPS – of course! It's in the back seat pocket. The satellites always know where to go. . . .'

re: think

Ellen White gets it! She understands our twenty-first-century heart-cry to experience God, to do something meaningful and enduring in our lives and to grapple with issues of poverty, alienation, health, education, diversity, inclusiveness, integrity and eternity.

Oh, yes, and she's dead.

No, we haven't been channelling a dead lady. The principles she taught transcend time and are just as pertinent and applicable today as when she lived. Writing on a wide variety of subjects over a period of nearly seventy years, Ellen White promoted principles that are consistent and timeless.

Though some of her counsel about knowing God, about prayer, Scripture study and character development parallels other nineteenth-century writers, her spiritual counsel bears a unique and over-arching world-view of the great controversy between Jesus and Satan, between good and evil. She always looked beyond the present to heavenly realities, and her writing reflects that projection.

Likewise, though some of her health and lifestyle counsel reflects ideas from some of her contemporaries, she never bought into those ideas wholesale. Sometimes her health principles were completely opposite to most of the popular ideas at that time. She believed that God and his Spirit were the source of her inspiration, not her own opinions or interpretations.

Whether they regard him as teacher, prophet or Messiah, most cultures value principles from Christ's teachings. Jesus used agrarian society as the backdrop for many of his parables; yet the principles from his stories endure even in societies very different from the culture of his original audience. Just the same, Ellen White made a significant contribution to the discovery and understanding of the meaning of life. I don't think that her principles on health, spirituality and lifestyle will ever become outdated, even with accelerating world change, because they have universal application.[395]

With global commerce, high-speed communication, terrorism, AIDS and family disintegration, our world has radically changed since the 1800s. Yet it is perhaps *because* of these accelerating changes that her counsel to cultivate a calm trust in God seems so surprisingly fresh.

In few areas does this particular author give more counsel than on the subject of caring for the poor, needy and marginalised. If our world leaders had no other counsel than this, Ellen White's enduring legacy and relevance to them would be assured. In today's unparalleled prosperity, neglect of the needy corresponds to spiritual poverty. Perhaps our perpetual search for meaning in the workplace might find resolution if we applied her suggestions about serving the poor.

Humanity's desire is to know God; God's desire is to restore humanity to reflect him. This restoration enables God to achieve companionship and communication with us. This kind of companionship includes our enthusiastic obedience in response to his love. The primary means through which God communicates that love and his will for individuals is through the Holy Spirit.

The Spirit works through various methods: Scripture, impressions on the heart that are tested by his Word,[396] the book of nature,[397] extrabiblical prophets[398] and the community of faith. So the discovery and practice of Spirit-inspired life principles in the writings of a prophet is one way for us to know and communicate with God himself.

Ephesians 4:11-13 indicates that the spiritual gift of prophecy will continue to exist until the church reaches full maturity and unity, and both 1 Corinthians 12 and Romans 12 identify prophecy as a gift of the Spirit.

Seventh-day Adventists[399] and Ellen White herself[400] base her call as a prophet on the prophecies of Joel 2:28, 29 and Revelation 12:17 and 19:10.

The Seventh-day Adventist Church believes that Ellen White's writings pass the biblical tests of confession in Christ[401] and harmony with Scripture.[402] Her messages do not contradict God's past revelation through prophets and through his Son, Jesus. Thus, Seventh-day Adventists consider Ellen White, though human, to be a divinely appointed spokesperson for God in the same way that Old and New Testament prophets were appointed as God's messengers.[403]

> Humanity's desire is to know God; God's desire is to restore humanity to reflect him.

Since Jesus foretold the emergence of false prophets as one of the signs of the imminence of his return, the implication is clear that there must also be true or genuine prophets at that same time.

While Seventh-day Adventists officially hold that Ellen White's writings are authoritative,[404] her writings are considered always subordinate to Holy Scripture. We believe she communicated messages from God[405] for the building up, encouragement and consolation[406] of the church.[407] Some Adventists maintain that Ellen White's gift was primarily for spiritual encouragement, but not for defining truth or correcting error. However, early Adventist leaders formally recognised God's revelations through Ellen White as having theological authority.[408]

Today the Seventh-day Adventist position continues to be that one of the purposes for Ellen White's writings is guidance in understanding the teaching of Scripture and application of those teachings.[409]

Ellen White herself saw her role as including the correction of error,[410] and 'to open the Scriptures to others as God has opened them to me.'[411] She stated, 'I have a work of great responsibility to do – to impart by pen and voice the instruction given me, not alone to Seventh-day Adventists, but to the world.'[412]

In times of historical crisis or calamity or deliverance, God often chose to declare his will through a prophet. Noah announced Earth's impending destruction by a global deluge; Moses brought deliverance to God's people from the Egyptians; Jeremiah and Isaiah warned of national calamity; and John heralded the arrival of the Messiah. Seventh-day Adventists believe that Jesus' return to this earth is coming soon. Isn't it unlikely that at Earth's final crisis God would leave his people without prophetic guidance?[413]

At the age of 17, Ellen White received her first vision and shortly after recognised her own calling by God to bear prophetic messages.[414] Through seventy years of public ministry, she maintained that her calling was human, but that the voice of God spoke to her through his Holy Spirit.[415]

Ellen White's roots were Methodist. She was baptised by immersion at 12 and accepted into the membership of the Methodist church. Methodists of the nineteenth-century placed a strong emphasis on disciplined living, and it was a Methodist minister who, when 14-year-old Ellen Harmon (her maiden name) was troubled by feelings of guilt and fear, reassured her of God's infinite love and mercy. She later described this event as pivotal in her Christian experience,[416] changing her view of God from demanding and stern to a kind and tender parent.[417] This early discovery of God as a loving deity became an encompassing theme in her writings.

Ellen White's world-view and theology were filtered through the lens of Scripture. She considered the Bible to be its own expositor.[418] The centrality of the Scriptures was a recurring motif in both her writings and public speaking. As early as 1851 she could say, 'I recommend to you, dear reader, the Word of God as the rule of your faith and practice.' She saw the details and insights in her writings as an agency to clarify the truths of the Word of God. In her view, the Bible provides all instruction necessary for believers to understand and accept salvation.[419] Her writings and testimonies were 'a lesser light to lead men and women to the greater light [the Bible].'[420]

Ellen White never claimed authority as intrinsic in herself. Her authority, she believed, came as a link in the chain of communication through which God gave instruction to his people.[421]

A Dudley and Cummings' survey of 2,848 readers of Ellen White's writings and 5,375 non-readers[422] came to some intriguing conclusions. The findings show that people who read Ellen White's writings:

(a) see their relationship with Christ as more intimate – a difference of 26% compared to the non-readers;

(b) have more assurance of salvation – a difference of 23%;

(c) re more ready to identify their spiritual gifts and to engage in the service of the Church – a 16% difference;

(d) are more supportive of investing funds in outreach or missionary projects – a 10% difference;

(e) feel better prepared for witnessing and outreach programmes – a 25% difference.

In addition, it seems clear and definitive that her readers are more likely to study the Bible daily, to pray for specific people, to view their church more positively and to share Jesus with more people by introducing them to their church.[423]

Another recent survey, conducted by The Barna Group in the United States on the subject of the reading habits of Protestant pastors, lists Ellen White as one of the most influential authors for today's younger clergy.[424] The survey states that 'the under-40 pastors championed several authors who were not ranked highly by older church leaders. Those authors included business consultant James Collins, seminary professor Thom Rainer, nineteenth-century Seventh-day Adventist icon Ellen White, and Pastor John Ortberg.'[425]

Members of the Seventh-day Adventist Church should be careful never to say, 'I believe it because the Bible and the writings of Ellen White say so.' We believe what we believe because the *Bible* says so – full stop. The Bible is our sole foundation and the final authority in Christian faith, and even Ellen White strongly and powerfully emphasised the centrality of the Bible.[426] The purpose of her writings is 'guidance in understanding the teaching of Scripture and application of these teachings with prophetic urgency to the spiritual and moral life.'[427]

She encouraged every church member, every Christian, to work for the salvation of those 'for whom Christ died.'[428] 'Lift up Jesus,' she wrote, 'lift him up in sermon, in song, in prayer.'[429]

re: consider

What would make you want to believe in prophecy more?

REFERENCES
395. In its 30 May 2005 electronic newsletter, *Update*, The Barna Group announced Ellen White as one of the authors, along with leadership theorist Jim Collins, who had the greatest impact on pastors under the age of 40.
396. John 16:14; Isaiah 8:20.
397. 1 Corinthians 11:14.
398. Joel 2:28-29.

399. *Seventh-day Adventists believe – a biblical exposition of 27 fundamental doctrines.* Ministerial Association, General Conference of Seventh-day Adventists, 1988, p. 252.

400. White, Ellen G. *Loma Linda Messages.* Leaves of Autumn, 1987, p. 33.

401. 1 John 4:1-3.

402. Isaiah 8:20.

403. Exodus 4:15, 16.

404. 'Affirmations and Denials.' 4 Apr. 2006. Biblical Research Institute. *www.adventist-biblicalresearch.org.*

405. 'Prophecies' has a broader meaning than mere foretelling of future events. The bulk of Ellen White's 'prophesying' is in the category of spiritual admonition, which appears to be the focus of 1 Corinthians 14:3.

406. 1 Corinthians 14:3.

407. White, Ellen G. *Early Writings.* Review and Herald Pub., 1945, p. 78.

408. Douglass, Herbert. *Messenger of the Lord.* Pacific P, 1998, p. 428; White, James. 'The Gifts – Their Object.' *Review and Herald* 28 Feb. 1856: 172..

409. Biblical Research Institute, (22 May 2006).

410. White, Ellen G. *Selected Messages. Vol. 3.* Review and Herald Pub., 1958, p. 31.

411. White, Ellen. *Testimonies for the Church. Vol. 8.* Pacific P, 1855-1909, p. 236.

412. Ibid.

413. Amos 3:7.

414. White, Ellen G. *Early Writings.* Review and Herald Pub., 1945, pp. 13-21.

415. 'A Message to the Churches.' *Review and Herald* 18 July 1907: 8.

416. White, Ellen G. *Life Sketches of Ellen G White.* Pacific P, 1915, 1943, pp. 36, 37.

417. Ibid p. 39.

418. White, Ellen G. *Counsels to Parents, Teachers and Students.* Pacific P, 1913, 1943, p. 511.

419. White, Ellen G. *Selected Messages. Vol. 1.* Review and Herald Pub., 1958, pp. 17-18.

420. White, Ellen G. *Colporteur Ministry.* Pacific P, 1953, p. 125.

421. White, Ellen. *Testimonies for the Church. Vol. 5.* Pacific P, 1855-1909, p. 661; White, Ellen G. *Selected Messages. Vol. 3.* Review and Herald Pub., 1958, p. 30.

422. Dudley, Roger L., and Des Cummings. 'Who Reads Ellen White?' *Ministry Magazine* Oct. 1982: 10-12.

423. Ibid.

424. See *www.barna.org/barna-update/article/5-barna-update/178-survey-reveals-the-books-and-authors-that-have-most-influenced-pastors*

425. Ibid.

426. 'The Inspiration and Authority of the Ellen G White Writings.' *Ministry* Magazine Aug. 1982: 21.

427. Ibid.

428. 'Christ's Commission.' *Review and Herald* 10 June 1880: 369.

429. White, Ellen G. *Gospel Workers.* 1915th ed. Review and Herald Pub., 1915, 1948, p. 160.

Affirmations[430, 431]

1. We believe that Scripture is the divinely revealed Word of God and is inspired by the Holy Spirit.

2. We believe that the canon of Scripture is composed only of sixty-six books of the Old and New Testaments.

3. We believe that Scripture is the foundation of faith and the final authority in all matters of doctrine and practice.

4. We believe that Scripture is the Word of God in human language.

5. We believe that Scripture teaches that the gift of prophecy will be manifest in the Christian church after New Testament times.

6. We believe that the ministry and writings of Ellen White were a manifestation of the gift of prophecy.

7. We believe that Ellen White was inspired by the Holy Spirit and that her writings, the product of that inspiration, are particularly applicable and authoritative to Seventh-day Adventists.

8. We believe that the purpose of Ellen White's writings includes guidance in understanding the teaching of Scripture and the application of these teachings with prophetic urgency to the spiritual and moral life.

9. We believe that the acceptance of the prophetic gift of Ellen White, while not a requirement for continuing church membership, is important to the nurture and unity of the Seventh-day Adventist Church.

10. We believe that Ellen White's use of literary sources and assistants finds parallels in some of the writings of the Bible.

Denials

1. We do not believe that the quality or degree of inspiration in the writings of Ellen White is different from that in Scripture.

2. We do not believe that the writings of Ellen White serve the same purpose as does Scripture, which is the sole foundation and final authority of Christian faith.

3. We do not believe that the writings of Ellen White are an addition to the canon of sacred Scripture.

4. We do not believe that the writings of Ellen White may be used as a basis of doctrine.

5. We do not believe that the study of the writings of Ellen White may be used to replace the study of Scripture.

6. We do not believe that Scripture can be understood only through the writings of Ellen White.

7. We do not believe that the writings of Ellen White exhaust the meaning of Scripture.

8. We do not believe that the writings of Ellen White are essential for the proclamation of the truths of Scripture to society at large.

9. We do not believe that the inspired writings of Ellen White are merely the product of Christian piety.

10. We do not believe that Ellen White's use of literary sources and assistants negates the inspiration of her writings.

REFERENCES

430. The following statement on the relationship of the writings of Ellen White to the Bible was prepared by the Biblical Research Institute and published in the *Ministry* magazine in August 1982. This statement represents an attempt to express the Seventh-day Adventist understanding of the gift of prophecy as an identifying mark of the remnant church.
431. *Ministry* Magazine Aug. 1982: 21.

ABOUT
MANAGEMENT

22. IT'S A PARADOX

God, humans in the past and present have often misunderstood what the Bible says regarding grace and rules. Please help me to understand their part in my relationship with you, so I don't grow unbalanced in how I live.

re: tell

Once there was a husband and wife who didn't really love one another. The man was so demanding that he prepared a list of rules and regulations for his wife to follow. He insisted that she read them every day and obey them to the letter. Among other things, his 'dos and don'ts' indicated such details as what time she had to get up in the morning, when his breakfast should be served, and how the housework should be done.

Then the husband died. Eventually the woman fell in love again, with a man who dearly loved her. When they married, this husband did everything he could to make his new wife happy, continually showering her with tokens of his appreciation.

One day, as she cleaned house, she came across the list of commands her first husband had required. As she looked it over, it dawned on her that even though her new husband hadn't asked her to, she was doing everything her first husband's list required anyway. This husband was so kind that her deepest desire was to please him out of love, not obligation.[432]

re: think

paradox: a statement or concept that contains apparently conflicting ideas

Faith, including Christianity, is full of paradoxes. In faith, *apparently* conflicting concepts are held to be true, in spite of the *apparent* logical contradiction.

Want examples?

God is one, yet he is three.

The Bible is written by human beings, yet it is the Word of God.

Jesus is God, yet he became man.

So we shouldn't get too worried when we find another fundamental paradox – that of *law* and *grace*.

God wants us to keep his law; it is a condition for our salvation. BUT salvation is through grace; it's free and cannot be earned.

Most people react negatively when they are confronted with 'the law'. It has connotations of coercion, fines, police, lawyers, even punishment and prison. Laws are often frustrating; they keep us from doing what we like and seem to challenge our freedom.

Yet we also recognise that 'law' is not only negative. The laws of nature give order and structure to our environment. We may not like all the laws of our land, but most of us agree that some system is needed. Laws may bring restrictions, but they also provide protection.

religious laws

Negative sentiments about laws are also reflected in the way many people view religious laws. They immediately think of religious laws as meaning restraint. 'He can't come because his religion forbids him,' they say, or 'Her faith doesn't allow her to do that.'

Some Christian denominations appear very strict, and their emphasis on scrupulously keeping God's law earns them the label of *legalistic*. Even to many Christians that sounds like a dirty word.

The Bible uses the term 'law' in many different ways. In some instances, especially in Paul's writings, it refers to the entire institution given to Israel some 1,500 years before Christ. In this sense, the law precedes Christ and was finished when Christ died on the cross. Those who follow Christ therefore 'no longer live under the requirements of the law', but instead 'live under the freedom of God's grace'.[433] The same idea was echoed in the gospel of John: 'For the law was given through Moses; grace and truth were realised through Jesus Christ'.[434] The apostle Paul described this Old Testament system of law as 'our tutor to bring us to Christ'.[435]

But does this mean that Christians today can ignore all laws that the Bible gives? No. Certainly some aspects of biblical law have lost immediate application. The *ceremonial laws* which regulated the services in the tabernacle and later the temple teach us a great deal about God's ways of dealing with sin, but they ceased to be binding or necessary when the curtain in the Jerusalem temple was ripped from top to bottom – at the very moment Jesus died his atoning death on the cross.[436]

Other Old Testament laws were *civil*; they applied to the government of ancient Israel as a nation. They still inspire us with certain principles but their immediate sphere no longer exists.

But other parts of divine law have no expiration date. Why would health principles given to God's people in ancient times suddenly be obsolete? Why should we disregard giving a tithe of our income, when we need a proven system of support for the church?

Most important is the core of this divinely given system of law known as the Ten Commandments.[437] These eternal principles have always been valid. They provide a basis for a well-oiled society, in which human rights are protected and God has his rightful place. These ten laws must, of course, be translated for every generation, so that they can speak to contemporary situations. After all, when one of the commandments tells me not to 'covet' my neighbour's donkey,[438] I realise that I should be happy to drive my Citroen Picasso and not drool over my friend's Lexus!

These ten rules offer protection and security. When the Bible states that we now no longer live 'under the law' but 'under grace' (NIV), it is ridiculous to suggest that these principles have suddenly ceased to apply as a governing code for human behaviour. Christ made that very clear when he stated that he had come to give us a perfect example of how this divine law should be observed. He was adamant that he had not come 'to abolish the law or the prophets'.[439] In fact, he underlined that 'even the smallest detail of God's law will remain until its purpose is achieved'.[440]

What is this purpose? First, it is a measuring stick against which we evaluate our conduct. 'It was the law that showed me my sin.'[441] This verse is talking about the Ten Commandments – the moral constitution for mankind. Second, the law offers a guideline for living a life to honour our Maker. It enables us to show our faith and love for God in a concrete manner by our actual deeds.[442]

gift of grace

God's law is still a vital aspect of the Christian faith experience. But here's the paradox: Salvation remains totally out of reach if we depend on the keeping of the law in order to obtain it. Salvation depends entirely on grace. 'For it is by grace you have been saved, through faith – and this not from yourselves, it is the gift of God.'[443]

> God wants us to keep his law; it is a condition for our salvation. BUT salvation is through grace; it's free.

The word grace is derived from the Latin *gratia*, which means 'free'. It has a rich meaning, but it has been cheapened. When people ask for a 'grace period' before an assignment is due, they fail to recognise the word's true meaning. Neither is 'grace' to be reduced to a little prayer you chant before eating. It is infinitely more. Grace is God's face turned towards the world. It is a new way of life.

One author struggled to find words to describe grace: 'Money cannot buy it, intellect cannot grasp it, power cannot command it; but to all who will accept it, God's glorious grace is freely given. But men may feel their need, and, renouncing all self-dependence, accept salvation as a gift. Those who enter heaven will not scale its walls by their own righteousness, nor will its gates be opened to them for costly offerings of gold or silver, but they will gain an entrance to the many mansions of the Father's house through the merits of the cross of Christ.'[444]

Grace is *free*. But it isn't *cheap*. Theologian Dietrich Bonhoeffer coined the term 'cheap grace' to refer to the kind of easy grace that just takes things for granted. True grace, he says, is costly, for it cost the life of Jesus. Take a concordance and check all the places where the word 'grace' is mentioned in the New Testament. You will find that in most instances it is directly connected with the name of Jesus. He is grace personified.

'God treats us much better than we deserve, and because of Christ Jesus, he freely accepts us and sets us free from our sins.' (Romans 3:24, CEV.)

Grace is a gift, not forced upon us. We have to realise that we need God's grace. And, once we receive it, we must ask him for the extra grace to live gracefully. To be guided by the instructions of his Word. What else is the church, but Christians modelling divine grace?

re: consider

How do you feel about the idea that grace is free but not cheap? Does it affect your mental picture of salvation?

REFERENCES

432. Author unknown. *www.sermonillustrations.com/a-z/g/grace.htm*. 12 April 2006.
433. Romans 6:14.
434. John 1:17, NIV.
435. Galatians 3:24, NKJV.
436. Matthew 27:51.
437. Exodus 20.
438. Exodus 20:17.
439. Matthew 5:17, NIV.
440. Ibid, verse 18.
441. Romans 7:7.
442. See James 2:18.
443. Ephesians 2:8, NIV.
444. White, Ellen G. *God's Amazing Grace*. Review and Herald Pub., 1973, p. 179.

23. TEN LITTLE RULES

God, it seems that your law is simple, beautiful and valid. Help me to understand the depth of its teachings and to integrate them into my daily life.

re: tell

A clever smuggler came to the border with a donkey. The donkey's back was heavily laden with straw. The official at the border was suspicious and pulled apart the man's bundles till there was straw all around, but not one valuable thing was found in the straw.

'But I'm certain you're smuggling something,' the official said, as the man crossed the border.

Now each day for ten years the man came to the border with a donkey. Although the official searched and searched the straw bundles on the donkey's back, he never could find anything valuable hidden in them.

Many years later, after the official had retired, he happened to meet that same smuggler in a marketplace and said, 'Please tell me, I beg you. Tell me, what were you smuggling? Tell me, if you can.'

'Donkeys,' said the man.[445]

re: think

Most of us don't like being told what to do. I'd rather sort out my own rules and decide my own actions, thank you very much. Even on small matters we resist: 'Go to bed early', 'Wash behind your ears', 'Write on only one side of the paper.'

A stretch of road I drive regularly has is a sign proclaiming a 30mph speed limit. Recently the local authority added a bright yellow board proclaiming, 'Obey the speed limit!' Yet many drivers take no notice. Laws are good, but if you can get away without obeying – who cares?

When the Bible talks about 'the law', we're already defensive. But a quick look reveals some surprises. The Bible describes God's law as a pleasure, a wonderful resource he has given to us.

'If your law had not been my delight, then I would have perished in my affliction.' (Psalm 119:92, NIV.)

'In my inner being I delight in God's law' (Romans 7:22, NIV).

Are these simply words from obsessive legalists, convinced of their own goodness? Hardly. Maybe they show how different God's law is from what we think.

The Ten Commandments came at an important point in Bible history. The Israelites had been slaves to the Egyptians for 400 years, abused and exploited, without freedom or hope. Then God rescued them. He freed them from injustice, released them from slavery and led them to a new future in the land of Canaan.

God had chosen Israel to bring blessing to the whole world.[446] God's desire to achieve that blessing was apparent in his love and faithfulness to Israel. God loved Israel so much that gave them the Ten Commandments after they were free.

The Ten Commandments start by reminding us that God freed his people from slavery,[447] when they were powerless to do anything for themselves. So these aren't commands that must be obeyed *before* God would rescue them. Rather, they demonstrate the quality of life to be enjoyed *because* of their new freedom. The Ten Commandments provide direction, a sense of belonging, an understanding of what it means to be a fulfilled human being.

'You must not have any other god but me.

'You must not make for yourself an idol of any kind or an image of anything in the heavens or on the earth or in the sea. You must not

bow down to them or worship them, for I, the Lord your God, am a jealous God who will not tolerate your affection for any other gods. I lay the sins of the parents upon their children; the entire family is affected – even children in the third and fourth generations of those who reject me. But I lavish unfailing love for a thousand generations on those who love me and obey my commands.

'You must not misuse the name of the Lord your God. The Lord will not let you go unpunished if you misuse his name.

'Remember to observe the Sabbath day by keeping it holy. You have six days each week for your ordinary work, but the seventh day is a Sabbath day of rest dedicated to the Lord your God. On that day no one in your household may do any work. This includes you, your sons and daughters, your male and female servants, your livestock, and any foreigners living among you. For in six days the Lord made the heavens, the earth, the sea, and everything in them; but on the seventh day he rested. That is why the Lord blessed the Sabbath day and set it apart as holy.

'Honour your father and mother. Then you will live a long, full life in the land the Lord your God is giving you.

'You must not murder.

'You must not commit adultery.

'You must not steal.

'You must not testify falsely against your neighbour.

'You must not covet your neighbour's house. You must not covet your neighbour's wife, male or female servant, ox or donkey, or anything else that belongs to your neighbour.'[448]

The first commandment, 'You shall have no other gods before me' (NIV), doesn't say that there *are* no other gods, just that we are not to worship them. We have competing commitments, success, power, money, entertainment, sex and more to distract our focus from God. This commandment means that those who have experienced the radical love of God will live a life dominated by their relationship with him. If God becomes our first priority, as in the first commandment, then the rest of the commandments are about the practical issues of *how* we live that committed life.

The second commandment prohibits images or idols. At first this may seem irrelevant to us now. But it isn't. When the commandments were originally given, idols were common. Idol worshippers didn't think the idol was actually a god. They thought their god made itself known through the idol. It was a way to experience their god. But the God of Israel isn't to be experienced through wood or metal idols. We know God through what he does in our lives.

> 'If your law had not been my delight, then I would have perished in my affliction.'
> (Psalm 119:92, NIV.)

And our God doesn't require images, because he already has an image – us. God created human beings 'in his own image'.[449] So in a way, this commandment invites us to live in a way that makes God known to the world through us. You might not be tempted to bow down before an actual idol. But we're all tempted to live lives which aren't examples of the love of God.

Incidentally, the 'third and fourth generation' who will suffer if we disobey this commandment refers to our family. What I do not only affects me, but those closest to me as well. They suffer because of my selfishness. In other words, God wants us to live in such a way that we give consideration to other people, not just ourselves.

The third commandment is straightforward enough; it guards against swearing and general profanity, but its purpose is significant beyond that. In Israel, God's name was used to support formal oaths. So by using God's name 'wrongfully', or telling lies, people were deceived. It also protects us from using religion to abuse others. There are plenty of examples of this in our world; people claim to know and serve the God of justice, yet are complacent about injustice. When we take God's name upon ourselves, we also take on responsibilities to represent him by the way we live.

The fourth commandment asks us to 'remember'. We don't need an incentive to remember our anniversary or the birthday of someone we love. (Except perhaps the forgetful husbands among us!) But this asks us to remember to keep the Sabbath as a day of rest because God created us. Deuteronomy 5 repeats the Ten Commandments and gives another motivation for observing the Sabbath – release from slavery. Sabbath rest is a reminder that God not only *created* us, but also *cares* for us. When we experience the joy that this brings, we will need no greater motivation to keep a weekly Sabbath. Observing the Sabbath is an act of gratitude to God and a means of pursuing a relationship with him.

The fifth commandment occupies a significant place. It is a bridge between the first four, which emphasise our relationship with God, and the last five, which emphasise our relationship with the world in general. In between these two sections is the command concerning parents and family. So here is the order of our responsibilities: first God (1-4); then family (5); then others (6-10).

This fifth commandment asks us to 'honour' our parents. This was originally given to adults, not young children, so this isn't asking young children to obey their parents. Rather, it points out the responsibilities that adults have towards their ageing parents. Here, 'honour' does not mean 'obey', but to care for them and show compassion. This is the attitude the elderly should receive from children who are committed to God. If we can't show compassion towards our ageing parents, we are unlikely to show it to anyone else. If we're committed to God, then we're committed to compassion.

The next three commandments are all very short, forming a group by themselves. They also appear to be arranged in order of importance. The sixth commandment, 'You must not murder', concerns *life*. The seventh, 'You must not commit adultery', is about *relationships*. The eighth, 'You must not steal', concerns *property*. All of them are important, but they are arranged in this sequence so that we can see their relative significance. Life has the highest priority, and placing relationships above property reminds us of the importance of commitment and faithfulness to those we claim to love.

We find another aspect of relationships in the ninth commandment, 'You must not testify falsely against your neighbour'. In a world where casual lies are commonplace, truth becomes vitally important in our relationships. The wording refers explicitly to giving false testimony in a court of law, where lies can be truly destructive; but can we live with integrity, can our word be trusted, can we refrain from undermining the reputations of others and can we treat others as we would want them to treat us?

Finally, we come to the tenth commandment. In some ways 'You must not covet' seems strange. It deals more with internal thoughts than outward actions, but that's just the point. Without this one, you could conclude that the Ten Commandments are only about our actions and behaviour, but this command reminds us that our relationship with God depends not only on what we *do*, but also on who we *are*.

The Ten Commandments are more than just a list of stale and outdated demands. Rather, they give direction about how to live a full life; they set out our priorities; give guidelines on how to respond to God in our lives and invite us to be the kind of people God would like us to be.

The Ten Commandments dare us to step away from the unremarkable to become representatives of this amazing God of love and commitment.

re: consider

Which commandment sounds like something you need more of in your life?

REFERENCES

445. www.storyarts.org/library/nutshell/stories/smuggler.html.
446. Genesis 12:3.
447. Exodus 20:1-2.
448. Exodus 20:3-17.
449. Genesis 1:27.

24. TAKE A BREAK!

God, you created time and you placed me in it. Often I feel I just don't have enough time for everything I want to accomplish! But now that I'm getting to know and love you, I want to acknowledge you with my time, just as much as I acknowledge you with my thoughts. Show me your plan for my time.

re: tell

One man challenged another to an all-day wood chopping contest. The challenger worked very hard, stopping only for a brief lunch break. The other man had a leisurely lunch and took several breaks during the day. At the end of the day, the challenger was surprised and annoyed to find that the other fellow had chopped substantially more wood than he had.

'I don't get it,' he said. 'Every time I checked, you were taking a rest, yet you chopped more wood than I did.'

'But you didn't notice,' said the winning woodsman, 'that I was sharpening my axe when I sat down to rest.'[450]

re: think

'Sorry, I just don't have the time.'

Do you ever hear yourself saying it? We have too much to do, earning a living, paying off debts, getting exercise, surfing the Internet, cleaning the house, shopping, washing the car. . . . There just aren't enough hours in the day or days in the week. Oddly, the more time-saving devices we buy, the less time we seem to have and the more stressed we get.

But more and more people are discovering that the Bible does have a solution. It's all about priorities, taking stock of how we use time so it doesn't abuse us. The Bible offers an oasis of calm for harassed lives; it's called the Sabbath.

When God created everything, he rested on the seventh day and set it apart. 'And God blessed the seventh day and declared it holy, because it was the day when he rested from all his work of creation.'[451] To put it literally, God *sabbathed*. It was the climax of creation. A time of rest and holiness, showing that the whole of life is spiritual. The world in which we live, and the time we have to enjoy it – both are gifts from God. Sabbath was given to us as a resource to enjoy both to the full.

The Bible is quite specific about the Sabbath. It isn't just one day in seven when we put work aside. Sabbath is that period between sunset on Friday and sunset on Saturday.[452] We choose to rest on this specific day, not simply because human beings need rest, but because we need a particular kind of spiritual rest.

Of course, if we are attuned to God, we spend every day of the week with him. But Sabbath has a different function; it helps us appreciate the presence of God on the other days of the week. It puts our lives in perspective, helps us set priorities and stick to them. In other words, Sabbath helps us manage our time so we can live fulfilled, ordered and satisfied lives.

We might as well admit it; sometimes Sabbath has received bad press. It has been resented as being a boring stretch of dull inactivity, but that's because it was hijacked by killjoys. The biblical Sabbath was a feast, not a fast. Something to anticipate and celebrate rather than dread.

So what can the Sabbath do for us? It gives us a fresh perspective on life.

Keeping the Sabbath challenges the questionable values of our society. We declare that life is more than work, money or production. We accept a radical set of values which places emphasis on the quality of being human.

Life is about more than *doing*. It is, most importantly, about *being*. By choosing to leave our work one day a week, we prove that we work to live, not live to work. Sabbath is a fantastic way to turn our backs on rampant materialism. We protest the view that a person's true worth is measured in what they contribute to the economy. It transforms our lives to a pace more in harmony with the natural world.

In keeping Sabbath, we don't reject everything from the technology age where life is lived twenty-four hours a day, seven days a week. We just refuse to let it dominate the God-given rhythm of work and rest. One of the advantages of observing a sunset-to-sunset Sabbath is that we return to the natural rhythms of the world, with the rising and setting sun. We embrace the natural world and rediscover our place within it.

I've observed a weekly Sabbath for some years now. I look forward to it every week and look back on each Sabbath with gratitude. Besides personal benefits, it's also helped me in my career. Sabbath gives me time away from professional goals and deadlines. I've learned that the world will not stop turning just because I'm not working.

Sabbath has also made a difference in my family life. I can spend unrushed quality time with those I love. More than anything, the Sabbath brings peace and order in my otherwise frazzled existence. Because I choose to keep the Sabbath, I've found it easier to focus on life's important questions, such as 'Why am I here?' and 'What do I value?'

Sabbath gives me time to reflect on my place in God's scheme of things.

But it's more than just personal benefits. Sabbath also emphasises my responsibility to the world. In the creation story, Sabbath is its crowning glory; human beings are not the be-all and end-all of the world. The Sabbath tells us that creation is ultimately a spiritual concern, so when we observe Sabbath we acknowledge our responsibility to God's creation. Concern for the environment is not a brand new issue. It's in the Bible, too, and it's connected to the Sabbath.

> Just as we benefit from the Sabbath, so we have a responsibility not to endlessly exploit creation's resources.

187

'Plant and harvest your crops for six years, but let the land be renewed and lie uncultivated during the seventh year. Then let the
poor among you harvest whatever grows on its own. Leave the rest
for wild animals to eat. The same applies to your vineyards and ol-
ive groves. You have six days each week for your ordinary work, but
on the seventh day you must stop working. This gives your ox and
your donkey a chance to rest. It also allows your slaves and the foreigners living among you to be refreshed.'[453]

Here we find two ideas side by side. Just as human beings should
work six days and rest on the seventh, so the land should be cultivated
for six years and rest for the seventh. To put it more explicitly, 'during
the seventh year the land must have a Sabbath year of complete rest. It
is the Lord's Sabbath.'[454]

Just as we benefit from the Sabbath, so we have a responsibility
not to endlessly exploit creation's resources. People who take their own
Sabbath seriously will desire nothing less for the world around them.

The Sabbath is also connected to social justice. It's the great leveller
of human society. Regardless of social status, on Sabbath everyone is
equal. In ancient Israel, Sabbath rest was everybody's inalienable right,
rich or poor, slave or master, native or foreigner. This reminder of social
justice every seven days was reinforced every seven years by the agricultural sabbatical.

Here is the prophet Isaiah's definition of true justice. 'Free those
who are wrongly imprisoned; lighten the burden of those who work
for you. Let the oppressed go free, and remove the chains that bind
people. Share your food with the hungry, and give shelter to the homeless.'[455] Then he encourages his hearers to 'enjoy the Sabbath and speak
of it with delight as the Lord's holy day.'[456] When we observe Sabbath,
we declare our passion for social justice.

Of course, keeping the Sabbath requires some adjustments to the
way we live our lives. But it's not so difficult once we realise the huge
benefits. We shouldn't start by compiling long lists of do's and don'ts.
We'll skip some things on the Sabbath, because they'd keep us focused

on work, competition, acquisition and performance. People with no interests other than their work can't help but be stressed and dull, because they don't see meaning in anything beyond the workplace.

Sabbath is an invitation to diversify our lives and also to celebrate. That's why many Sabbath-keepers welcome its arrival and departure with small rituals – lighting candles, a special meal, Sabbath prayers – whatever is meaningful to them. Just simple actions which set the Sabbath aside from the rest of the week. We actually prepare for the Sabbath on Friday, so that we can avoid as much work as possible during Sabbath hours. We do the extra cooking, cleaning and ironing during other week days, so that when Friday sunset comes, there's no better feeling than a clean house, a fresh supper and the comfort that we don't have to think about work for a full twenty-four hours!

Since Sabbath can be such a delight, you might well ask, 'Why we don't hear more about it?' The early Christian church observed Sabbath. And it is tragic that Christians in general have lost track of it. There have been Sabbath-keepers all through Christian history. But in more recent times it's been rediscovered by a growing number of Christians. There's no better time than Sabbath to worship God with other people whose lives have been turned around by his love.

Perhaps you'd like to rediscover it, too? Try to see how it helps you to get your life in order, take stock, make priorities. It'll bring quality time to think through your life, and how God can make a difference to it.

You'll discover one of the greatest resources God has provided for us.

re: consider

How would keeping the Sabbath change the way you live?

REFERENCES

450. Source unknown. *www.sermonillustrations.com/a-z/r/rest.htm*. 25 July 2006.
451. Genesis 2:3.
452. In the Bible, days begin and end at sunset. See Leviticus 23:32, 'from evening to evening you shall celebrate your sabbath.' NKJV.
453. Exodus 23:10-12.
454. Leviticus 25:4.
455. Isaiah 58:6-7.
456. Isaiah 58:13.

ABOUT
SPIRITUALITY

25. GROWING UP

God, this whole journey with you has been an experience in learning practical spirituality. Help me to learn what your Word says about spiritual growth and how I can make my walk with you even deeper and more practical.

re: tell

Søren Kierkegaard, the Danish philosopher, once told a story about a flock of barnyard geese in Denmark. Every Sunday the geese would gather in the barnyard near the feeding trough. One of their number, a 'preaching goose', would struggle up on to the top rail of the fence and lecture the geese about the glories of goosedom.

He would honk about how wonderful it was to be a goose, rather than a chicken or a turkey. He reminded them of their great heritage and told them of the marvellous possibilities in their future.

Occasionally, while he was preaching, a flock of wild geese winging their way south from Sweden across the Baltic Sea on their way to sunny France would fly overhead in a marvellous V formation thousands of feet in the air. All the geese would excitedly look and say to one another.

'That's who we really are! We are not destined to spend our lives in this stinking barnyard. Our destiny is to fly.'

But then the wild geese would disappear from sight, their honking echoing across the horizon. The barnyard geese would look around at their comfortable surroundings, sigh and return to the mud of the barnyard.[457]

re: think

We expect growth: we believe our children will grow; we hope the seeds in our garden will grow; we assume young adults will gain understanding as they advance through university.

The Christian life is no different. In the Bible, spiritual growth is an expected process. Paul talks about it,[458] telling us about the gifts Jesus gave to help the church. These gifts equip the saints (believers) to build up the church (the body of Christ) to grow towards maturity and so avoid deception and childish behaviour. 'Speaking the truth with love, we will *grow up* in every way into Christ, who is the head.'[459]

God not only desires growth, but he has made provision for it. Spiritual growth protects us from false doctrine and helps us towards maturity and Christ-likeness.

three key words

- Belief/believer.
- Follower.
- Disciple.

To see the overall process we must understand these three words.

The gospel of Mark succinctly summarises the message Jesus taught. 'The time is fulfilled, and the Kingdom of God is at hand; repent and believe in the gospel.'[460] When the Philippian jailer asked, 'What must I do to be saved?' Paul told him to 'believe in the Lord Jesus, and you will be saved – you and your household.'[461] I begin Christian growth by repenting (turning away from) my past way of life and believing in Jesus; I become a *believer*.

At this point the other two words come into the picture. Jesus often called people to follow him.[462] When someone truly believes, he or she becomes a follower of Jesus. A similar Bible word is *disciple*. Disciple means 'student' or 'learner' and occurs 269 times in the New Testament. To understand this word we must know something about the cultural approach to education in the time of Jesus.[463]

A *disciple* was like an apprentice who attached himself to a teacher. He actually gave his personal allegiance to the teacher and in many cases lived with the teacher or rabbi. A disciple was not a come-and-go student with many instructors. Rather, the teacher-disciple relationship was personal, all-encompassing and exclusive. This is the biblical vision of what a *believer* should become – a *follower* and *disciple* of Jesus. In such a relationship growth happens naturally.

> Spiritual growth protects us from false doctrine and helps us towards maturity and Christ-likeness.

the growth process

Let's trace the discipleship cycle as the Bible presents it. After you receive a message and become a believer, you proceed to be a follower/disciple. You grow in discipleship and, in turn, become a disciple-maker who mentors others. Christ's final command to his disciples was, 'Go and make disciples of all nations, baptising them in the name of the Father and of the Son and of the Holy Spirit, and teaching them to obey everything I have commanded you. And surely I am with you always, to the very end of the age.'[464]

Jesus literally commanded his disciples to go and make more disciples. They'd been closely following him for more than three years, and now he told them to begin helping others to become believers and disciples.

This growth process is just that – growth and a process. It isn't some legalistic rule to follow. It isn't an onerous task to perform. It's a growing relationship with a gracious mentor. It's a process filled with challenge because growth always brings change. But it's a path also full of joy and satisfaction – joy in the presence of love; satisfaction that life has purpose.

Will each disciple be perfect? Of course not! The Bible is full of stories about the failures of the disciples. But a student doesn't need to get 100% on every test. The aim is not perfection but perseverance in the learning process. The teacher cares most that the learner stays close, because in that kind of intimate relationship growth becomes inevitable.

principles for growing in Christ

What general principles govern the Christian growth process?

We must be convinced of the value of the Christian experience and life.

It's especially difficult for people from a western cultural background to move beyond the cultural viewpoint which sees doctrine, intellectual belief and philosophy as the centre of faith. But biblical religion is holistic and maintains the spiritual experience as central.

Intellectual belief is a key part, but personal experience, including a life of devotion in relationship with God, must be added to it. Jesus said that the greatest commandment in the law was to 'love the Lord you God with all your heart and with all your soul and with all your mind'.[465] This love involves all we are – heart, soul and mind.

Eugene Peterson's contemporary paraphrase, *The Message,* says that we must love with 'passion and prayer and intelligence'. Without experience and growth, the Christian life is neither authentic nor whole.

We must be honest with ourselves and God.

The longer I live, the more I see in myself and others the capacity for self-deception. It's often unpremeditated; it just happens naturally. But we need deliberately to set barriers against self-deception in our lives.

We can do this in several ways. Look for people who will keep us honest about our lives. They might be family members, spiritual counsellors, mentors or pastors. Join a small group, if you haven't done so already, for fellowship and accountability. People who know us and care about us help us to maintain our honesty.

Take time to reflect on your life at regular intervals. Some daily quiet time can give honest self-evaluation. A strong sense of God's grace and forgiveness helps us to be transparent with him, knowing that he forgives freely, loving us in spite of our faults and problems.

We must recognise the key role of the Holy Spirit.

After Jesus' resurrection, his first followers (disciples) were to wait and pray for the Holy Spirit.[466] Later on, the apostles expected the early believers to have the same experience of receiving the Holy Spirit.[467] The Holy Spirit is the dynamic behind all spiritual life and growth.

When are prayer and worship effective in the divine-human relationship? It is when the Holy Spirit is with us. If we want to grow spiritually, we must invite the Spirit to live with us every day. Just quietly and seriously ask the Spirit to come. Be persistent, because your spiritual growth depends on it.

Becoming a *believer* is a big step, but it doesn't suddenly make you a mature Christian *disciple*. It merely initiates a growth process. It's like a new birth – the growing process is challenging but tremendously rewarding.

This path of growth is your opportunity to mature and grow, find joy for yourself and become a source of help and healing for the world.

re: consider

In what ways would you like to see yourself grow?

REFERENCES

457. *http://elbourne.org/sermons/index.mv?illustration+1411*.
458. Ephesians 4:11-15.
459. Ibid, verse 15, NCV (italics supplied).
460. Mark 1:15, NKJV.
461. Acts 16:30, 31, NIV.
462. See Matthew 4:18-22 and 19:21, 22.
463. See *Harper's Bible dictionary*. Harper & Row, 1985.
464. Matthew 28:19-20, NIV.
465. Matthew 22:36-38. NIV.
466. Acts 1:8; 2:1-4.
467. Acts 2:37, 38.

26. SPIRITUAL DISCIPLINES

God, I am here now because I want to learn how to connect my heart with yours. Show me what I can contribute to this relationship between myself and my Creator, and how this most intimate of all relationships can stay strong.

re: tell

Adam checks his heart rate as his shoes pound the pavement. The sun has not yet risen as he begins his daily workout, punctuated with stretching, sit-ups, pull-ups and a few rounds with the punch-bag. After a carefully calibrated breakfast of fresh fruit and a protein shake, he heads out to work, surprising no one when he walks up all nine flights of stairs to his office.

Sliding into his ergonomically designed workspace, Adam grabs his phone and starts giving orders while scanning the latest reports. As the day wears on he feels his muscles tensing, the tension creeping up his shoulders and neck, wrapping around his head. As he tells his secretary to inform his wife he'll be home late, he wonders why he just can't shake off his daily headaches.

re: think

Ever since God spent time with Adam and Eve in the Garden of Eden, Christians have recognised the value of maintaining a personal connection with God. Some call it devotional time or quiet time; others say they're practising spiritual disciplines. But no matter what you call it, the important thing is to take that special time for yourself.

spiritual disciplines = building relationships with God and believers through communication, reflection and service

It's based on three key principles:

1.   Jesus is alive and active through the Holy Spirit in the world.[468] After Jesus died and was resurrected, he came back and spent time with his disciples and followers. The New Testament clearly demonstrates that contact with Jesus can be an ongoing reality.

2.   Jesus desires a relationship with his followers. He wants to communicate with us. The New Testament demonstrates this in several ways. Jesus specifically calls us to 'Remain in Me'.[469] That's how we bear spiritual fruit.[470] He promises to be with us until the end of time.[471] And he calls us his 'friends'.[472] It's a real relationship.

3.   God gives us ways to build and strengthen this relationship with him. That's where the spiritual disciplines come in. They aren't legalistic commands or monastic requirements. They're avenues to nurture our relationship with Jesus.

prayer

The first spiritual discipline is *prayer*. There's only one story in the Bible where Jesus prayed for twenty-four hours straight through.[473] He began on a Sabbath morning and finished some time on Sunday. 'Very early in the morning, while it was still dark, Jesus got up, left the house and went off to a solitary place, where he prayed.'[474]

Even with his crazy schedule, Jesus took time to pray alone. Jesus also prayed daily, but sometimes he intensified that prayer time; for example, when he had to choose the twelve disciples[475] or when pressure from the crowd became intense[476] or when his trial and crucifixion were approaching.[477] Sometimes he invited the disciples to be part of that prayer experience with him.[478]

In the early Christian church, followers of Jesus were expected to pray. They were even characterised by their devotion to prayer.[479] 'Pray continually!' Paul wrote to the Thessalonian believers.[480]

It's nice, you may be saying to yourself, that they prayed so much. But what is prayer? How do I pray? What does it mean for my life today, hundreds of years later?

Remember our definition of the spiritual disciplines? They build relationship. And healthy relationships require communication and dialogue. So prayer is communication and dialogue with God. Good relationships work in both directions. We usually think of prayer as our chance to talk, but it includes listening in silence as well. The ancient psalmist reminds us to 'be still, and know that I am God'.[481] Stillness involves taking time to listen to what God might have to say to you.

> Pray simply, tell God what you feel in your heart and then listen quietly while he whispers to you – that is the heart of prayer.

Prayer is communication and dialogue with God. Two great Bible teachings on prayer are the book of Psalms and the model prayer of Jesus. Psalms was Jesus' prayer book, and he often quoted from it in the New Testament. Jesus also gave his followers a model prayer, called the Lord's Prayer.[482]

'Our Father in heaven,
hallowed be your name,
your kingdom come,
your will be done on earth as it is in heaven.
Give us today our daily bread.
Forgive us our debts,
as we also have forgiven our debtors.
And lead us not into temptation,
but deliver us from the evil one.'[483]

199

Christian prayer is different from prayer in other belief systems. We don't see God as a tyrant or dictator. Instead, we call him 'Father'. It's really a very personal and relational intimacy. Jesus addressed God as 'Abba'– the familiar Hebrew word meaning 'papa' or 'daddy' – and he suggests we do the same.[484] This intimacy affects the way we talk to God and how we pray.

Honesty in prayer is also important. When we pray, we can express a whole range of positive and negative human emotions, even anger or despair. While we always seek to respect God's power, he wants us to express our true feelings when we talk to him – just as we would with a best friend.

Prayer is a broad category. Sometimes we treat it like a wish list to Santa Claus. But it's so much more than that. Personal requests are a big part of prayer, but so are praise and worship, confession, concern for God's will and questions about what we don't understand.

Pray simply, tell God what you feel in your heart and then listen quietly while he whispers to you – that is the heart of prayer. There are as many ways to pray as there are people praying, but try it in a quiet place where you can reflect without interruption.

bible study

A second spiritual discipline is *Bible study*. God can speak to us during prayer, but his messages are usually more clear and complete during our study of the Scriptures.

During his ministry, Jesus often showed his deep knowledge of the Old Testament Scriptures. His use of Scripture supports the idea that the Bible is inspired, or God-breathed.[485] We have already studied about the inspiration of the Bible; the important thing is how we apply it. If the Bible really is God's Word we must study it and use it in our lives. After all, it is good for teaching, reproof, correction and training in right doing and it helps us become complete, equipped for good works.

There are so many good Bible translations that it doesn't have to be hard to understand what the Bible is saying. You can also find simple Bible guides (like these studies) to help you get started.

quiet time

Church and/or a small group are good places for Bible study, but it's also very important to make some personal time each day to fellowship with God.

My suggestion is a quiet time of fifteen to thirty minutes every day for talking and listening to God. This is where real growth happens.

Here are some practical ideas. They're not hard rules but suggestions to help as you start your discipleship journey.

- **Find a quiet place that you can use regularly.** Try to make some space in your schedule so that your quiet time is at the same time every day. A good structure helps us to be in a frame of mind to meet God. When things get busy, it's easy to give up this spiritual oasis, but if you miss it sometimes, don't just give up. Do the best you can and start growing a new habit.

- **Spend part of this quiet time listening to God's word in the Bible.** Use a translation you enjoy and remember that there is no need to hurry through a set number of verses. Thoughtful pondering of one verse is better than speed-reading through a chapter or two. Maybe you can memorise some verses to remember during the day. Other devotional books can be helpful, but the Bible should be our basic emphasis.

- **Pray.** Speak to God and also listen. Again, there is no need to rush. As God gives you the words, talk to him and, in between, listen to him. Prayer is more like a quiet, thoughtful conversation with a very good friend than a required ritual or a set formula.

- **Write notes. It can really help to keep a journal, charting your spiritual journey.** Jot down what you learned from your Bible reading. Write down for whom you prayed or what God brought to your mind as you reflected on Scripture. Note down a concern or fear that you shared with God. You can go back to these later and see just how much you have grown.

- **Begin with fifteen to twenty minutes; for some thirty minutes feels better.** Don't make the time so long that it becomes a burden. Over a period of time, you'll find that you naturally spend longer, but don't force it.

God wants to commune with you. Are you willing to reach out to him? Try this plan for a month and if it is not what you had hoped for, talk to a friend or your pastor about how you might find ways that help you meet God.

re: consider

When would be the best time for you to fit some quiet time with God in your daily routine?

REFERENCES

468. Read 1 Corinthians 12.
469. John 15:4, NIV.
470. John 15:5, 6.
471. Matthew 28:20.
472. John 15:15.
473. Mark 1:21-38.
474. Ibid, verse 35, NIV.
475. Luke 6:12.
476. Mark 6:45, 46.
477. Matthew 26:36; Mark 14:32; Luke 22:41.
478. Luke 22:40.
479. Acts 2:42.
480. 1 Thessalonians 5:17, NIV.
481. Psalm 46:10.
482. Read the Lord's Prayer in its lengthier form in Matthew 6:8-13 and its shortened form in Luke 11:2-4.
483. Matthew 6:9-13, NIV.
484. Mark 14:36 and Galatians 4:6.
485. 2 Timothy 3:16, 17, NIV.

27. YOUR GOD CONNECTION

God, they say angels bow to worship you, and that makes me think I should worship you, too. But I don't even know where to begin! Please show me how to worship you with my whole heart.

re: tell

Xavier worshipped work and its by-product, money. The harder he worked, the more money he earned, the more he invested, the more he gained and the more he could buy. Soon he owned houses, corporations, cars, yachts and anything else that caught his eye. He took lavish vacations from Austria to Zanzibar. He poured all his energy into maintaining his over-the-top lifestyle, but all the excess left him empty, a buzz that faded ever faster.

Theron worked hard, played hard and loved with ferocity. His life centred round his God, his family and anyone he saw who needed a helping hand. He faced more than his share of struggles and burdens, but with his life centred on something far greater than and beyond himself, he felt a fulfilment he could scarcely describe or contain.

re: think

In twenty-first-century culture, worship is a difficult word. It often seems strange to us to reverence or honour the divine. Worship goes beyond simple acknowledgement and moves into a very personal recognition of God. For many it feels inappropriate or unnatural.

But the Bible makes worship central – the predominant spiritual activity of believers, even more than prayer. Scripture has more than 400 references to worship.

The call to worship is the most basic biblical command. When an expert lawyer asked, 'Of all the commandments, which is the most important?'[486] Jesus gave a clear answer. ' "You must love the Lord your God with all your heart, all your soul, all your mind, and all your strength," ' he said. 'The second is equally important: "Love your neighbour as yourself." '

loving by worship

What does it mean to love God? Some say you show love to God by loving other people, but that turns the first commandment into the second, so that can't be true. Loving God should *lead* to loving one's neighbour, but it's got to be more than that.

The Bible says that we actually love God by worshipping him. When we understand that Jesus is our Creator and our Saviour, we are led to worship him in response and, as a result, we also love others whom God loves. The starting point is always the same – our worship is a response to God's presence in our lives.

The Ten Commandments[487] also show the centrality of worship. Commandments 1-4 tell us how to love God, number 5 talks about family, and 6-10 teach us how to love our neighbour. Look carefully at the first four and see how they define worship.

'You shall have no other gods before me.'[488] In a culture with multitudes of gods and rampant polytheism, Israel was to worship only the Redeemer God, Yahweh of creation.

The second commandment forbids making or worshipping idols.[489] Since worshipping other gods is already covered in the first commandment, this one focuses on the *means* and *method* of worship. Yahweh is too big and universal to be limited to a man-made representation.

He can be worshipped anywhere, not just through material representations.

Number three forbids misusing God's name.[490] Traditionally, many Christians have interpreted this commandment as prohibiting swearing, cursing and profanity. This includes using God's name to curse another person or uttering angry expletives. But the commandment also refers to using God's name under oath. We bring disrespect to God and fail to worship him when we use his name to back up our false words, because his name represents his character.

The fourth one[491] reminds us to keep the Sabbath holy, honouring God as our Creator. This commandment safeguards our *time* for worship.

All four of these commandments are about worship. They're about *whom* we worship, our *means* and *method* of worship, guarding against the *misuse* of the God's name and character, and safeguarding the *time* for worship. Pretty comprehensive, don't you think?

reason why

Worship isn't only an activity here; it's the preoccupation of heaven, too. The book of Revelation graphically illustrates a divine realm where praise is central. Why is biblical worship so carefully safeguarded? The reason is simple: Worship demonstrates that we understand and feel God's free grace and love.

When I earn my salary, I don't worship the one signing my cheque, because I've worked for that money! Writing my cheque is the treasurer's job; but worship is so central, because it vividly demonstrates our response to something *undeserved*.

> Worship isn't only an activity here; it's the preoccupation of heaven, too.

God doesn't deliver us from sin based on our goodness. We don't deserve grace, and there's no way we can repay it. Our God-given response is to worship, acknowledging the tremendous love and grace God gives to us. To fail to worship is to misunderstand or ignore grace, the very core of Christian belief.

So we define worship as our response to God's acts and presence. Worship is holistic – we respond with our mind, heart, emotions, body and voice, and real divine-human interaction takes place. It can be in our prayer closet, in a small group or in the large corporate context of church worship.

paths to worship

If you understand religion mostly from a rational viewpoint, this can be a challenge. Worship isn't only a doctrine or belief; it's an experience which flows from an encounter with love and grace. How does this happen?

Reflect on or seek a new experience of grace, love and the awesomeness of God. All true worship springs from a sense of who God is, which then reveals our own condition. The experience of the prophet Isaiah is a good example.[492] His vision of the holiness of God led him to worship and to a deep sense of his own uncleanness. This, in turn, led to a statement of God's forgiveness and cleansing and a commission from God to be his divine messenger. This realisation about God isn't doctrine or theology, but an insight that affects everything we are.

Deliberately take time to act and react in response to your experience of God. Do it personally; kneel and thank God for his goodness; sing a song or write a poem about his grace; stand in awe and bow your head at the beauty of a sunset or sunrise; lift your hands and offer all you are; do whatever comes naturally as you respond fully to God.

Let your body, heart and mind work together to respond to him. Remember that what you are doing is not a preliminary to something else. Let your joy and your feeling flow out in praise. You might be surprised by your response to God's presence.

Let your experience of personal worship transform your corporate experience. One young person who studied worship shared how a deeper understanding of personal worship had transformed her corporate worship experience. Even though nothing in the order of service changed, *she* had been transformed, and that had transformed her worship.

How does this happen? Try to pause before entering your church and thank God for this place of praise; ask him to let you feel his presence during the programme. Enter with joy, thanking God for another week of life; view other parishioners as your family in worship and thank God for them. When you find your seat, maybe kneel and pray briefly to start your worship experience immediately. Seek to enter fully into every part of the service; listen to the prayers; sing from your heart. Do all of this as an offering to God.

You are there not to *get* a blessing, but to *give* a blessing. You are there to bless and worship God and join in corporate worship celebration. Not everyone will know what you are doing, but your experience in worship will be enriched and fresh.

changed hearts

As I teach many eager young students, some feel that a certain order of service or type of music will bring renewal to corporate worship, but I don't think that is true. We need to focus on the reason we are there – the purpose of worshipping God as he has asked us to worship him. When we truly meet God, worship changes naturally. The human heart that has been touched by God is the greatest key to amazing worship.

Our initial human response to God's presence is worship, and that never changes, not even when we get to heaven. For true believers, worship never ends; it's one thing we can enjoy forever.

re: consider

What would enhance your personal worship experience this week?

REFERENCES
486. See Matthew 22:34-40 and Mark 12:28-31.
487. Exodus 20:1-17; Deuteronomy 5:6-21.
488. Exodus 20:3, NIV.
489. Exodus 20:4-6.
490. Exodus 20:7, NIV.
491. Exodus 20:8-11; Deuteronomy 5:12-15.
492. Isaiah 6.

28. LIFE WITH PURPOSE

God, I've started going to your Word for answers to the meaning of my life. I need to know how I fit into the intricate and vast plans you have for the universe. Please let your Spirit guide my reading and direct my life to its highest purpose.

re: tell

The Dead Sea is a fun place to visit (and a great source of beauty treatments), but you might not want to live there. Bordering Israel, Jordan and the West Bank, it receives less than four inches of rain a year. Located 400 metres below sea level, its shores are as low as you can get without scuba gear. However, diving is the last thing you'd think about doing in the Dead Sea – with a salt content over eight times greater than the ocean, it's well nigh impossible to sink in it. No fish swim in its waters and no plants can grow in it. For all but the jovial tourists bobbing on its surface, the Dead Sea lives up to its name.

'He remembers when the Dead Sea was only sick,' may be a funny line at birthday parties, but the area was once known for its fertility. So what 'killed' it? All that salt flows in, but has no way to get out. Water escapes through evaporation, but the lake just gets saltier and saltier. Without an outlet, what once was lush dries up.

re: think

It's important to have a clear purpose in life, and when you're free to pursue it you feel vitalised and invigorated. Life, your life, becomes significant, and this is what Jesus wants for us.

'I came so they can have real and eternal life, more and better life than they ever dreamed of.'[493]

So maybe you're asking yourself, *What is God's will for my life? What is my purpose? How can I find out his desires for me? What is God's plan or will for my life as a follower of Jesus?*

Sometimes these questions come to us in a very specific form. *Should I marry and, if yes, whom? What should I do for my job? Where should I live?* At other times the questions are more general. *Now that I'm a believer, how does God want me to live my life?*

Christians find that a strong sense of knowing and doing God's will brings hope, peace and meaning. Even Jesus talked about this feeling: 'My food . . . is to do the will of him who sent me and to finish his work.[494] God's purpose gave Jesus more satisfaction even than eating! If this was the basic plan of Jesus, might it be ours as well?

Jesus answered that question, too. 'Whoever serves me must follow me; and where I am, my servant also will be. My Father will honour the one who serves me.'[495] Here Jesus uses the word *servant* as a synonym for *follower* or *disciple*. So he's saying that his disciples (you and I) will follow him and work where he is working. And God will honour those who follow him.

SEVEN REALITIES OF EXPERIENCING GOD

- God is always at work around you.
- God pursues a continuing love relationship with you that is real and personal.
- God invites you to become involved with him in his work.
- God speaks by the Holy Spirit through the Bible, prayer, circumstances and the church to reveal himself, his purposes and his ways.

- God's invitation for you to work with him always leads you to a crisis of belief that requires faith and action.
- You must make major adjustments in your life to join God in what he is doing.
- You come to know God by experience as you obey him and he accomplishes his work through you.[496]

To have a growing experience with God is to see where Jesus is working and join him there. Spiritual disciplines are key – especially prayer, worship and study of the Bible. They are ways in which we can specifically seek God's will and hear his voice guiding our lives. It also reminds us that the real question is not *whether* God is working, but *where* is he working at this very moment, and how can I join that work? It's a wonderful experience to know that we are working with God on something.

results of God's will

When you've begun looking for opportunities to work with God, you might then wonder what's next. *What are the final results of God's will? What end does he have in mind?*

First, the New Testament tells us that if we commit to growth we are promised eternal life, and we can *know* that we have it. 'I have written this to you who believe in the name of the Son of God, so that you may know that you have eternal life.'[497]

> To have a growing experience with God is to see where Jesus is working and join him there.

Second, God asks us to make disciples of others.[498] But how do we do this? By becoming *witnesses*. 'But you shall receive power when the Holy Spirit has come upon you; and you shall be my witnesses both in Jerusalem and in all Judea and Samaria and to the end of the earth.'[499] The power to witness comes from the Holy Spirit, and we are to be witnesses.

In any court, witnesses aren't allowed to repeat hearsay as testimony. You can't say what somebody else said or experienced. A witness has to testify to his or her own personal, first-hand experience. It's the same with disciple-making, too. If we don't have a personal experience with God, then there's no point in claiming to be a witness.

We are able to share only what we have directly experienced, and this comes from a quiet time and personal relationship with God. Only then can we tell our own testimony of God's action in our lives. We invite others to discipleship so that they can find the joy we have found. God's will for us always involves us as witnesses to his love and grace. Disciples are made when people respond to our testimony of God's love.

Third, the testimony or witness of the Christian is to be given everywhere. Christians are to bring this good news to the entire world. This is the basis for worldwide mission outreach in every form.

Every disciple has the life purpose of giving personal testimony to God's action in our lives. It doesn't mean we all become preachers or teachers, but we can testify in any occupation or role that we have in life. Being a witness has more to do with who we are as disciples than with our position, job or salary.

our gifts

You're a disciple and you're also a witness, sharing your personal experience of God's actions. But how exactly do you do it? Do we all do the same thing?

The biblical answer highlights your spiritual gifts.[500] The Holy Spirit gives different gifts to different people, and somehow they all work together to enhance the witness of all his disciples.

Take a minute to read three specific passages about spiritual gifts:

- Romans 12:6-8
- 1 Corinthians 12:4-11, 27-31
- Ephesians 4:11, 12

The lists of gifts are more illustrative than exhaustive, and none of the four lists is the same, but each gift comes from God to be used in his service.

These gifts are more than just our natural abilities or talents; they're more than skills, roles and functions. Sometimes our spiritual gifts might employ some of our natural abilities, but at other times they might not. These gifts are intended to make us more effective witnesses in order to build up the body of Christ, but if we don't take the time to recognise them, our gifts can lie dormant.

Spiritual gifts are given to the disciples within the body of Christ. Different gifts perform different ways, just like the various organs of any living body.[501] Each organ is important and irreplaceable and has its own function, and the body could not work without it.

This is a good reason for being part of the church family instead of just connecting with God alone. The church is composed of people with different spiritual gifts; each person is part of the total organism (the church body) and necessary for its efficient function. Independently functioning organs don't work as well.

It is important to discover our individual spiritual gifts, and often your church leader or small group can help with this. Your gifts were given to you to be discovered and used. To function most productively, use them in connection with other disciples who are all working together, then everyone draws strength from each other.

Discovering our place in God's work can bring incredible meaning and purpose. When we witness God's work in our lives and share that witness with others, then we can understand God's purpose for us.

re: consider

What has God done for you that you can tell to others as a witness?

REFERENCES
493. John 10:10, MGE.
494. John 4:34, NIV.
495. John 12:26, NIV.
496. Blackaby, Henry T., and Claude V. King. *Experiencing God*. Broadman and Holman, 1994, p. 50.
497. I John 5:13.
498. Matthew 28:19, 20.
499. Acts 1:8, RSV.
500. See chapter 18 in this book.
501. 1 Corinthians 12:12-26.

ABOUT
PREDICTION

29. COURT IN SESSION

God, you have given us the prophetic book of Daniel, and I've learned enough about you to know that you always have a purpose in everything you do, so please let me understand and learn from it. I know I'm not some fancy theologian, but would you please give me the keys to unlock its meaning?

re: tell

The headaches kept coming, but everybody told her it was just stress. Twenty-eight-year-old Angela Cooper knew there had to be more to it. Then she saw an episode of the television drama *ER* where one of the characters, Dr Greene, bites his tongue and when a colleague tells him to stick it out it goes over to one side. 'No, stick it straight out,' the other doctor says, and Greene tells her, 'I am.' The on-screen diagnosis – brain tumour!

Angela stuck out her tongue in front of a mirror – then headed to her local A&E to tell them about her own identical symptom. A CT scan found a tumour behind her nose. Radiation and chemotherapy followed and, thanks to aggressive treatment, she survived her cancer.

re: think

Take your Bible and go with me to the book of Daniel. We're going to take a look at his apocalyptic prophecies. Daniel's prophecies make three points clear:

- There is good and evil in this world, which each of us experiences every day. But good will one day overcome evil.

- History isn't a cycle of meaningless events or repeated failures. Instead, it's actually heading somewhere. And God decides where it will go.

- One day God will bring things to an end. That's when Jesus returns and, despite all appearances to the contrary, God is in charge.

Read Daniel chapter 2. This dream, given to King Nebuchadnezzar of Babylon, is of a statue made of several metals standing on feet of iron and clay which was suddenly demolished by a stone missile.

Daniel tells the king that the image represents a broad outline of human political history and the stone represents the kingdom of God. It's fascinating that the prophecy predicts, hundreds of years in advance, the exact sequence of kingdoms throughout history from Babylon to Rome! Then the stone, the kingdom of God, comes and demolishes all the human empires. It's like a judgement from God.

Judgement is actually a major theme in this book; even Daniel's name means *God is my judge*. When the Bible talks about God's judgement, it illustrates what judgement was like in ancient times, not today. In today's judicial system, the judge must be impartial, hearing evidence from both defence and prosecution, but in the Bible the judge wasn't impartial; he was also the *defending attorney* for the person facing charges. The judge was biased in favour of the accused and defended him from accusations until the weight of evidence demanded a guilty verdict.

This would explain why biblical writers ask God to judge them. For example, 'Save me, O God, by thy name, and judge me by thy strength.'[502] Today we think of judgement as a condemnation, but here the psalmist sees it as deliverance, because he knows the judge, who is also his advocate.[503]

So, with that in mind, let's look at another apocalyptic vision in Daniel chapter 7.

Here Daniel himself has a dream: he sees the Mediterranean Sea whipped up by a storm. From the water come four monstrous beasts, unlike anything in real life. The first is a lion with eagle's wings; then a bear raised up on one side with three ribs (or tusks) in its mouth; next a leopard with four wings and four heads; and the fourth is indescribable, absolutely terrifying, with iron teeth and ten horns on its head. Then one of its horns takes on a life of its own, removing some of the other horns, sprouting eyes and speaking arrogantly.[504] What a dream! And it doesn't end there – but let's talk about this for now.

A dream like this raises many questions, but Daniel provides only some of the answers. He tells us some of the content of the dream,[505] then gives an interpretation,[506] followed by more content[507] and even more interpretation.[508] Yet nowhere are any of the beasts identified. It seems as though there is something more important in this dream than identifying the beasts. And that key piece is about understanding the importance of the judgement.

A judgement takes place in this vision and it is painted just as imaginatively as those beasts are described. A figure known as the Ancient of Days (obviously God) sits on a throne, wearing brilliant white clothing and having snow white hair. Flames flash out from his throne, it is surrounded by fire, and untold numbers of attendants surround it. This is significant, Daniel says, because 'the court began its session, and the books were opened'.[509]

The whole vision centres on this judgement, but look at how the vision is presented:

A: The lion, bear and leopard (vv. 3-6)

    B: The indescribable beast (v. 7)

        C: The little horn who speaks arrogantly (v. 8)

            D: The court sits in judgement (vv. 9-10)

        C`: The fate of the arrogant-speaking little horn (v. 11a)

    B`: The fate of the indescribable beast (v. 11b)

A`: The fate of the lion, bear and leopard (v. 12)[510]

Notice how the judgement is the hinge in this vision. Everything leads up to it and then leads away in reverse order. But why is it central? What does the judgement achieve?

Some answers to these questions had already been given in Nebuchadnezzar's dream back in Daniel 2. There Daniel moves quickly through the metals of the image (he mentions only that the first is Babylon), but he emphasises the stone missile, which represents the kingdom of God. When the stone grinds the whole image to dust, it illustrates just how temporary is our human history. Exactly the same happens in chapter 7; once the court sits in judgement, the arrogant horn and beasts are either destroyed or deprived of their power.

> We can use our ambitions, talents and gifts to make a difference for good.

Neither of these visions indicates that human achievement is worthless. Of course not. We can use our ambitions, talents and gifts to make a difference for good. We can work in any field to make the world a better place. But both of these visions show that there is a limit to God's patience with arrogant human pride, the kind of blind ambition that perpetuates economic injustice or religious intolerance for selfish ends. The visions of Daniel 2 and 7 show that God's ultimate aim is to bring that sort of thing to an end.

In fact, the two chapters run parallel: the gold of chapter 2 and the lion of chapter 7 both represent Babylon; the silver and the bear are Medo-Persia; the bronze and the leopard are Greece; the iron and the indescribable ten-horned beast are Rome; and just as the feet of iron and clay are a continuation of the iron, so the little horn is a continuation of the horned beast. So, if you've already understood chapter 2, then you've also understood most of chapter 7. Chapter 7 just expands on the judgement and what it achieves.

This judgement highlights the good news of the apocalyptic prophecies of the Bible.

- First, that good will triumph over evil. The little horn represents the earthly powers who persecute and blaspheme their way to godless power and influence. But in God's judgement the arrogant little horn gets its just rewards. Not only that, but judgement is given in favour of 'the saints of the Most High'.[511] In other words, those with integrity, faithfulness and justice will see the fulfilment of their dreams.

- Second, that history is not meaningless, but is heading somewhere – to a day when God's justice is finally established.

- Third, despite current appearances to the contrary, God is in charge, because God is the judge.

This vision in Daniel invites us to take a courageous moral stand. It sets out clearly that there is a battle raging between good and evil. Whether this is represented by metals and crushing stone missiles (Daniel 2) or by fearsome beasts and boasting horns (Daniel 7) makes no difference. The varying details are merely to help us see different aspects of the main picture.

Both dreams are saying: since good will one day triumph, commit yourself to goodness, integrity and faithfulness in a world which prefers size, power and arrogance. Evil isn't just theoretical, it's real. It ranges from gross injustice such as racism, religious persecution and child abuse to the more subtle prejudices which prevent us from showing the compassion God requires.

God's final judgement will certainly right all wrongs. But, in the meantime, we need to show which side we're on.

re: consider

If your life choices are the equivalent of showing your team loyalty, how are you showing the world which team you're on?

REFERENCES
502. Psalm 54:1, KJV.
503. Turner, Laurence A. 'Judgement: A Friend of the Judge.' *Signs* Aug. 1992: 3-5.
504. See Daniel 7:1-8.
505. Daniel 7:1-14.
506. Ibid 7:17-18.
507. Ibid 7:19-22.
508. Ibid 7:23-27.
509. Ibid 7:10.
510. Ferch, Arthur J. *The Son of Man in Daniel 7*. Andrews UP, 1983, pp. 136-137.
511. Daniel 7:22, NIV.

30. RIGHT ON TIME

God, you talked about the prophecies of Daniel and made them relevant to your disciples then and to us who are living in these last days before you return to Earth. But even Daniel himself didn't understand everything you showed him at first, so I'm asking for your Holy Spirit to interpret the symbols and time prophecies of Daniel's book.

re: tell

A devout believer in astrology, French king Louis XI was deeply impressed when an astrologer correctly foretold that a lady of the court would die in eight days' time. Deciding, however, that the too-accurate prophet should be disposed of, Louis summoned the man to his apartments, having first told his servants to throw the visitor out of the window when he gave the signal. 'You claim to understand astrology and to know the fate of others,' the king said to the man, 'so tell me at once what your fate will be and how long you have to live.'

'I shall die just three days before Your Majesty,' answered the astrologer. The shaken king cancelled his plans![512]

re: think

Let's visit our friend Daniel once more. Read Daniel 7, 8 and 9.

Remember he's an exile in Babylon, away from his home with no temple, no priests, no sacrifices. He is cut off from his roots, the centre of his world and what gave his life meaning. In other words, he's a lot like us.

The world in which we live just doesn't seem as certain as it once did; it changes every day; there are no absolutes anymore. This might sound great – until we hit a crisis and need a definite answer.

In this lonely state of mind, Daniel has a vision of a ram and a goat.[513] These beasts are less spectacular than those he saw in his previous vision. But once again they represent world superpowers, showing the world as it appears to be. Notice how they're described. They're charging, powerful, strong, savagely forceful, enraged. They strike, throw down, trample, become enormously great and so on.

In all of that, there is not a single mention of God. Just like the world in which we live, this is a world of swaggering political powers, cynical governments and crazed terrorists; a world often difficult to make sense of, and God *apparently* absent, but only apparently so as Daniel's vision shows. These beasts aren't the first prophetic characters to be powerful, enraged or despotic.

In real life, King Nebuchadnezzar was like this. He overthrew Jerusalem, ransacked the temple, took Daniel into exile, threatened to execute all his wise men, threw Shadrach, Meshach and Abednego into a furnace and pranced around on his palace roof, proclaiming, 'Is not this great Babylon I have made!'[514] Nobody seemed to oppose him, until one day, during a personal crisis, he finally realised that God was in control after all.[515]

Let's get back to our dreams, though. From among the beasts a peculiar little horn comes on the scene and continues the arrogance of the ram and goat, but to an even greater degree. It opposes God, persecutes those who've committed themselves to him and tries to eliminate all worship.[516] Things seem to be getting worse rather than better. What will happen next?

This vision follows Daniel 7, which developed and supported the message of Nebuchadnezzar's dream in Daniel 2. The vision of Daniel 2 set the pattern for the rest of the Daniel's book. It passed quickly over the metal and clay kingdoms, but focused on the stone that smashed the image. In other words, it was mostly interested in *the end*. It's the same here, 'the vision concerns the time of the end'.[517] And, as we've seen already in Daniel, our present lives have meaning because there will be a meaningful end.

But in the meantime, however, it seems that the beasts are in control. That was certainly Daniel's experience. He'd been taken into exile by the Babylonians; then he'd lived long enough to serve the next superpower of Medo-Persia (the ram). In this vision he sees the coming kingdom of Greece (the goat), its disintegration and beyond that to the end. If God's own people could be exiled in Daniel's time and the temple destroyed and the worship of God abolished – then is God in control *anywhere*? If beasts swagger like this in prophecy, then does God really rule in heaven? Is God really in charge?

For many people, the Bible is a book of answers. But it is also a book of questions. And Daniel 8 is no exception. Far more than we might think, people have questions for God. Such as, '*Why* do you hide yourself in times of trouble?'[518] or '*How long* will you hide your face from me?'[519] Daniel asks a similar question: '*How long* will the vision be?'[520]

We ask that question – *How long?* – when life doesn't live up to our expectations. So how long will these beasts flaunt their power? How long before the human kingdoms acknowledge the kingdom of God?

> The world in which we live just doesn't seem as certain as it once did; it changes every day; there are no absolutes anymore.

Those are the questions; now here is the answer: 'For two thousand three hundred evenings and mornings; then the sanctuary shall be restored to its rightful state.'[521] The answer is as symbolic as the beasts that prompt the question and, strangely, the answer makes no reference to the beasts. It simply states that the sanctuary will be 'restored to its rightful state', but what is its rightful state?

Originally the sanctuary or temple was a place where people worshipped God, where he symbolically lived among his people.[522] If the sanctuary is restored to its rightful place, then God will also be restored to *his* rightful place in our lives. The attacks on the people of God, the worship of God and the reputation of God – presented in all their detail in the vision – will finally stop because, despite all appearances to the contrary, God is in control.

In order to appreciate the full impact of this vision and to understand one or two of its details, we must take a look at the next chapter. Here we see Daniel considering a prophecy by Jeremiah (another ancient prophet) that Judah (the ancient Israelite tribe of God's followers) would spend seventy years in exile.[523] As Daniel is thinking about Jeremiah's *seventy* years, God reveals a prophecy concerning *four hundred and ninety* (70 x 7) years.

What is the significance of these numbers? Ancient Israel lived on a cycle of sabbatical years, where every seventh year agricultural land was left unplanted, slaves were freed and debts were cancelled.[524] Jeremiah's prophecy was based on this principle;[525] the seventy years meant a cycle of ten sabbatical years (10 x 7). In addition, there was a cycle of *jubilee* years, every seventh sabbatical (or every forty-nine years).[526] This cycle of seven sabbaticals or forty-nine years inaugurated a jubilee in the fiftieth year,[527] when all property reverted to its original owner.

So Daniel 9 begins with Jeremiah's seventy years, or *ten sabbatical years*, and concludes with a new prophecy concerning 490 years, or *ten jubilee cycles*. Just as the jubilee year had greater significance than the sabbatical year, so Daniel's 490 years has broader scope than Jeremiah's seventy years.[528] Jeremiah's ten sabbatical years resulted in the literal release of the people of Judah from exile in Babylon, but Daniel's prophecy of the 490 years provides a time 'to finish transgression, to put an end to sin, to atone for wickedness, to bring in everlasting righteousness', and it points to the arrival of 'the Anointed One' or Messiah.[529] It's a far greater release than people returning from Babylon – it's the ultimate jubilee.

In addition, the prophecy provides an indication of when this expected Messiah would arrive. Daniel outlines a period of 483 years (69 x 7), starting from the decree to restore Jerusalem until the coming of the 'Anointed One'.

If we start from the Persian decree to rebuild Jerusalem in 457BC and count forward 483 years, we come to AD27. The prophecy continues that 'in the middle of the [seventieth] "seven" he [the Messiah] will put an end to sacrifice and offering'.[530] The seventieth cycle of seven years concluded in AD34. So this ultimate act of the Anointed One would occur sometime between AD27 and AD34. That is precisely the point in history when Jesus Christ was crucified, died and rose from the dead.[531]

We can see how Daniel 9 adds detail to Daniel 8 and its prophecy of the 2,300 'evenings and mornings' or days. Just as the beasts were symbolic creatures, so is the time period.

The Bible uses days to represent years,[532] just as 'weeks' are used to represent cycles of seven years in Daniel 9. It's likely, then, that the period in Daniel 8 was actually 2,300 years and that the prophecy of the seventy weeks (490 years) in Daniel 9 provides its starting point. Two thousand three hundred years from 457BC brings us to AD1844. At this point in history, the process of restoring the sanctuary 'to its rightful state' began.

Daniel 9 helped us understand Daniel 8, and so does Daniel 7. Just as the judgement in Daniel 7 is good news, announcing the end of injustice, persecution and evil, so the restoration of the sanctuary will clarify who has chosen to be on God's side.

Who takes commitment to God seriously and lives as if that commitment makes a difference? Daniel's prophecies appeal for us to take the side of honesty, compassion and justice. They also provide an answer when we ache for God to overturn the injustices in our world. Living as we do, after the seventy weeks and the 2,300 days have ended, the world's injustices continue to test our patience and make us ask God, 'How long?'

God's answer is, 'Not much longer!'

re: consider

What do you most want to understand about the future?

REFERENCES

512. Today in the Word, 16 July 1993. *www.sermonillustrations.com/a-z/p/prediction.htm*. 13 April 2006.
513. Daniel 8:3-7.
514. Read Daniel 1-4 for the details.
515. Daniel 4:33-37.
516. Daniel 8:9-12.
517. Daniel 8:17, 19, NIV.
518. Psalm 10:1, NIV.
519. Psalm 13:1, NIV.
520. Daniel 8:13, NKJV.
521. Daniel 8:14, ESV.
522. Exodus 25:8.
523. Jeremiah 25:11-12 and 29:10.
524. Exodus 23:10-11; Leviticus 25:1-7; Deuteronomy 15:1-2 and 11-12.
525. See 2 Chronicles 36:21.
526. Leviticus 25:8.
527. Leviticus 25:10.
528. Doukhan, Jacques. 'The Seventy Weeks of Daniel 9: An Exegetical Study.' Andrews University Seminary Studies 17 (1979): pp. 1-22.
529. Daniel 9:24-25, NIV.
530. Daniel 9:27, NIV.
531. The previous two paragraphs are adapted from: Turner, Laurence A. 'The Coming of Jesus Anticipated.' *The Essential Jesus: The Man, His Message, His Mission*. Ed. Bryan W. Ball and William G. Johnsson. Pacific P, 2002, pp. 71-73.
532. Numbers 14:34; Ezekiel 4:6.

31. ONE THOUSAND YEARS

God, you are the one who gives me a sense of justice and lets me perceive the absolute lack of justice in this world. But the waters get muddy when it comes to thinking about judgement on me. Please show me from your Word what happens when all is said and done.

re: tell

A beggar found a leather purse that someone had dropped in the marketplace. Opening it, he discovered that it contained 100 pieces of gold. He then heard a merchant shouting: 'A reward! A reward to the one who finds my leather purse!'

Being an honest man, the beggar came forward and handed the purse to the merchant, saying, 'Here is your purse. May I have the reward now?'

'Reward?' scoffed the merchant, greedily counting his gold. 'Why, the purse I dropped had 200 pieces of gold in it. You've already stolen more than the reward! Go away or I'll tell the police.'

'I'm an honest man,' said the beggar defiantly. 'Let us take this matter to the court.'

In court the judge patiently listened to both sides of the story and said, 'I believe you both, and justice is possible! Merchant, you stated that the purse you lost contained 200 pieces of gold. Well, that's a considerable cost, but the purse this beggar found had only 100 pieces of gold. Therefore, it couldn't be the one that you lost', and, with that, the judge gave the purse and all the gold to the beggar.[533]

re: think

When some people hear the words 'judgement' or 'justice', they automatically think of punishment. In everyday understanding, 'justice' means 'to get what one deserves'. Famous American writer and cynic H. L. Mencken once said: 'Injustice is relatively easy to bear; what stings is justice.'

God says that one day he is going to judge the world.[534] Everybody will receive a reward according to what he or she has done in life.[535] And that is what scares us. We know it would be very unpleasant if God's perfect justice apportioned to us what we deserve.

So is the biblical teaching about God's judgement something that we should be scared of or is it good news?

Historically, God's judgement consists of three phases.

judgement on the cross

Jesus said about judgement: 'Now is the time for judgment on this world; now the prince of this world will be driven out.'[536] He connects the judgement with his being 'lifted up from the earth' on the cross.[537] This will result in the throwing down of Satan[538] and the drawing of all men to Christ.[539]

On the cross God judged the whole of mankind in the person of Jesus Christ. Jesus came 'in the likeness of sinful flesh'[540] and took on himself all the sins of all people from all times.[541] At Christ's death Satan lost his right to claim people as his (Satan's) own on account of their sins.[542] Christ defeated the devil.

On Easter Sunday, God resurrected the 'one who knew no sin'[543] and who could not be accused of any sin.[544] Thus, all promises given to mankind were fulfilled in him.[545] While on the cross, Christ was condemned for all mankind, and in his resurrection all mankind was given new life.

All people are included in this judgement.[546] The cost of sin was paid for every one of us on the cross in the person of Jesus, our substitute. Our condemnation is his condemnation. His justification is our justification, and his resurrection is a guarantee of resurrection for those who identify themselves with Jesus Christ.

preaching the gospel

According to John, the second phase of judgement is the preaching of the gospel. This phase is a direct continuation of the first phase. In preaching the gospel people are called to identify with the judgement that took place on the cross. Every time Christ and his cross are presented to people, judgement takes place,[547] and their response is a matter of life and death.[548]

Every one of us makes a choice when we hear the gospel message: either to identify with sin, knowing that it was condemned on the cross, or to identify with Christ, who was glorified in resurrection. By making our decision regarding Jesus Christ, we pronounce judgement upon ourselves.

judgement at the end of time

The third and last phase of God's judgement takes place at the end of time.[549] But this judgement is just a confirmation and manifestation of the result of the first two phases of judgement. If we reject the words of life now, we will see the final result on the day of judgement.[550] Those who are 'in Christ' now will be found in him also at the final judgement.

This end-time final judgement consists of three parts:

pre-advent judgement

The first part of the eschatological (end-time) judgement takes place before the second coming of Jesus. Jesus said that there would be a 'resurrection of life' and a 'resurrection of condemnation'.[551] Because resurrection to life takes place at the second coming of Jesus,[552] and resurrection is the pronouncement of a verdict, some judgement process must have taken place beforehand.

Jesus spoke about those who would be 'considered worthy of taking part in that age and in the resurrection from the dead'.[553] Resurrection to life and/or transformation 'in a flash, in the twinkling of an eye, at the last trumpet'[554] is the result and a proof of a judgement that preceded it.

We spoke more about this pre-advent judgement when we talked about Daniel chapters 7 and 8. Its purpose is not for God to determine who will be saved,[555] but to provide the evidence to the created beings of the universe that the redeemed are 'safe to save'.

judgement during the millennium

With the second coming of Christ, words from Daniel 7:27 will be fulfilled: 'Then the sovereignty, power and greatness of the kingdoms under the whole heaven will be handed over to the saints, the people of the Most High. His kingdom will be an everlasting kingdom, and all rulers will worship and obey him.' (NIV.)

The activity of the redeemed during the millennium is described with these words: 'I saw thrones on which were seated those who had been given authority to judge.'[556] The wicked dead are killed at the second coming of Jesus by 'the breath of his mouth', and are destroyed by 'the splendour of his coming'.[557] Now, during the millennium, they are judged by the redeemed. Together with the wicked, the fallen angels are also judged.[558] This judgement does not decide who will be saved, as that issue was settled during the pre-advent judgement.

So, then, what does this judgement decide? The second coming of Jesus causes final and irrevocable separation of mankind into two groups. Marriage partners, families, friends, co-workers may be separated.[559] The questions that will inevitably be on the minds of those who are saved is: 'Why are they not with us here? Why are they not saved?'

Because God runs an open government, based on evidence, he will allow all the redeemed to inspect the evidence (the books).[560] The redeemed have plenty of time (1,000 years) to see that God respected the free decision of every human being. For future peace in the universe it is vital that every one of the redeemed is convinced that God could not have done more for the salvation of these people.

judgement after the millennium

The millennium both starts and ends with a resurrection. 'The rest of the dead did not come to life until the thousand years were ended.'[561] This is the resurrection that Jesus calls the 'resurrection of judgement.'[562]

Christ descends to Earth with his redeemed and the holy city.[563] And now the last part of the last judgement takes place. A 'great white throne' is revealed and 'the dead [who were resurrected], great and small, [were] standing before the throne, and books were opened. . . . The dead were judged according to what they had done as recorded in the books . . . and each person was judged according to what he had done.'[564]

'There will be weeping there, and gnashing of teeth, when you see Abraham, Isaac and Jacob and all the prophets in the kingdom of God, but you yourselves thrown out.'[565]

As a result of this judgement, 'at the name of Jesus every knee . . . [will] bow, in heaven and on earth and under the earth, and every tongue [will] confess that Jesus Christ is Lord, to the glory of God the Father.'[566] Even the condemned will have to acknowledge that God treated them fairly.

When the wicked, in spite of all the evidence presented to them, march 'up on the broad plain of the earth' and surround 'God's people and the beloved city',[567] they show that nothing can be done to help them. The direction of their thinking and their actions cannot be changed; they have no restraint in their desire to harm and kill. Then 'fire came down from heaven . . . and consumed them.'[568]

> During the course of history, many people have been exploited and made victims of distorted justice.

The question of God's justice is forever settled; all the angels, the redeemed and the wicked have acknowledged that God was not partial and that he governed the universe with justice, fairness and integrity. It is a strange act for God, but there is nothing more he can do to help those who do not want to be helped.[569] The whole judgement process was put in place to make sure that when evil is finally eradicated, God has the approval of all his creatures.

purpose and meaning of God's judgement

1) In relation to humankind

During the course of history, many people have been exploited and made victims of distorted justice.[570] These people cried out, 'Why? How long?'[571]

At the end, all injustice will be dealt with and the meek will 'inherit the earth', even though it may have seemed unlikely throughout history.[572] We may not always experience joy here, but 'in keeping with his promise we are looking forward to a new heaven and a new earth, the home of righteousness'.[573]

The purpose of judgement is not punishment but restoration.[574] All who want to be part of the kingdom where there is no more evil or pain can be there.

The primary purpose of God's judgement in relationship towards us is to save us, defend us and make us free.[575] Thus, in light of God's method of judgement, we can experience joy.[576]

2) In relation to God himself

When Revelation 14:7 announces the beginning of God's last judgement, it says: 'the hour of *his* judgement has come.' (NIV.) The judgement goes beyond deciding our fate.[577] The apostle Paul says that God 'will be judged'.[578] God is not judged because someone summoned him to court. God himself graciously allows his created beings to pronounce a judgement on how he has run his universe and dealt with sin and sinners throughout history.

Salvation would be meaningless if Satan could prove God to be cruel, unloving, unkind or an arbitrary ruler who uses fear tactics to reach his goals.[579] God has been accused of everything that takes place on this planet; therefore, judgement must vindicate *his* character as well.

God could not refute these accusations by using his power. That would only prove Satan's point and make things worse, because God wants people to serve him on the basis of love for him, not fear.[580]

The last judgement will reveal the essence of Satan's rebellion and evil. By revealing the dimensions of the cosmic controversy regarding his character, God will be able to gain the admiration and worship of all his children. All created beings will at the end admit that God has treated them fairly.

3) In relation to intelligent beings in the universe

Satan and one third of the angels decided to use their free choice against God,[581] and in order to preserve peace in heaven they had to leave their positions.[582] The unfallen beings have seen the pain and confusion that sin has brought to the universe: the Bible tells us that they carefully follow what is happening on this planet.[583]

Satan criticises God's mercy towards his people: he is called the 'accuser of . . . brethren'.[584] Christ's death on the cross answered this accusation once and for all before the whole universe.[585]

When Satan accuses God's people, he begs the question: If God 'welcomes sinners, and eats with them',[586] why were Satan and his angels thrown out of heaven while other sinners would be accepted into heaven?

The last judgement reveals to the whole universe why God has made the decisions he has made regarding the salvation of humankind. The purpose of God's last judgement is not to inform God about who can be saved; he knows them very well.[587] It is to give evidence to the intelligent beings of the universe about the relationship of the redeemed with Jesus Christ. This way, God will remove any suspicion or fear that the redeemed people could be the cause of a new conflict in the universe.

This understanding of the biblical doctrine of judgement makes it possible for us to have a better relationship with God. If our behaviour is motivated by fear of judgement and/or its outcome, then whatever we do will be tainted with guilt and fear and we shall not have the right relationship with God. Judgement is a revelation of God's love, and God wants us to love him, because he first loved us.[588] 'There is no fear in love. But perfect love drives out fear, because fear has to do with punishment. The one who fears is not made perfect in love.'[589] When we have a proper understanding of the judgement, we can then experience joy in our lives and a better relationship with God.

re: consider

How does it feel to know that judgement is an ongoing process in which you participate? How does that responsibility affect you?

REFERENCES

533. *www.storyarts.org/library/nutshell/stories/purse.html.*
534. Acts 17:31.
535. 2 Corinthians 5:10.
536. John 12:3, NIV.
537. Ibid verse 32.
538. Revelation 12:7-9.
539. John 12:32.
540. Romans 8:3, NKJV.
541. 1 Corinthians 15:3; 2 Corinthians 5:21.
542. John 12:31.
543. 2 Corinthians 5:21, NKJV.
544. John 8:46.
545. Acts 13:23-33.
546. John 12:32.
547. John 3:14-21.
548. John 5:24-25.
549. John 5:27-30; 12:48.
550. John 5:28-29.
551. John 5:29, NKJV.
552. Matthew 16:27; John 12:48.
553. Luke 20:35, NIV.
554. 1 Corinthians 15:52, NIV.
555. 2 Timothy 2:19.
556. Revelation 20:4, NIV.
557. 2 Thessalonians 2:8, NIV.

558. 1 Corinthians 6:2-3.
559. Luke 17:34-36.
560. Matthew 7:22; Luke 13:26.
561. Revelation 20:5, NIV.
562. John 5:29, NASB.
563. Revelation 20:9.
564. Revelation 20:11-13, NIV.
565. Luke 13:28, NIV.
566. Philippians 2:10-11, NIV.
567. Revelation 20:9.
568. Ibid.
569. Isaiah 28:21.
570. Luke 18:1-3.
571. Daniel 8:13; Revelation 6:10.
572. Matthew 5:5, NIV.
573. 2 Peter 3:13, NIV.
574. Zechariah 3:1-7.
575. Daniel 7:27.
576. Psalm 7:9; 20:1; 35:24; 43:1; 54:3.
577. 2 Corinthians 5:10.
578. Romans 3:4, from the Greek language.
579. Genesis 3:1-6.
580. 1 John 4:18, 19.
581. Revelation 12:4; 2 Peter 2:4.
582. Jude 6.
583. Exodus 25:20; 1 Peter 1:12; Ephesians 3:10; 1 Corinthians 4:9.
584. Revelation 12:10, NKJV.
585. John 12:31, 32; Revelation 12:10.
586. Luke 15:2, NIV.
587. 2 Timothy 2:19.
588. 1 John 4:19.
589. 1 John 4:18, NIV.

32. PLANET FRESH

God, what I have been learning about your future plans for this earth makes me want to know even more. Please open my spiritual eyes so I can see whether the next life will be more than just one long endless holiday. What will happen there?

re: tell

An anonymous writer tells of an American tourist's visit to the nineteenth-century Polish rabbi, Hofetz Chaim. Astonished to see that the rabbi's home was only a simple room filled with books, plus a table and a bench, the tourist asked, 'Rabbi, where is your furniture?'

'Where is yours?' replied the rabbi.

'Mine?' asked the puzzled American. 'But I'm a visitor here. I'm only passing through.'

'So am I,' Hofetz Chaim replied.[590]

re: think

What will heaven be like? This question has intrigued me from my earliest youth. I learned from my parents and my church that if a person lives a good life, he or she will go to heaven.

What age shall we be when we live eternally in heaven? My little brother died when he was 8. I was just one year older when it happened, and my grandfather died a little later. So would my brother be resurrected as an 8 year old and then grow into full manhood, and would my grandfather regain his hair and full mobility and turn into a much younger version of the man I had known?

Ask ten different people what heaven will be like and you may get ten different answers. Speculation runs wild about paradise in the hereafter. Papias, a second-century Christian writer, got rather excited when he thought about Isaiah's prophecy of the hereafter, where it is predicted that all will have their private vineyards.[591] According to the church father Irenaeus, Papias believed that all vines will have 10,000 stems, and that each stem will have 10,000 branches, and each branch will have 10,000 shoots. Each shoot will have 10,000 clusters, with 10,000 grapes on each cluster. Each grape, when pressed, will produce twenty-five measures of wine.

He is just one of many Christians who have dreamed about eternity. Many dreams of heaven even surpass those of the Muslim martyrs who expect that, among other blessings, paradise will guarantee an ample supply of virgins to satisfy all male desires!

a real place

Not everyone agrees that heaven would be such a great blessing if it were simply an extension of the rather dubious pleasures of this world. But some people aren't attracted by some of the traditional Christian ideas either. Christians talk about singing eternal praises, shouting endless hallelujahs and playing heavenly harps. But won't that be rather boring? What sort of God would actually want that kind of endless adoration?

Let's start at the beginning. According to the Bible, there's no question about the reality of a hereafter. Heaven is real. There will be 'a new heaven and a new earth'.[592] The first glimpses are found in the Old Testament, in the prophetic book of Isaiah. 'Look! I am creating new heavens and a new earth – and no one will even think about the old ones anymore.'[593] It will be a place where 'my people will live as long as trees, and my chosen ones will have time to enjoy their hard-won gains'.[594] Isaiah talks about a New Jerusalem that will overflow with peace and prosperity.[595]

The New Testament fills this sketchy picture with more details. Jesus declared that upon his ascension to 'heaven', he was going to prepare places for us. There will be many rooms for his disciples in his 'Father's home'.[596] Peter tells us to anticipate eagerly the day when God will set fire to this present world and will create 'new heavens and a new earth.' He then adds one crucial detail; it will be a world 'in which righteousness dwells'.[597]

The most complete picture is found in the last two chapters of the Bible, Revelation 21 and 22. The very position of these two chapters emphasises that the new world exists after this present one has ended – after Jesus returns to Earth and the resurrection has taken place.

Revelation chapter 20 clarifies that there will be a thousand-year interlude during which the saints will be in heaven, where they reign with Christ[598] and participate in the work of judgement. Paul says that at this time 'the saints will judge the world'.[599] After all this has taken place, 'the old heaven and old earth [will have] disappeared'.[600]

Take some time to read and re-read the last two chapters of the Bible. The language is highly symbolic, but that doesn't make this new earth any less real. What does it mean that the capital city of this new world, 'the New Jerusalem', is 'pure gold, as clear glass'?[601] How can the city walls be 216 feet thick?[602] It may be easier to understand what this new world isn't than to get a clear picture of what it actually is. But I definitely know that I want to be there!

> According to the Bible, there's no question about the reality of a hereafter.

end of everything negative

There won't be any more death because, after the final judgement, 'God himself will be with them. He will wipe every tear from their eyes, and there will be no more death or sorrow or crying or pain.'[603]

Just imagine! No more death. No more accidents. No more sickness, not even a little fatigue. No more Alzheimer's or heart attacks. No more sudden infant deaths or ageing; no more handicaps or farewells or separations. Truly, that is a new world.

Our present life is always linked with death. Every newspaper has obituaries. Every beautiful medieval cathedral has tombstones. When we visit the maternity ward in the hospital, there is a chance that on our way we will see a sign for the morgue. No matter how we try to ignore death, to fight it and beat it, it always catches us up. But in heaven it won't exist!

And the good news continues: those who inherit this new world won't have to worry about safety, because only God's people will be there. 'Cowards, unbelievers, the corrupt, murderers, the immoral, those who practice witchcraft, idol worshipers, and all liars' will be noticeably absent.[604] Can you imagine a world with only honest and decent people?

There won't be any reason to be afraid of darkness or drowning either. 'And there will be no night there – no need for lamps or sun'[605] and there will no longer be any sea.[606] For the superficial reader this may not sound too promising. Where do you go for your vacation if there are no more sunny beaches? We have to remember that this is symbolic language and ask ourselves how the original reader may have understood this.

In ancient times the night was dark. In today's world, wherever we go at night we can easily see light somewhere, or we can bring artificial light. But before modern technology made our light sources possible, darkness meant danger and threat. The ocean, too, was formidable and dangerous.

These statements about the sea and the night are not necessarily statements about geography or environment. Rather, they form a declaration of God's eternal love and care. When the old world is replaced by a new creation, anything that ever posed a threat will disappear. For the ancient people, the absence of darkness and ocean was comforting. For us, they imply that those elements which threaten our existence will be removed. No longer will there be the threat of nuclear war, of chemical pollution, environmental disaster or swine flu. God's new world will be the safest place imaginable – for everyone.

There's one more important aspect: the skyline of this new earth is dominated by a majestic capital city – the New Jerusalem – and it beats every man-made structure in history. 'Its length and width and height were each 1,400 miles.'[607] It forms a perfect cube.

When we read about the dimensions of the Old Testament sanctuary, built according to divine instructions, we discover that its most holy room was also a cube.[608] This was the place where God's presence was manifested in a unique way. On the new earth, we find another cube, far exceeding the one in Old Testament times; for the first time since the Garden of Eden 'God's home is now among his people! He will live with them, and they will be his people'[609] for eternity!

'The great controversy is ended. Sin and sinners are no more. The entire universe is clean. One pulse of harmony and gladness beats through the vast creation. From him who created all, flow life and light and gladness, throughout the realms of illimitable space. From the minutest atom to the greatest world, all things, animate and inanimate, in their unshadowed beauty and perfect joy, declare that God is love.'[610]

re: consider

What could you do to help make your bit of the world more like heaven now?

REFERENCES
590. Christopher News Notes. *www.sermonillustrations.com/a-z/h/heaven.htm*. 13 April 2006.
591. Isaiah 65:21.
592. Revelation 21:1.
593. Isaiah 65:17.
594. Ibid verse 22.
595. Isaiah 66:12.
596. John 14:1-3.
597. 2 Peter 3:12, 13, NKJV.
598. Revelation 20:4.
599. 1 Corinthians 6:2, NKJV.
600. Revelation 21:1.
601. Revelation 21:18.

602. Ibid verse 17.
603. Ibid 21:3, 4.
604. Ibid 21:8.
605. Ibid 22:5.
606. Ibid 21:1.
607. Ibid 21:16.
608. 1 Kings 6:20.
609. Revelation 21:3.
610. White, Ellen G. *The Great Controversy.* Pacific P, 1971, p. 678.

ABOUT
NEW LIFESTYLE

33. CHRISTIAN, CULTURE, WORLD

God, I'm learning how you have a special purpose for my life, not only to live in heaven, but also for how I live now on Earth. Please give me a better understanding of this purpose and help me to figure out what life means for me.

re: tell

She had amassed a small fortune, but the last thing Oseola McCarty wanted was fame. The elderly African-American had spent her life washing clothes for a living. (She'd bought a washing machine and dryer in the '60s but found its performance not up to her standards.)

Earning a small but steady salary each week, she deposited half that salary in the bank, living on the rest and never withdrawing a cent. She never owned a car, lived in a house inherited from her uncle and never even upgraded her tattered Bible.

By the age of 87 the sixth-grade dropout had accumulated nearly a quarter of a million dollars, $150,000 of which she donated to the nearby University of Southern Mississippi – a place she'd never visited. She asked that scholarships be established for students who would otherwise not be able to attend college.

Her stunning gift inspired many others around the country to donate as well, and McCarty laughed as local business people, her former customers, tried to match her gift.

re: think

In 1951 the American theologian H. Richard Niebuhr wrote the influential book *Christ and Culture*. Decades later, this book still demands attention during discussions about Christianity and culture. Niebuhr listed five options:

Christ against culture
the Christ of culture
Christ above culture
Christ transforms culture, and
Christ and culture in paradox.

Many Christians, especially of the *stricter* and more *orthodox* variety, choose the 'Christ *against* culture' approach. However, I believe the Bible does not support their choice, but tells us that 'Christ *transforms* culture'.

culture – what is it?

What is culture? Is it primarily our literature, music, museums or theatre? Or are there more elements that make up how we relate to our culture?

Every textbook on cultural anthropology offers its own definition, but here's a fair summary of most of them: 'Culture is the accumulated habits, attitudes and beliefs of a group of people that define for them their general behaviour and way of life; [it constitutes] the total set of learned activities of a people.'[611] That's not a bad place to start.

We have to agree that elements of culture are not necessarily to be classified as good or bad; often they are morally neutral. Most Europeans eat with a knife and fork, while many Americans just use a fork. People in Japan may use chopsticks, while others around the world just eat with their fingers. One method isn't better than another; they're just culturally different.

It's the same with greetings; with 'appropriate' dress when we go to church; the architecture of our homes; our sense of humour and the way we do business. In most cases, moral issues aren't involved; it is simply a matter of the behaviour that we learned as we grew up in a particular society.

> Some people pray on their knees, others stand with their hands stretched heavenward.

In many ways this cultural diversity, which isn't necessarily good or bad, also applies to religion. Some people pray on their knees, others stand with their hands stretched heavenward. For some people, the best worship is singing psalms to sixteenth-century tunes, while others use musical instruments unheard of or considered distinctly irreligious in our own culture or country. Much of our religious expectations are shaped by history, geography, ethnicity and even climate.

a critical mind

Having said all that, it's also true that some aspects of our acquired behaviour or culture cannot pass the test set by followers of Christ. Believers must always make choices and reject anything that draws them away from God or sabotages their spiritual growth. 'Fix your thoughts on what is true, and honourable, and right, and pure, and lovely, and admirable. Think about things that are excellent and worthy of praise.'[612]

When Christians live in cultures where activities or habits are against the divine commandments, no compromise is possible. For example, to worship idols or statues merely to follow one's culture is an act of rebellion against the only true God.[613]

So when we look at our own culture or enter a new culture, we should carefully measure what we see against the principles of God's Word. At the same time, we must carefully distinguish between *form* and *content*. The cultural dress (form) of the phenomena we encounter may be acceptable, while the thing itself (content) may be totally unacceptable, or vice versa.

Let me illustrate: Followers of Jesus may disagree with many elements of Islamic theology and desire to introduce Muslims to Jesus Christ and salvation, but we should have no strong burden to change all the ways in which they worship. What is wrong with praying five times a day or respectfully removing your shoes before entering a house of worship?

Why should Western worship habits be forced on to people who have shown reverence in a different way for centuries, as long as they now worship the true God of the Bible? Although Paul introduced totally new ideas about God and salvation, he had no problem worshipping in the cultural context of the Jewish synagogue.[614] And while he preached a very specific and revolutionary message to an audience of unbelievers, he intentionally quoted their poets, knowing if he showed respect for their culture they might choose to listen.[615]

This goes even further when we apply it to our lives today. In biblical language, we don't just live in our own culture; we live in the world. We cannot move beyond culture, nor can we totally withdraw from the world; we are always part of it. And there's nothing inherently wrong with this.

However, we must remain critical about what the world has to offer. The operative word is not *negative*, but *critical*. This comes from a Greek word that means *to judge*. In other words, Christians should always examine the culture around them – whether it's the culture of their childhood or one they've crossed into – on the basis of the gospel, and they must always determine whether or not it meets God's standard.

When praying for his disciples, Jesus said, 'My prayer is not that you take them out of the world but that you protect them from the evil one.'[616] Many Christians haven't taken this text to heart and believe we should withdraw from the world as much as possible. They hold that we shouldn't engage in 'worldly' things and that we must avoid 'worldly' places or 'worldly' friends. But they often have a very subjective view of what 'worldly' means. They tend to draw up long lists of Christian dos and 'worldly' don'ts.

living as a christian

Drawing up lists is usually not a good idea. It can easily lead to *legalism* instead of a relationship with God.

legalism – noun, excessive adherence to law or formula

It's better to think through issues one at a time, identifying and applying biblical principles. Of course, Christians will be selective and discerning. The apostle Peter puts it very succinctly: 'Be careful to live properly among your unbelieving neighbours.'[617] Notice that he doesn't say: Avoid your unbelieving neighbours at all costs.

How do we do this? Figuring this out can be a lifelong process. It demands a close, growing journey with God. Only when we grow spiritually, only when we listen to our conscience, only when we find encouragement in a community of like-minded people, shall we be able to be in the world while not being part of it. We live here, but the world – our culture, our milieu, the external and material aspects of our existence – is not our ultimate focus.

While we live in the world, interact with the world and discerningly enjoy many things the world has to offer, we do not 'belong' to the world.[618] That is, our ultimate allegiance is to God and serving him is the underlying motive of all aspects of our daily life.

We can only contribute good things to the world if we stay in it; and only when we connect with people in the world, can we witness to our faith and invite others to start the same faith journey that has brought us satisfaction. Jesus made it clear that he didn't come to *condemn* the world. He came to *save* the world.[619] As his followers, that's also our operating principle.

In his famous Sermon on the Mount, Jesus provided a blueprint for the life of his disciples. He said: 'You are the salt of the earth.'[620] Salt has a unique quality in that it penetrates the entire dish: even a small amount brings flavour. That's the challenge for every Christian – to be present and change the taste of the environment so that people notice the difference, so that without this Christian presence in their community it feels as though something is missing.

Jesus added: 'You are the light of the world.'[621] When it's dark, a little light goes a long way to help us get around. This spiritual metaphor reminds us that we can be like lights to people near us, helping them to find their way in life. Jesus added another aspect: Put your light where it is in full view. Don't hide it and keep it to yourself. In other words, if you want to be a Christian, you've got to be visible to everyone.

Do you like these visual metaphors? Here's another one: as we grow more like Jesus, our lives become 'a Christ-like fragrance rising up to God'.[622] We must never remain anonymous, inaudible, invisible, unnoticed. Within our own world – in our culture – we're called to be like perfume, a good smell that brightens a room and leaves traces even after we leave. As we are transformed, so the culture around us – the world in which we live – will be transformed. It won't be complete until Jesus returns, but the change will be noticeable.

re: consider

How do you see your culture affecting your daily habits? How does it affect your faith?

REFERENCES

611. *www.geographic.org/glossary.html*.
612. Philippians 4:8.
613. Jeremiah 25:6.
614. Acts 17:1.
615. Acts 17:28.
616. John 17:15, NIV.
617. 1 Peter 2:12.
618. John 17:16.
619. John 3:17.
620. Matthew 5:13.
621. Matthew 5:14.
622. 2 Corinthians 2:14-16.

34. HEALTHY LIVING

God, I've been getting the message loud and clear throughout this book and in my study of the ancient scriptures that you want the absolute best for me. It's no surprise that you would include advice on how to live a healthy lifestyle. Help me to understand how these principles apply to my life.

re: tell

Writer Arthur Gordon once asked a doctor for the most effective prescription he knew.

'Well, I'll tell you,' the doctor said. 'One of my colleagues once had a patient who suffered from depression. It got to the point where she stayed at home all the time, listless, apathetic, indifferent to everything. Her usual medications didn't seem to help.

'One day the doctor delivered a package to her home. "Take what's in this package," he said, "and spend ten minutes every day looking through it at some object in this room."

'In the package was a magnifying glass. The woman began looking through it at the fabric on her sofa. Then she examined the veins in a flower from her garden, the colour dots in an old photograph, even the texture of her own skin. That was the turning point of her illness. She began to get well because this *prescription* aroused the most curative of all emotions – gratitude.'

Sharpening your sense of gratitude may be the best health insurance of all![623]

re: think

The World Health Organisation defines health as 'a state of complete physical, mental and social well-being and not merely the absence of disease'.

Other definitions imply that *health* is about total well-being: 'sound bodily condition, soundness, condition of wholesomeness,'[624] or 'physical soundness, mental soundness, spiritual soundness'.[625]

This concept of wholeness runs through the Bible. And since we know that God wants us to be happy, it's no big surprise that he's concerned with our welfare. He even gives us guidance about how to live in a healthy way:

- It started at creation when God outlined the diet for Adam and Eve and their future offspring.
- It was defined in detail to the Jewish nation (as promised to Abraham).
- It continued in the context of the body – to be considered as a temple of God's Spirit – in all succeeding generations to the present day.

at creation

At creation we were made in the image of God,[626] implying – among other things – that we have the same purpose and sensibilities as he does. He also provided for our nourishment, saying, 'Look! I have given you every seed-bearing plant throughout the earth and all the fruit trees for your food.'[627]

This strictly vegetarian diet was modified later, after all the vegetation was destroyed during the Flood. When Noah and his family were saved, God said, 'Everything that lives and moves will be food for you. Just as I gave you the green plants, I now give you everything.'[628] But there were still a few restrictions, such as avoiding meat with any trace of blood in it.[629]

Many Christians today choose to live the original creation diet, not just being vegetarian (which includes eggs and dairy products), but vegans (or pure vegetarians). This has been shown scientifically to be the optimal diet for human health. Other people also become vegetarians for economical or moral reasons, too.

a new nation

Due to the destruction of plant life after the Flood, God allowed meat to be eaten. Later natural human curiosity and the plentiful availability of so many 'moving things' led to people eating anything, and human health declined, along with the general lifespan.

When the Israelite nation was formed, God gave instructions on health and hygiene in order to safeguard their health. These are often referred to as *Mosaic* laws (since they were written down by Moses) or the rules regarding clean and unclean foods.

Many of these health codes are still the basis of sanitation and quarantine measures today. They were all-encompassing in their content and covered:

diet

- flesh torn by beasts was prohibited[630]
- boiling young goat meat in its mother's milk was prohibited[631]
- eating animal fat and blood was prohibited[632]
- clean and unclean meats were listed in detail (unclean foods primarily include meats from animals who are scavengers)[633]

disease

- laws pertaining to leprosy[634]
- laws concerning abnormal male conditions[635]

land conservation

- land to rest every seventh year, called 'jubilee' or 'sabbatical year'[636]

drugs

- priest not to drink alcohol before serving in religious ceremonies[637]

hygiene

- period of post-natal uncleanness[638]
- circumcision of boys on the eighth day[639]
- male conditions and sex[640]
- menstruation and observations[641]
- prevention of sickness[642]

quarantine

- for leprosy[643]

rest

- Sabbath rest and renewal[644]

sanitation

- tattooing prohibited[645]
- excreta disposal[646]

These wide-ranging rules were obviously intended to preserve health and cleanliness for individuals and the community.

In addition to any natural benefit derived from following these health-giving instructions, God placed a blessing on obedience to his leading, a blessing so important it was stated twice.[647] God told his people, 'If you listen carefully to the voice of the LORD your God and do what is right in his eyes, if you pay attention to his commands and keep all his decrees, I will not bring on you any of the diseases I brought on the Egyptians, for I am the LORD, who heals you.'[648]

the body temple

God asks us, his children, to obey him even in our health habits, but it's because he wants us to be healthy and strong. In the Bible God often calls us to be holy, just as he is holy.[649] Since God promises to live in us, our bodies are like a sanctuary for him.[650]

In his letter to the Ephesians Paul said, 'In him you too are being built together to become a dwelling in which God lives by his Spirit.'[651] The concept of the body as a temple is also discussed in his letter to the Corinthians: 'Don't you know that you yourselves are God's temple and that God's Spirit lives in you? If anyone destroys God's temple, God will destroy him; for God's temple is sacred, and you are that temple.'[652]

The New Testament emphasises internalising biblical principles, using self-control as the basis for thinking and behaviour. This attribute is described in a few ways:

- mastery of action[653]
- moderation[654]
- sanctification[655]
- soberness,[656] sobriety,[657] sober-minded[658]

This is why many Christians avoid using alcohol, drugs or addictive substances. Our whole life is affected by whatever we choose to eat and drink. Susannah Wesley wrote to her son John Wesley (founder of Methodism) concerning this: 'Whatever weakens your reason, impairs the tenderness of your conscience, obscures your sense of God, decreases the strength and authority of your mind over your body – that thing is wrong, however innocent it may be in itself.'

full health

Dr John Wilkinson, physician and theologian, highlights four New Testament definitions of health[659] as: *Life, Blessedness, Holiness* and *Maturity*. When Jesus said that he came to give life, he used the Greek word *zoe* which means[660] a life that continues into eternity without horizon or time limit. The word for "blessedness" (Greek: *makarious*) implies blissful happiness extending into eternity. Maturity is another word that extends into eternity and it is a work we engage in now as we improve our health.[661]

All these health definitions speak of a God who loves us and is interested in our personal health and well-being, not in order to control us, but because he wants us to be happy and feel good. We may be unaccustomed to these definitions, but they fit well with the idea of holistic well-being. It's important to recognise that God has gone to extraordinary lengths to make his people happy, healthy and holy and, as we have seen, these are part of the salvation that he offers.

Surely, as our designer and Creator, God knows what is best for us. When we don't observe his requirements or we're careless with our health and become ill, this is not so much about God being angry with us, but that we are just suffering the natural consequences of our lifestyle choices. People often argue that God has done away with these 'outdated' dietary requirements, but there is no biblical evidence for this, and Jesus himself lived within the dietary expectations of the Jewish customs.

What *has* become a burden and encouraged the 'outdated' attitude towards biblical food rules are all the extra conditions and regulations added to the scripture by the Jews in their law commentary, the *Mishnah*.

Mark writes in his gospel about hand washing and ritual cleanliness (Mark 7:19). Jesus' remark in verses 14 and 15 is often taken out of context to show that any restrictions on food intake are done away with. Acts chapter 10 comes in for the same kind of misinterpretation. The context of these texts reveals the error of forcing them to mean something different.

> People who pray, attend church regularly and read their Bibles enjoy better health than those who don't.

Would Jesus Christ, who 'is the same yesterday and today and forever,'[662] want us to be any less healthy today than hundreds of year ago? How does that fit with God's words about himself, 'I, the LORD, do not change'?[663]

health and longevity

Want further evidence that God gives good health when we follow his plan? Take a look at medical literature worldwide.

People who pray, attend church regularly and read their Bibles enjoy better health than those who don't. They live longer and have a lower incidence of almost every disease and condition known to medicine. When they do contract illness, they typically recover more quickly or survive longer.

Part of this health protection comes from living a low-risk life: not drinking alcohol or smoking, not having casual sex, avoiding drugs or other risky behaviours. As a result, records show that Seventh-day Adventist men live up to 8.9 years longer, and Adventist women up to 7.5 years longer than their peers. But even these measures aren't the whole story.

God blesses his people over and above this basic protection. He promises that when we interact in a positive way with our communities, there is a special blessing: 'Then your light will break forth like the dawn, and your healing will quickly appear.'[664] Behavioural biologist Paul Martin states:

'Brain scanning has revealed that when someone trusts and co-operates with another person, certain areas of their brain become more active; and the brain areas that light up are those known to be involved with the emotional experience of feeling good (the so-called reward centres).'[665]

In hundreds of experiments and trials, people who have total commitment to their faith (described as *intrinsic religiosity*) have been shown to be healthier than those who attend a place of worship for purely social reasons (to make friends or gain other benefits) in hundreds of experiments and trials. As health educator Don King says:

'The gospel of total health covers a broader spectrum of activities than scientific experiments on rats, vegetarianism, and meatless cookery, and it certainly does not entertain the idea that healthful living is some starvation marathon, sentencing one to a life of lettuce leaves and cottage cheese. Rather, the gospel of health is the gospel of making mankind whole and ready for the second coming of Jesus Christ.'[666]

Morris Okun and William Stock, from Arizona State University, note, 'The two best predictors of well-being among older persons were health and religiousness. Elderly people are happier and more satisfied with life if religiously committed and active.'[667]

And health advantages are not only for the elderly.

'Belonging to a religious community offers the individual a powerful source of social support through opportunities to *meet regularly,* the *sharing of commitments and beliefs,* and *their expression* in the established rituals and liturgies. . . . People holding religious beliefs and regular church-goers enjoy better health than nonbelievers and non-attenders.'[668]

So what have you got to lose – besides a bit of extra weight, your lethargy and your stress?

re: consider

How would you most like to improve your health?

REFERENCES

623. Daily Guideposts, October 1983. *www.sermonillustrator.org/illustrator/sermon2/ best_health_insurance.htm.* 13 April 2006.
624. See *Chambers twentieth century dictionary.* Littlefield, Adams, 1973.
625. See *Concise Oxford English Dictionary.* Oxford UP, 2002.
626. Genesis 1:27.
627. Genesis 1:29.
628. Genesis 9:3, NIV.
629. Genesis 9:4.
630. Exodus 22:31.
631. Exodus 23:19.
632. Leviticus 3:17; 7:26, 27; 17:10-16; 19:26; Deuteronomy 12:23-25.
633. Leviticus 11; 20:25; Deuteronomy 14:3-21.
634. Leviticus 13; 14; Deuteronomy 24:8.

635. Leviticus 15:2-15; 22:4; Numbers 5:2.
636. Exodus 23:10, 11; Leviticus 25:2-22.
637. Leviticus 10:9, 10.
638. Leviticus 12:2.
639. Leviticus 12:3.
640. Leviticus 15:16-18.
641. Leviticus 15:19-30.
642. Exodus 15:26; 23:25; Deuteronomy 7:15.
643. Numbers 5:2-4.
644. Exodus 20:8-11 and 23:12.
645. Leviticus 19:28.
646. Deuteronomy 23:12, 13.
647. Deuteronomy 28:1-14, Leviticus 26:1-13.
648. Exodus 15:26, NIV.
649. Leviticus 11:44, 45; 19:2; 20:7, 26; Deuteronomy 26:19.
650. Exodus 25:8.
651. Ephesians 2:22, NIV.
652. 1 Corinthians 3:16, 17, NIV.
653. 1 Corinthians 9:25.
654. Philippians 4:5.
655. Acts 20:32.
656. Acts 26:25.
657. 1 Timothy 2:15.
658. Titus 2:6.
659. Wilkinson, John. *Health and Healing*. The Handsel P, 1980, pp. 13-16.
660. John 10:10.
661. Colossians 1:28.
662. Hebrews 13:8, NIV.
663. Malachi 3:6, NIV.
664. Isaiah 58:8, NIV.
665. Martin, Paul. *Making Happy People*. Harper Perennial, 2006, p. 83.
666. King, Donald G. 'Sabbath Policy Brings Blessings to Hospital.' *Adventist Review* (International Edition) 11 (1981): 23.
667. Koenig, Harold G., Michael EM McCullough, and David B. Larson. *Handbook of Religion and Health*. Oxford UP, 2001, pp. 106-109.
668. Totman, Richard. *Mind, Stress and Health*. Souvenir P (E&A) Ltd., 1990, pp. 151, 152.

35. HANDLING MONEY

God, I'm learning that this relationship with you as Creator is meant to pervade my entire existence, and I have a feeling that, as I study your guidelines for handling money, it will all come back to the same underlying theme: your love and protection.

re: tell

Two men were marooned on an island. One man paced back and forth, worried and scared, while the other man sat back and was sunning himself. The first man said to the second man, 'Aren't you afraid we are about to die?'

'No,' said the second man, 'I earn $100,000 a week and tithe faithfully to my church. My pastor will find me.'[669]

re: think

I think I know less in my 50s than I did in my 20s. Back then I knew everything – or I thought I did. I had an answer for every question. But I now realise I know very little, that life isn't black and white.

I had planned to retire at 50. Well, that didn't happen. In fact, I think I'm poorer now than I was in my 20s. After seeing three children through university and two weddings, there isn't much left to call my own. But the years have taught me that happiness isn't found in wealth and material things.

Strange as it may sound, I've found greater happiness in giving away than in receiving. I can't forget the joy I felt when I saw my children play with the toys I brought home. It's the same thrill I get from giving money to someone in need or doing something kind.

'O divine Master, grant that I may not so much seek to be consoled as to console; to be understood as to understand; to be loved as to love. For it is in giving that we receive; it is in pardoning that we are pardoned; and it is in dying that we are born to eternal life.' (St Francis of Assisi.)

'Happiness comes from giving, not receiving.' (Acts 20:35, *Clear Word*.)

God urges us to give of ourselves – our money, our time, our talents and our lives – for the benefit of others. 'What right does God have to tell me how to live?' you ask. Well, he is the owner of the world and our Creator.

creator

'In the beginning God created the heavens and the earth.'[670]

'The heavens are yours, and yours also the earth; you founded the world and all that is in it.'[671]

Not only did God create the world, he also created human beings. We're part of the created world. 'God created man in his own image, in the image of God he created him; male and female he created them.'[672]

Because God is Creator, nothing in the world really belongs to us, not even our own lives. God allows us to use his creation – our lives, the trees, the animals, the oceans, the rivers, the silver, the gold – so we're accountable to him for everything. This makes us his custodians, and we're acting on his behalf.

owner

Because God is the Creator, he owns the world and everything in it. So he owns us humans as well. 'For every animal of the forest is mine, and the cattle on a thousand hills. I know every bird in the mountains, and the creatures of the field are mine. If I were hungry I would not tell you, for the world is mine, and all that is in it.'[673]

This was written in an agricultural age when wealth was measured by the number of animals you owned. We could paraphrase it something like this: *All the oil and gold in the world are mine. The buildings, motor vehicles, stocks and shares are all mine. I have given skills, talents and knowledge to people. Everything that you can think of belongs to me.* If everything in the world belongs to God, then we actually own nothing.

C. S. Lewis's character Screwtape, a senior devil, says, 'Humans are always putting up claims to ownership which sound equally funny in heaven and in hell.'[674] It's almost laughable to think that human beings actually own anything. We might not enjoy the idea of being God's custodians of the world, but we can't change reality.

The word *custodian* means steward. It describes the person in charge of the domestic affairs of a household. In relation to God, it refers to one who has control over God's house or things that belong to God.

What about what we earn? Doesn't that belong to us? No, God claims our earnings as well: 'Remember the LORD your God, for it is he who gives you the ability to produce wealth.'[675]

A child living in his parents' home has the freedom of the house. He calls one room 'his', but it actually belongs to his parents. The parents are the real owners of the room, even though the child has temporary charge of it and is responsible to make the bed and keep it clean. Likewise, we are responsible for the resources we use, but they still belong to God.

our lives

'Life is just for living!' is a popular concept in some circles. Essentially it means that there is no real purpose to life and we don't need to account for how we live. But the Bible says we should live in harmony with God, since he gave us life in the first place. His purpose for our lives becomes our purpose for living. 'Whether you eat or drink or whatever you do, do it all for the glory of God.'[676]

God's act of creating us and then rescuing us through the death of Jesus makes us accountable to him for how we live and the choices we make. We are each called to be accountable to God and to the world he gave us.

'We can make plans and design our life to achieve our personal goals and ambitions. We can invent our own purpose for living. We can even live our life with no particular purpose in mind. We can live from day to day with no intent and no direction. We can live our life being guided by others and guided by the influences of the world around us. However, we are to live our life with God's purpose as our purpose. Sometimes we do not know what God wants from us in specific terms but we always know what God wants from us in general terms. God's purpose for our life is written in his Word. God's purpose for our life should be our purpose and our only purpose. Every thought, word, and action on our part should be a reflection of God's purpose for our life.' (Patrick Kelly, Daily Devotionals, Shepherd's Care ministry.)

our money

The Bible talks about money quite a bit. Maybe that's because our attitude to wealth and possessions tells God more about our trust in him than anything else. Because God is our Creator and owns everything, he also owns our money. And he has a plan for the best way to use what we earn. Since we're living to serve him, it might be good to check with him about that plan.

'Yet true godliness with contentment is itself great wealth. After all, we brought nothing with us when we came into the world, and we can't take anything with us when we leave it. So if we have enough food and clothing, let us be content. But people who long to be rich fall into temptation and are trapped by many foolish and harmful desires that plunge them into ruin and destruction. For the love of money is the root of all kinds of evil. And some people, craving money, have wandered from the true faith and pierced themselves with many sorrows.' 1 Timothy 6:6-10.

Helping other Christians: As Christians, we belong to the family of God and we should use our money to help members of this family, in the same way that we'd assist members of our human family: 'Share with God's people who are in need. Practise hospitality.'[677]

Helping the poor and needy: The way we treat the poor and needy speaks volumes about our attitude towards God. When we show kindness to those in need, we are in effect showing kindness to him. 'Then the righteous will answer him, "Lord, when did we see you hungry and feed you, or thirsty and give you something to drink? When did we see you a stranger and invite you in, or needing clothes and clothe you? When did we see you sick or in prison and go to visit you?" The King will reply, "I tell you the truth, whatever you did for one of the least of these brothers of mine, you did it for me." '[678]

'He who is kind to the poor lends to the LORD, and he will reward him for what he has done.'[679]

Giving to God: An acquaintance of mine and I were chatting recently about money. He looked shocked when I told him that my wife and I gave more than 10% of our income to our church.

'That's a lot of money!' he said. 'Is it some kind of tax that you have to pay to the church?'

'Not really. It's more like a recognition that all my money belongs to God. In fact, all my possessions belong to God, too.'

'But think what you could do with all that money.'

'Yes, I know,' I replied, 'but my wife and I are no worse off as a result of giving a part of our income to the church. We think we're much better off for doing so.' He shook his head and wondered how that could be. But it's true.

In recognition of God as the owner of our money and material possessions, God asks us to return to him one tenth of our increase. The Bible calls this *tithe*. Millions of people around the world return a tithe to God, just like my wife and I.

The Bible talks very plainly about this idea of giving back some money to God. 'Bring the whole tithe into the storehouse,'[680] one prophet said. King Solomon wrote, 'Honour the LORD with your wealth, with the firstfruits of all your crops; then your barns will be filled to overflowing, and your vats will brim over with new wine.'[681]

God isn't dependent on our money. He doesn't need our tithe, but he gives us a chance to share in his work of sharing the gospel with the world. And giving our tithe is an act that tangibly reminds us that everything belongs to God.

In addition to giving a tithe, Christians also donate offerings from the remaining nine-tenths of their income. This was part of the practice of God's ancient people and is a requirement in the Bible itself.

'Will a man rob God? Yet you rob me! But you ask, "How do we rob you?" In tithes and offerings.'[682]

God promises to bless those who give him a tithe and an offering as well. You'd be amazed to see that after we give God our tithes and offerings, the remainder goes much further.

One friend of mine jokes, 'There's just no way that we can make ends meet on my salary. When I add up the bills, there shouldn't be two pennies left. But, somehow, we always manage fine on 80%!' My friend gives a full tithe and an extra offering of 10% from every paycheque. But every month they have enough and often a little extra.

Stephanie, a college student, just glowed as she told me about her decision to pay tithe with the last money she had in hand. However, she also needed a winter jacket, and the cold weather was coming. So, with only a few dollars left after the tithe was paid, she went coat shopping.

'God, you know I need a coat, and I'm trying to be faithful to you,' she prayed. When she got to the store, she saw huge sale signs everywhere. She found a coat for a fraction of the price she'd expected, then found a wool turtleneck and a new pillow – all of which she desperately needed. At the sales counter, the clerk added up her purchases, and they cost the exact amount she had in her purse. So she had paid her tithe and then was able to buy more than she needed for less than she'd planned.

> 'Will a man rob God? Yet you rob me! But you ask, "How do we rob you?" In tithes and offerings.'

Marie, a mother of six, went to church and pulled out her cheque-book. Her tithe should be $300 to give to God. But it was also the last money in her account. If she wrote the cheque, she would have no money to feed her children until the next paycheque two weeks later. She struggled with the thought.

'God, my fuel tank is almost empty. I won't be able to drive back and forth to work. And I'll have no food for my family. This isn't what you want, is it?' Deciding to be faithful anyway, Marie wrote the cheque. Her heart was heavy as she prepared to work the night shift that evening. 'If you have any cash in your pocket, please don't spend it,' she told her husband. 'I need it for petrol, and the account is empty.'

'Oh, didn't I tell you?' he replied. 'A cheque came in the mail today while you were resting. It's $1,000 for us to use for expenses!'

God promises to reward our faithfulness: 'Bring the whole tithe into the storehouse, that there may be food in my house. Test me in this, says the LORD Almighty, and see if I will not throw open the floodgates of heaven and pour out so much blessing that you will not have room enough for it.'[683]

God's blessings for giving faithfully and generously take various forms. It might be a blessing of good health, an increase in income or profit, or your children's clothes not wearing out. God chooses the blessings that he bestows upon us to match our needs and capacity.

As custodians of God's creation, we have a responsibility. God sees us not only as managers of his planet, but as his sons and daughters. His ultimate purpose is to reconcile us with himself and each other, and all he asks in return is that we give him our loyalty and love. When we give ourselves completely to God, he transforms our lives.

Tithe-payers discover that when they give their tithe to God and add an offering, the leftover money tends to last much longer than if they had kept the 100% for their use. Someone said that it seems that whenever we give a spoonful, God gives back a shovelful. But it's a test of our willingness truly to place God first.

re: consider

What would it mean for you to give God back a tithe? What kind ofsacrifice would that be for you?

REFERENCES
669. *www.kluth.org/church/quips&quotes.htm#Biblical%20Generosity%20&%20Tithing.*
670. Genesis 1:1, NIV.
671. Psalm 89:11, NIV.
672. Genesis 1:27, NIV.
673. Psalm 50:10-12, NIV.
674. Lewis, C. S. *The Screwtape Letters*. HarperOne, 2001.
675. Deuteronomy 8:18, NIV.
676. 1 Corinthians 10:31, NIV.
677. Romans 12:13, NIV.
678. Matthew 25:37-40, NIV.
679. Proverbs 19:17, NIV.
680. Malachi 3:10a, NIV.
681. Proverbs 3:9-10, NIV.
682. Malachi 3:8, NIV.
683. Malachi 3:10, NIV.

ABOUT
CHURCH

36. PURPOSE AND MISSION

God, I want to learn more about how to relate to others who share my passion for you. Show me how to be a part of the community you created for all of us, and where I fit in both to serve and learn.

re: tell

There you are, visiting your mum at dinner, when suddenly her left cheek begins to droop. Her words slur and food spills from her mouth, and you realise that she can't move her left arm. You reach for your mobile phone and dial 999. The operator calmly takes your information and sends the paramedics right away.

The emergency crew lift your mum onto a stretcher and place her in the ambulance, monitoring her vital signs and keeping her safe until she reaches the hospital. Upon arrival she's transferred to a room, and a flurry of activity begins.

A radiologist takes X-rays while a nurse hooks her up to monitors. Telemetry specialists monitor heart rhythm, and a medical receptionist starts building a file. Meanwhile, doctors begin to examine and treat her for an acute ischemic infarct of the right middle cerebral artery.

During her ten-day stay in the hospital, speech, physical and occupational therapists begin working with your mother; dieticians ensure she's getting the right nutrients; and a case manager facilitates her transfer to a rehab facility. The road to recovery has been difficult, but a dedicated team has brought all their talents together to help her on her way.

re: think

Relationships are essential. We've established that. This interaction between individuals – couples or families, groups or organisations, even nations – drives the world! Society is obsessed with the lives of celebrities, whether you read Jane Austen's *Pride and Prejudice* or watch re-runs of *Friends*.

Life is about relationships, for better or for worse; it's deeply ingrained in humanity. We seek positive relationships to make our lives meaningful and fulfilled.

In addition, our bodies were made for relationships; we can communicate – both verbally and physically. Relationship is about being connected, and communication is the way we get there. Naturally, we each manage relationships in different ways and with varying degrees of success. For lots of people, the difficulty of building constructive relationships is overwhelming.

Have you ever wished for a proven relationship model to assist, guide and support you? I have, and I'd like to show you what I've found.

biblical model

In the biblical creation story, God acknowledged that 'It is not good for the man to be alone.'[684] God showed concern over the human beings he created, from man's creation in his image[685] to the Sabbath rest[686] to his desire to communicate with us.[687] The Bible establishes three dimensions of human relationships:

- me > God (relationship by faith)
- me > my neighbour (relationship by mutual trust or love)
- me > my mind (relationship by sound self-dignity)

Jesus summarised these three dimensions as the essence of faith and life: 'You shall love the Lord your God with all your heart, and with all your soul, and with all your mind . . . and . . . love your neighbour as yourself.'[688]

Based on this, Paul said that 'love is the fulfilment of the law'[689] and that 'what is important is faith expressing itself in love'.[690]

God's love is described in the famous love chapter.[691] Take a few minutes to read it sometime. It's a beautiful snapshot of what real love looks like.

'Love is patient and kind. Love is not jealous or boastful or proud or rude. It does not demand its own way. It is not irritable, and it keeps no record of being wronged. It does not rejoice about injustice but rejoices whenever the truth wins out. Love never gives up, never loses faith, is always hopeful, and endures through every circumstance. Prophecy and speaking in unknown languages and special knowledge will become useless. But love will last forever!'[692]

The Bible teaches that the way God demonstrated his love to us forms the model for making our relationships fruitful and good.

church as a model

In defining the nature and purpose of the church, Jesus said: 'By this everyone will know that you are my disciples, if you have love for one another.'[693]

Church isn't only about internal relationships between the members and external relationships with the outside world. It's also about the relationship between us and God. While God has a special relationship with his followers, he wants everyone to be part of his church. The church should be open to all people. It can't be an exclusive club for members only. It represents God's open arms to the world.[694]

My faith in God can't grow without being integrated in relationships with other people of faith who have decided to take a stand for God. In my personal experience, whenever I lost my connection with church fellowship, my relationship with God also weakened. Since we were created for relationships, even our faith in him needs the companionship of others to help it grow. So what is the church's purpose?

belong – believe – behave

From our individual points of view, the church experience is three things: believing, behaving and belonging.[695] You *belong* to a certain community, you *believe* certain things and you *behave* according to certain principles.

In the church you *belong* to God's people, meaning that you belong to him. And you gradually feel at home in this community of believers, worshipping God together with them. Belonging to God's people always implies belonging to God, because the unity and essence of the church is our common submission to the Spirit of God in worship.

As a member of the church, you choose to *believe* in God. You believe that he loves you and accepts you as you are, offering forgiveness so you can live a new life in his Spirit. You believe that God wants to change you and make you a better, stronger person who is more like him. You also believe in the Bible, seeking to follow its instruction in every part of life.

> 'We were all baptised into one body – Jews or Greeks, slaves or free – and we were all made to drink of one Spirit.'

Your new life also includes learning to *behave* according to God's will, knowing that when you fail, God continues to offer forgiveness whenever there is genuine repentance. It also means that you actively participate in the mission and service of the church.

These three aspects are of equal importance. One is not more important than the others,[696] and you won't feel truly part of your church if one of them is missing.

community belonging to God

As the Christian church develops among God's chosen people, God is present through the Spirit of Jesus Christ and a renewed emphasis on community. 'For where two or three come together in my name, there am I with them.'[697]

It's the work of the Holy Spirit that makes the church a warm spiritual community – collectively and in the heart of each believer. When we fellowship in the church, we share the gifts and the fruit of the Spirit with each other. This binds us together in an intimate belonging to God, a process of coming closer to him, even being unified with him.[698]

We're encouraged to get close to God and to build each other up towards love and good deeds in our worship and community meetings.

'And so, dear brothers and sisters, we can boldly enter heaven's Most Holy Place because of the blood of Jesus. By his death, Jesus opened a new and life-giving way through the curtain into the Most Holy Place. And since we have a great High Priest who rules over God's house, let us go right into the presence of God with sincere hearts fully trusting him. For our guilty consciences have been sprinkled with Christ's blood to make us clean, and our bodies have been washed with pure water. Let us hold tightly without wavering to the hope we affirm, for God can be trusted to keep his promise. Let us think of ways to motivate one another to acts of love and good works. And let us not neglect our meeting together, as some people do, but encourage one another, especially now that the day of his return is drawing near.'[699]

We can't just define the church community in the same way that we define other human communities – families, tribes or social groups. In the church, the sense of community is spiritual; it comes from God and unites us in him. This unity is especially evident when the church unites in worship.

Church community is built around worship. And worship is based on experiencing God's love in Jesus Christ, through the Holy Spirit. So it doesn't really matter who sits next to me in the church – whatever their status, character, personality, race, ethnicity or nationality – we're all united by the Spirit in worshipping God. The Bible says it this way:

'In Christ Jesus you are all children of God through faith. As many of you as were baptised into Christ have clothed yourselves with Christ. There is no longer Jew or Greek, there is no longer slave or free, there is no longer male and female; for all of you are one in Christ Jesus.'[700]

The Spirit directs us collectively and individually to the gospel, while we keep our diverse gifts, backgrounds, thoughts and interests. This diversity transforms into resources and values in the church, if we allow unity of the Spirit to prevail.

body of Christ

Just as your fingers, toes, ears and nose all have their own specific job to do, so the church is like a body, all the people working together for the common cause – to glorify God. Sometimes the Bible calls the church the 'body of Christ'.

> 'For just as the body is one and has many members, and all the members of the body, though many, are one body, so it is with Christ. For in the one Spirit we were all baptised into one body – Jews or Greeks, slaves or free – and we were all made to drink of one Spirit.'[701]

Paul went on to say that 'there should be no division in the body, but that its parts should have equal concern for each other. If one part suffers, every part suffers with it; if one part is honoured, every part rejoices with it.'[702]

I remember one occasion when Christians from several different countries were making their way to an international congress. Some arrived a few days ahead of their luggage, thanks to the airline. Because they were poor, they had no insurance to cover their loss, and they didn't have enough to buy fresh clothes or underwear for the duration of the meetings. So a few fellow believers donated enough money to enable the travellers to purchase the necessities.

This is community in the body of Christ. And it has been happening in the church from the beginning: 'All who believed were together and had all things in common; they would sell their possessions and goods and distribute the proceeds to all, as any had need.'[703] It's no surprise that the first attempts at organised social relief in early nineteenth-century England came from Christians or that the push to abolish slavery started with Christians.

This body of Christ symbolises the unity and fellowship of the church. When we value every member, we witness about Jesus Christ and are empowered by the Holy Spirit. The church community becomes a school for relating to people. As Christians, we need that training, because we have a mission to connect with others and share Jesus.

community with a mission

The church exists to carry out God's mission in the world. Jesus told us to go out and make disciples and bring healing to people. This is called the 'Great Commission'.[704]

Many passages in the Bible speak of this. Read Ephesians 2:11-22. This is telling us: *The basic purpose of the church and its mission is to bring church members and all other people closer to God! It is to live, serve and grow. It is not static, passive, or dead, but a living organism – one that multiplies itself.* Our unity and fellowship with each other is intimately dependent on our closeness to God: 'For through [Christ] we both have access to the Father by one Spirit. . . . And in him you too are being built together to become a dwelling in which God lives by his Spirit.'[705]

Still have questions? Keep studying and talking to fellow believers. And maybe try participating in the church or even joining it. You might find yourself growing in new ways, like:

- Growth in your inner spiritual life, which is demonstrated by the fruit of the Spirit, to show others the love of God and the grace of Christ in your life;
- Growth in your experience of unity and maturity in Christ, together with other believers in your church community;
- Growth in discovering your spiritual gifts and being willing to use them to serve God and other people;
- Growth in understanding God's mission to the world, the needs of people everywhere, and your own willingness to share the gospel with other people.

So the question for you and me? Do we really wish to come closer to God and bring others along to spend time with him?

re: consider

Can you think of ways that you could help and serve others around you? How could you share in someone else's joy or sadness?

REFERENCES
684. Genesis 2:18.
685. Genesis 1:26.
686. Genesis 2:2-3.
687. Genesis 3:9.
688. Matthew 22:37-39, NRSV.
689. Romans 13:8-10, NIV; cf. Galatians 5:14.
690. Galatians 5:6.
691. 1 Corinthians 13.
692. 1 Corinthians 13:4-8.
693. John 13:35, NRSV.
694. Ephesians 2:16-19.
695. Rice, Richard. 'Believing, Behaving, Belonging: Finding New Love for the Church.' Association of Adventist Forums 2002. 13.
696. NOTE: I do not fully share Rice's view that 'belonging is the most important of them all' (p. 15). According to scripture we don't 'belong' unless we have faith in Christ ('believe') that expresses itself through love ('behave') (cf. Galatians 5:6).
697. Matthew 18:20, NIV.
698. See B. Wiklander, 'The People of God: Foundations of a Biblical Ecclesiology', paper read at the Trans-European Division's Pastors' Council in Budapest, August, 1995.
699. Hebrews 10:19-25.
700. Galatians 3:26-28, NRSV.
701. 1 Corinthians 12:12-13, NRSV.
702. 1 Corinthians 12:25-26, NIV.
703. Acts 2:44-45, NRSV.
704. Matthew 28:18-20; Mark 16:15-18; Luke 24:45-49; John 14-17.
705. Ephesians 2:18, 22, NIV.

37. THREE SPECIAL MESSAGES

God, the apostle John loved you deeply when he travelled with you for three years, and it changed the course of his life. When he was an old man, exiled and alone, you came to comfort him and gave him a message for your people through all time. Help me to understand that message, because I desire to be yours in this present time. Send your Spirit to enlighten me and to plant these things deep in my heart.

re: tell

Charles Taylor ruled the African nation of Liberia with despotic fervour. As the dictator clashed with rival warlords, the country warped into civil war. Lives shattered as thugs fought for control; even children were forced to fight. The chaos looked as if it would go on forever, until a group of ordinary women banded together to demand their country, their lives, their families and their children back.

Leymah Gbowee, a Christian, founded Liberian Mass Action for Peace, stirring the women in her church to action. Asatu Bah Kenneth, a Muslim policewoman, soon joined her, and women from both faith communities staged peaceful demonstrations to demand an end to the violence and a new start for Liberia.

When Taylor, fearing arrest for war crimes, refused to attend peace talks, the women staged a mass sit-in at the conference site in Ghana. Their courageous resilience ended the war and toppled a dictatorship, and in 2006 Ellen Johnson-Sirleaf became the first female president of Liberia – and in all of Africa.

re: think

Have you ever seen an angel flying? I don't mean those winged figures dangling from Christmas trees or the chubby plaster sculptures embellishing baroque churches. And I'm not talking about creatures from old fairy tales and mythology. I'm talking about *real* angels, the ones you can actually see with your own eyes.

No? You haven't? Neither have I. Although I did see a photograph recently that was supposed to be an angel – or what the photographer thought was one. (To be honest, I couldn't recognise anything on the picture.)

However, there are millions of people today who believe in angels, and I'm one of them. Some people claim to have seen or talked to them. I don't. Angels are the topic of countless books and seminars which attempt to tell us who angels are, what they do and how we can contact them. In spite of modern science, naturalistic philosophy and rationalistic thinking, belief in angels is popular in our postmodern world.

Even the Bible speaks of angels, nearly 400 times. It says that angels are spirit beings created by God to protect, warn and comfort us and to convey God's will.[706] The Greek word *angelos* means 'messenger', which fittingly describes their divine mission. So, while angels are mysterious and intriguing, it's really the messages they bring that are most important.

an attack on freedom

In contrast to the guardian angels of my childhood faith, the final book of the Bible tells a rousing story about three angels who proclaim a unique message to the inhabitants of the world.[707]

Remember that prophecy often uses fantastical images and dramatic descriptions to make a point. The characters in a prophetic story may be larger than life, but everything symbolically represents something else.

The appearance of these angels marks the climax of this apocalyptic drama, vividly describing a fierce attack led by Lucifer himself against God and his people. Through political oppression, military force, religious deception and miraculous signs, they bring almost the entire world under their control. Only the faithful people of God resist and, because they refuse to submit, 'the remnant' as they are called, face rejection, persecution and death.[708]

For people who live in relative peace and prosperity, democracy and freedom, these prophecies may seem like Hollywood disaster movies – bouts of angst within the comfort zone of our TV or cinema. However, if you've experienced political oppression, social injustice, religious persecution, physical abuse or other infringement of your basic human rights, the Apocalypse might sound more realistic.

What hope does the Bible offer? How will God protect his people? And how should we react when totalitarian powers threaten us? The prophet John's answer is intriguing: God and his people fight evil, not by schemes or coercion, but by the power of Scripture! They simply utter a warning and proclaim the ultimate victory of God and his people.[709]

urgent message

This is where the three angels are an important part of the story. As divine messengers, they announce to the world how God himself sees the situation and how he's going to respond. Their message is addressed 'to those who live on the earth – to every nation, tribe, language and people'.[710] A global threat calls for a global answer. Everyone on this planet – including you and me – has to make a life-or-death decision. That's why the angels are flying in mid-air, calling out: 'Fear God and give him glory, because the hour of his judgement has come. Worship him who made the heavens, the earth, the sea and the springs of water.'[711]

Our society worships its own intellectual, cultural, scientific and technological achievements. We're more comfortable trusting our own abilities and potential and obeying human authorities. But God is making an urgent call for us to worship him as Creator and Lord. This way we don't put creation above the Creator, don't adore ourselves rather than God, don't become slaves to each other instead of serving God out of love. It's really a call to freedom, an invitation to be liberated from all self-styled lords and false gods.

The serious relevance of the angels' announcement is underlined by a reference to the divine judgement about to take place – if it hasn't already begun.

'Fear God and give him glory, because the hour of his judgement has come,' the first angel shouts. This judgement is then described in graphic language by the other two. The second angel announces the moral fall and final destruction of mystical Babylon, that great city that has oppressed God's people and infatuated the whole world with 'the maddening wine of her adulteries',[712] luring them into worshipping and serving Satan rather than God.

Next, the third angel warns that those who worship these beastly powers 'will drink of the wine of God's fury, which has been poured full strength into the cup of his wrath'.[713] In the strongest language possible, the Bible tells the consequences of ignoring these angels. Refusal to honour God leads to a loss of liberty and justice and, ultimately, to destruction and death. Nothing in all eternity can undo this fate.[714]

eternal gospel

Hardly any other passage in the Bible has such stern warnings in such strong language. These verses are a striking prelude to a series of judgement visions, which describe the downfall of rebellious and destructive forces (the old symbolic Babylon) and the establishment of God's eternal kingdom (the New Jerusalem) on this earth.

> Our society worships its own intellectual, cultural, scientific and technological achievements.

These angels proclaim a threefold judgement message, which captures the entire book of Revelation in a nutshell. But how can we reconcile such a judgement with a God of love and a gospel of grace?

This question is actually answered in the vision of the three angels itself. The most striking part of this passage[715] is its opening sentence, where the judgement is introduced as an 'eternal gospel'.[716] But how can an announcement of judgement be 'good news'? Wouldn't a loving God forgive? Or offer a new opportunity instead of 'fire and brimstone'? So how can this judgement message be an 'eternal gospel'?

To answer this crucial question, we need to remember that the Greek term *euangelion* was used at the time to proclaim victories by the Roman army. John uses this same term to denote a very different message of victory – the final triumph of Jesus Christ over sin, evil and death. This victory will ultimately be won when Jesus comes back to redeem his followers.[717]

That means that Christians can live in hope, waiting for the fulfilled promise of 'a new heaven and a new earth, where righteousness dwells'.[718]

While the announcement of this judgement is bad news for those connected with oppression and injustice, it is good news for everyone who wants to be free from those evil powers. In an earlier vision in Revelation, the blood of innocent Christian martyrs cries out for justice and redemption.[719] According to Paul, all of creation is eager for freedom from suffering and pain, decay and death.[720] For all of us, this final judgement can be a day deliverance.

call for faithfulness

It isn't really judgement but deliverance which is at the heart of this message to the world. The central vision of the book of Revelation, with its flying angels and their crucial messages, is ultimately about a call for faithfulness and endurance – not a cry for punishment or revenge. It focuses on the suffering people of God and their encouragement. 'This calls for patient endurance on the part of the saints who obey God's commandments and remain faithful to Jesus.'[721]

How do you react to challenge and crisis? Are you the one who won't give up, who resists hurting whoever hurt you? Do you remain faithful to God at all costs? History has had many heroes of faith, who gave up their life of freedom rather than change their principles. These men and women are worthy examples.

It's easy to become discouraged and fearful in the face of difficulties. We feel weak and unable to resist the pressure to act against our conscience. That's how the forces of evil win. But this prophecy tells us it won't be forever!

Some people choose to trust God, 'who is able to keep you from falling and to present you before his glorious presence without fault and with great joy'.[722] These true saints – the Bible also calls them 'the remnant'[723] – remain faithful to Jesus by declining to serve or worship other gods. Their love and loyalty strengthen their determination to live as God has asked (obeying his commandments), no matter what others expect.

Instead of being overwhelmed by evil, they overcome evil with good.[724] Jesus gives us a great promise: 'To those who are victorious and do my will to the end, I will give authority over the nations.' '[They] will inherit all this, and I will be their God and they will be my children.'[725] This means that wielding evil power now will leave you weak in the end, but the apparent losers will eventually turn out to be the real winners!

re: consider

When this particular prophecy asks for faithfulness to God's promises, how does it make you feel? How will that feeling affect your life and choices?

REFERENCES

706. Psalms 91:11; Matthew 18:10; Acts 12:15; Hebrews 1:14.
707. Read Revelation 14.
708. Revelation 12-13.
709. Revelation 14:6-12.
710. Ibid 14:6 NIV.
711. Ibid verse 7, NIV.
712. Ibid verse 8, NIV.

713. Ibid verse 10, NIV.
714. Ibid verse 11.
715. Revelation 14:6-12.
716. Ibid 14:6, NIV.
717. Revelation 14:14-20; 19:11-21.
718. 2 Peter 3:13, TNIV.
719. Revelation 6:9-11.
720. Romans 8:18-23.
721. Revelation 14:12, NIV.
722. Jude 24, NIV.
723. Revelation 12:17, KJV.
724. Romans 12:21.
725. Revelation 2:26 and 21:7, TNIV.

38. COVENANT CELEBRATION

God, I want to follow you every step of the journey through this life. Please continue to show me the ways in which I can do this, so that I can show the world my commitment to you.

re: tell

A party of Methodist ministers was attending an annual conference at a private countryside resort. Several of them set off to explore the area and presently they came upon an old bridge that crossed a quiet pond.

Unfortunately, they didn't notice a sign declaring the bridge to be unsafe. As they crossed it, the caretaker came running after them. 'Hey! You there! Get off that bridge!' he protested.

'It's all right,' declared one of the ministers, 'we're in this resort with permission. We're Methodists from the Conference.'

'I'm not worried about *that*,' replied the caretaker. 'But if you don't get off that bridge, you'll all be *Baptists*!'[726]

re: think

Personal experience has never been more relevant than it is in today's society.

Past generations have focused on set times, specific places and local jobs. They were defined by huge institutions and authoritarian governance, and they gave unremitting commitment and loyalty. For them it was enough to clock in and out, in a specified location, in a specialised job at a factory or corporation. Then they could boast about their reward – a gold watch for unstinting lifetime service to the company.

However, in that working environment, their personal experience, their achievement of ambitions and dreams was deferred to the next generation. And the next. . . .

We could call the experience of the past generation *quantitative*, where focus was on keeping time, setting up monumental buildings and the sanctity of roles. In that context, faith was abstract, an intellectual compulsion of belief in God.

Today, the kind of experience we yearn for could be called *qualitative*, because time and workplaces and roles are more fluid. In other words, we now tend to place emphasis on *how* time is experienced rather than *what specific* time is experienced. We focus on the personal use of space rather than the specific location of space, and on the function of roles rather than who has the role. This fluidity, flexibility and interchangeability pose challenges for Christians in today's postmodern world.

For one, the postmoderns wish to see evidence of our faith *now*. It isn't enough just to go through a series of Bible studies on faith. It isn't enough to quote the logic of rational, albeit biblical truth. Postmoderns want, and some might argue that they have the right, to see what our personal faith is made of and where it has got us *today* – how our living relationship with God gears us to deal with reality. No doubt, this power is most visible in the transformed life of the Christian witness, the individual.

Postmoderns also wish to see a God who is not confined to time, space or a job description. This God can't be copyrighted as though only one organisation gets all the access rights or has all the answers. God must be presented as one who is larger than human institutions. He is the spiritual, transcendent God. Yet he is personal. He can be accessed and experienced by one and all at any time and in any place.

Perhaps most challenging, the postmodern wants to see a God that is representative and yet inclusive of all kinds of peoples – male, female; black, white; heterosexual, homosexual; religious, non-religious; rich, poor; able-bodied, disabled; educated, uneducated. He is the sinner's God, our neighbour's God. This every-human's God makes his many followers into one people, attributing spiritual gifts not exclusively to an elite class, but indiscriminately to all.

It is in this social context – the context of a boundless (whether in time or space), spiritual (as opposed to religious), multi-people (not just a peculiar people) God – that this chapter on the teaching of baptism must be presented to today's postmoderns. It may seem incongruous at first glance, especially if commitment is viewed doctrinally through the windows of loyalty, authority and public witness – values that were upheld by a seemingly bygone era.

So before we look at two very important and specific doctrines of baptism and communion in this chapter and the next, it might be helpful to add a comment on loyalty, authority and public witness.

In the case of loyalty, baptism is a biblical teaching of lasting commitment to God forever. Postmoderns tend to speak of loyalty only in terms of functionality: if it works, then it may last. This can have a veneer of expediency when postmoderns look to God: 'If my affiliation to God is convenient and practical, then it will last; if not, then I will move on.'

With regards to authority, baptism is a ceremony of authoritative approval and recognition by the church. Postmodern commitment, on the other hand, stands out for its absence of ceremony and authoritative seal – when people are in a committed relationship, for instance, they simply cohabit. Further, the ceremony of baptism is a public witness. Postmodern commitment, in contrast, is an entirely personal and private affair. And so there is quite a divergence between the typical postmodern world-view and the biblical teaching of baptism.

In the past century, when values of loyalty, tradition and ritual were extolled, baptism and Holy Communion as practised by the church were seamlessly explained and biblically referenced, as, indeed, they had been for hundreds of years. But now it's different. Loyalty, tradition and ritual are seen as passé. So we need another framework to explain these timeless biblical teachings. One framework that might answer the postmodern's challenge about baptism and Holy Communion is the concept of *symbol*.

A symbol is something that represents something else. The power of a symbol is that it not only embodies a particular meaning, but it is also dynamic in its representation. It can respond to different cultures in different ways, showing different ways to see the same thing, the same truth. That's why symbols last, because they are adaptable to different explanations, even while remaining the same – yesterday, today and tomorrow.

For this reason, symbols can appeal equally to postmoderns as to those from past generations, because they speak to the postmoderns in their own context. Thereby, the meaning of the symbol is not only embraced but also re-evaluated and adapted in light of our own context, our personal circumstances.

baptism

'Baptism is a symbol of our union with Christ, the forgiveness of our sins, and our reception of the Holy Spirit.'[727] It is done in the name and under the authority of the Trinity: the Father, the Son and the Holy Spirit.[728] The very word *baptism* means *immersion in water*, and this act is a very powerful symbol.[729] Let's look at four personal experiences that the symbol of baptism generates in scripture.

NEW beginning

Baptism marks a new beginning of a new commitment to God. Expressing a stand the postmodern is making deliberately to commit allegiance to God, it is a natural step in response to the work of God on the heart. The new believer is saying to God, 'We've had a personal, intimate relationship for a while now. It's time for me to tell everyone how much I care about you. I am not ashamed of you. I'm willing to go public!'

The emphasis of baptism here isn't on finishing a lifetime relationship; it's on the beginning of a committed relationship. It's similar to the emphasis of a wedding, which marks the beginning of a meaningful journey into marriage. Baptism, as a new beginning, does not place undue focus and pressure on how the future partnership with God might pan out, but instead marks a fresh start with God.

Nicodemus was a powerful Jewish ruler who came to Jesus by night to ask questions about spiritual life and renewal.[730] When Jesus said, 'unless you are born again . . . by water and spirit . . . you cannot truly experience God's reign,'[731] he was essentially saying, 'We've had a relationship for a while, Nicodemus; it's time to be honest; time to take a stand. It's the next logical step.'

When Jesus himself was baptised, it was a personal and intimate affair. He was baptised by his cousin, John the Baptist, in front of fellow believers. He heard the voice of God and saw a representation of God.[732] The symbol of his baptism was pragmatic, with existential relevance there and then. God was marking his presence with Jesus.

Likewise, at every baptism since, God is present through the symbol in a pragmatic, personal, yet spiritual way. This is reinforced through the first person of the Trinity stated at baptism, 'in the name of the *Father . . .*' Thus, a new allegiance is signified.

spiritual reNEWal

Baptism is also a symbol of spiritual renewal, spiritual healing. People today are often very open to experience in the spiritual realm. We want to fill this gap in our lives. Romans 6:1-4 speaks of baptism as a death, burial and resurrection of the new believer. We can't downplay the importance of this. Paul doesn't speak of it as a once-for-all event, as if we become sinless and flawless in a single moment. Yes, baptism is an event, symbolising spiritual death-burial-resurrection. But it also serves as the beginning of a process, an ongoing life-change, the onset of a spiritual journey at a new and heightened level.

Here we focus on our personal experience, just as with other meanings of the symbol. The new believer mystically experiences God through the symbol. We experience the immense meaning of dying, being buried, being resurrected to a newness of living. God impresses upon our spirit a soul-cleansing watershed. Thus, we rise out of the water with new expectations.

It's a mystical experience where our hearts open to God's supernatural presence, and this allows for and anticipates new possibilities. It celebrates our movement from slavery to sin into freedom in goodness.

The emphasis of baptism here isn't on finishing a lifetime relationship; it's on the beginning of a committed relationship.

Baptism is a deep, life-changing event. It marks the birth of a new heart receptive to a new outlook, new values, tastes and desires, and new possibilities. While the Holy Spirit has already started this process in the individual, baptism signifies it with evocative power.

NEW belonging

Baptism symbolises a new belonging to a new family. It's about joining a NEW community, which the Bible calls the body of Christ, the church.[733] The witness of the local community lends intimacy and shared joy to the baptismal experience. It's encouraging to know that your entire Christian family joins in your spiritual walk. It means, 'You are not alone. You are being celebrated. We affirm you.'

Note that this family, as a body, is organic. It's not like a secular corporation. Then it would be obsessed with tradition, hierarchy, uniformity and self-preservation. Rather, it is a spiritual powerhouse that is dynamic, flexible, people-yet-other-centred and growing. It is a living organism.

Here the Seventh-day Adventist Church gets very interesting. It isn't just an institution. Rather, it is at best a *living organism* and at the very least a *movement*, an advent movement.

Adventists, although human and imperfect, are always headed forwards and looking towards the second coming of Jesus Christ. That is, we are always going somewhere – moving, changing, adapting, accepting, co-opting, multiplying. When you are baptised, this is the body that you are joining through baptism. And when you submit your life to Jesus, it is the unity and harmony of this dynamic body that you're uplifting.[734] This is why we are baptised in the name of the Son, who is the head of the body.[735]

NEW gifts

Baptism is also a symbol of anointing. When we are baptised in the name of the Father, the Son and the *Holy Spirit*,[736] a new authoritative power is released to help us serve people.[737] Hence, we are also baptised 'in the name of the *Holy Spirit.*'

This is part of being anointed; the Holy Spirit gives unction (divine or sanctifying grace). It states that we are not only wanted, but also needed and trusted by God. We're not left on our own.[738] The challenge is to enable new believers to see this as part of the baptismal heritage, especially at a time when they are excited and enthusiastic about the transforming power of God.

It's an empowering experience to see how God can give us supernatural, spiritual gifts for the purpose of service.[739] At baptism the church body recognises the new gifts that it can support and from which it can benefit. Then the newly empowered gifted one can flourish in ministry as he or she co-operates with other ministries, and through loving relationships helps to grow the church physically, spiritually and emotionally.

At baptism, your sphere of service isn't only the family of God but also the community, the place of your witness. This continuum between the marketplace and the worship place helps to keep you relevant, not only to your new church family, but also to friends and society.

In summary, baptism marks a new beginning with a personal, dauntless and boundless God. It's a spiritual renewal of life, even with all its complexities and contradictions. It's a new sense of belonging to a diverse and varied community and a new re-sourcing of spiritual power manifested through spiritual gifts and communication.

Like a cascade, the baptismal symbol can unleash a fresh and adventurous journey with God. Because symbols are so adaptable, there are many creative and meaningful ways to make baptism fulfil its vari-

ous meanings while still speaking to those of us who yearn for a qualitative, inclusive experience with God.

re: consider

What do you think about joining a faith community through baptism?
How would it affect you to know that everyone is rooting for you and
supporting you?

REFERENCES
726. *http://elbourne.org/sermons/index.mv?illustration+902.*
727. *www.adventist.org/beliefs/fundamental/index.html.*
728. Matthew 28:19, 20.
729. The words 'baptise' and 'baptism' come from the Greek root *baptizo*, 'to immerse'. A
related root is *bapto*, 'to dip in or under'. Not only does the word used support the
idea of baptism by immersion, the details of baptismal stories in the NT clearly indicate immersion. For example, Matthew points out that 'when Jesus was baptised, he
went up immediately from the water' (Matthew 3:16), and John baptised at Aenon
near Salim, 'because there was much water there' (John 3:23). In Acts 8:38-39, both
Philip and the eunuch went down into the water and came up from it.
See: Kiesler, Herbert. *Handbook of Seventh-day Adventist Theology.* Ed. Raoul Dederen. Vol. 12. Review and Herald Pub., 2000, p. 583.
730. Read John 3.
731. John 3:3-8, author's paraphrase.
732. Matthew 3:16, 17.
733. 1 Corinthians 12:12, 13.
734. Ephesians 4:2-6.
735. Ephesians 4:15.
736. Matthew 28:19.
737. Matthew 3:16; Acts 19.
738. Matthew 28:20.
739. See 1 Corinthians 12:27-30 for a list.

39. RITUALS OF SPIRITUALITY

God, as I learn how to integrate you into the deepest parts of me, I am amazed at the intimacy you desire us to share. Help me to embrace this intimacy as I discover more about the spiritual ritual of Holy Communion.

re: tell

After nearly two weeks in a desert beach town in Chile, three dozen firm friends, citizens of four countries and numerous states, sat in the candle-light around the church they'd just built. Sweat, tears, sand fights, cold nights, laughter, scraped knuckles . . . barking dogs, sore backs, spontane-ous songs, long lines at the shower . . . all added up to this sacred moment.

Cointe leaned back and pondered how a few pieces of bread, a few cups of Chilean grape juice and song after song knit them together and spoke of intangible bonds that would linger long after the candles burned out.

re: think

The ritual of Holy Communion, also called the Eucharist or the Lord's Supper, is another example of the power of symbols. It's a spiritual practice of renewing our covenant relationship with God, celebrating the love-sacrifice Jesus gave us when he died on the Roman cross. This symbol penetrates and transcends all culture, language and ages.

Within God's community, Holy Communion serves as a binding agent across all kinds of boundaries – gender, sexuality, age, ethnicity, spirituality, disability, class and education on one dimension, and time and distance on another – through the sheer force of Christians washing each other's feet and sharing the same bread and wine. These acts are symbols of contrition, humility and renewal of faith.

Jesus himself instituted Holy Communion when he said, 'Do this in remembrance of me.'[740] This story is told in all four gospels – the books of Matthew, Mark, Luke and John. From the earliest accounts, Christians were admonished to do this regularly.[741]

Historically, Holy Communion is similar to the Jewish Passover. Cited variously as originating between the nineteenth and thirteenth centuries BC, this is an annual anniversary that still commemorates the great deliverance (Exodus) of the people of Israel (then called Hebrews) from Egyptian bondage.[742] In fact, it was at his last Passover meal that Jesus instituted the Holy Communion as a spiritual ritual to symbolise that ever after he would *pass-over* (forgive) and *hover-over* (guide and protect) – words etymologically derived from Passover – whenever Christian believers practised this new communion. In essence, that night Jesus replaced the Passover meal with the Last Supper.

The Passover	The Last Supper
God remembered his covenant	a new covenant is enacted
slavery in Egypt	slavery to sin
deliverance from Egypt	forgiveness of sins (Matthew 26:28)
blood of Passover lamb	blood of Christ (our Passover: 1 Corinthians 5:7; lamb of God: John 1:29, 35)
call for annual celebration	call for continual celebration

It is no wonder that at the moment of this new ritual Jesus said, 'Do not let your hearts be troubled. Trust in God; trust also in me. . . . I will come back and take you to be with me that you also may be where I am.'[743] Here Jesus connects his promise of returning for his community with the symbol of the Holy Communion.

So when Christians celebrate Holy Communion, we have one eye on the way of the cross (humility and sacrifice) and the other eye on the way home to heaven (exaltation and reunion) through expecting Christ's return in the future.[744] It is through this periodic celebration that the bond of family ties between believers is reinforced and strengthened.

This religious ritual of Holy Communion is not just a historical relic of a bygone era that ought to be replaced. It has relevance even to our iPod-Facebook-YouTube-MTV generation. For instance, Holy Communion for believers traditionally represents a recommitment to their baptismal vows. It also reminds us that everyone is equal before God, irrespective of gender, sexuality, age, ethnicity, spirituality, disability, class or education; and it is in this context that we can pursue the symbolic meanings of Holy Communion.

prelude: foot washing

Washing someone else's feet may sound a bit medieval, but this is actually a rich and beautiful symbol that comes directly from scripture.

To re-commit or re-surrender your life to God in the communion service requires an approach that is humble, and the service of *foot washing* is an appropriate prelude to the service of eating the bread and drinking the wine. It humbles our hearts.

It takes a sincere humbling of heart to kneel before someone and wash his or her feet, especially if things are not entirely right between you. It is a tangible, physical way of saying sorry; it's a means of reconciliation! So when the entire body of Christ engages in foot washing, a strong bond is forged between all individuals, and unity reigns supreme preparatory to the communion table.

In this open space there is no gender, sexuality, age, ethnicity, spirituality, disability, class or education boundaries.

It is important to understand the specific symbolic meaning of foot washing as found in John 13. This ritual began when Jesus first washed the disciples' feet in the upper room. Peter, after realising the cleansing significance of this ritual, actually requested to have his whole body washed by Jesus.[745] But Jesus didn't want it to be yet another typical cleansing rite to separate his disciples from everyone else. He wanted to maintain the imagery of foot washing as a lesson of humility.

Today, globally, foot washing still has an association with humility. Before believers participate in foot washing, it is important that they initiate forgiveness and reconciliation with anyone with whom there is a disagreement. Many believers will seek out other people to ask for forgiveness, or to offer it, before the ceremony of Holy Communion takes place. We want our hearts to be clean and pure before God, without anger or resentment in the air.

That's why foot washing is still a fitting prelude to Communion – just like humility is a prelude to unity. It cannot be an end in itself, but it guards against entering the communion service in an 'unworthy manner' with pride and self-centred arrogance against God or others in our hearts.[746]

unleashing a people

The communion table, around which humbled believers sit and from which we share, is full of symbolic meaning. The principal items (called *emblems*) are the bread and wine. Jesus referred to the bread as a representation of his own incarnated and now sacrificed body, and to the wine as his spilled blood – thus invoking the memories of Exodus 24:8 where the blood of a sacrificed animal was sprinkled over the people of Israel for their sins. Now Jesus' blood globally atones for the sinners' sins.[747]

The communion service reminds us of Jesus' sacrificial death as our atonement for sin. Thus, it is a sort of re-enactment of the sacrificial lamb that ancient Israel understood to be their atonement for sin. This is why the symbol is so powerful; it recalls the force and power of Jesus' death. Every time a believer partakes of the bread and wine, he or she is re-covenanting his or her life with Jesus, but it's not merely an individual experience, it is also corporate; it's richer, because everyone experiences it together.

There's something of a sense of belonging between kindred minds and spirits, when the soul is revived and enabled, when sins are forgiven and a newness of life is shared. A new and formidable community is unleashed and this community is unstoppable. The strength is in the newness, and also in the bond of unity.

in an open space

Today's postmoderns understand the human need for private space where rituals can be experienced for personal benefit, yet we are increasingly suspicious of secret spaces. Holy Communion isn't practised in secret for a privileged few; it is an open communion; there are no walls of partition; it is done in an open space.

So is this a service in which the public may participate? When someone believes in the atoning power of Jesus' blood, he or she may come into this open space and partake of the emblems. Then his or her participation is one of joining and enlarging the body of Christ.

In this open space there is no gender, sexuality, age, ethnicity, spirituality, disability, class or education boundaries to separate us from each other. There is solidarity at the table and our challenge is to make this open space available to one and all.

In summary, Holy Communion with its prelude of foot washing creates an open space in which today's believer may engage humbly and forge solidarity within the community of Christ as each one of us recommits our lives to God in response to Jesus' sacrifice.

re: consider

What would change in your life if you experienced a ritual of forgiveness and reconciliation with those in your circle on a regular basis?

REFERENCES
740. Luke 22:19, NIV.
741. 1 Corinthians 11:21-26.
742. Exodus 14.
743. John 14:1-3, NIV.
744. I Corinthians 11:26.
745. John 13:9.
746. I Corinthians 11:27.
747. Matthew 26:28.

ABOUT
COMMUNITY

40. KNOWING MY NEIGHBOUR

God, I want to have your eyes and your heart when I see those around me. So often I rush through my day, forgetting that I am surrounded by people who need my encouragement and support. Help me to recognise them, and thank you for making me aware of the care and concern you have for every single person.

re: tell

Two men were travelling together, when a bear suddenly met them on their path. One of them climbed up quickly into a tree and concealed himself in the branches. The other, seeing that he must be attacked, fell flat on the ground, and when the bear came up and felt him with his snout and smelt him all over, he held his breath and feigned the appearance of death as much as he could.

The bear soon left him, for it is said he will not touch a dead body. When he was quite gone, the other traveller descended from the tree and jocularly inquired of his friend what it was the bear had whispered in his ear.

'He gave me this advice,' his companion replied. 'Never travel with a friend who deserts you at the approach of danger.'

re: think

People were amazed at how the community of Christ's followers grew after his death. When faced with this new social phenomenon – Christianity – many felt a sense of deep wonder and reverence, as they were witnessing something supernatural.[748] It was obvious to them that here was something which transcended all existing human experience, something that went beyond the laws of human logic and the natural flow of things.[749]

Individuals from all different ethnic, religious and social castes were suddenly united together in one cause, one love, one divine relationship. There were two reasons for the uniqueness of this community.

First, this movement revolved around the conviction that it *was created and sustained by a divine initiative*.[750] The notion of God being present and active within the human social body was a scandalous idea to the Greco-Roman culture. Their view of the universe didn't allow any contact between the perfect divine world of ideas and humanity's imperfect material reality.

According to the Greco-Romans, the divine force lived isolated in the eternal realm and simply could not enter or approach the corrupted and sinful life of humans. But this emerging community of Christ-followers openly proclaimed and demonstrated the fact that divinity could live among its members and actively engage in the affairs of their everyday life.[751] This phenomenon toppled the contemporary social and religious paradigms and was regarded in history as scandalous.[752]

Second, the emerging community was divergent from any other social model because of the *distinct way in which its members related to each other*.[753] Saint Ignatius of Antioch, for instance, describes the reaction of pagans when they came in contact with the first Christian community. The people remarked, 'See how they love each other!' Amazed by the vibrant quality of the relationships within the early Christian community, which were characterised by genuine mutual love and care, many wanted to be part of this rich and authentic experience.[754]

This Christian community seemed to have captured a better vision – a higher ideal – of what it means to be fully human. The community valued the individual, *not according to what one had, but according to what one was* – a unique, unrepeatable being created by God himself, and thus an irreplaceable member of his cosmic family.[755]

This community did not define its members in terms of their social status, ethnic roots, material possessions, personal achievements, gender or racial differences. The type of love reflected in their mutual relationships went beyond the barriers of prejudice, misconceptions and stereotypes, which cause many to label others as inferior and less important. Human beings were instead defined by their existence and uniqueness.[756]

Though imperfect, this emerging community of believers represented a powerful reminder of the high ideals that were an integral part of God's dream for humanity when he first moulded Adam from the clay of the new-formed earth.[757] It also served as the foretaste or the anticipation of the future mutual personal indwelling of God the Father, Son and Holy Spirit within their disciples.[758] It was clear that this wasn't merely a social club of like-minded people joined by their common goals, values and interests. Neither did it resemble typical business or political organisations.

The quality of mutual interaction in the Christian community attracted those who longed for something more than human manipulations, conspiracies or unrealistic and artificial utopian social constructs. It attracted those who strove for deeper, truer and more authentic relationships where[759] they could find their ultimate fulfilment and happiness.

> The ultimate goal of the community was to follow Christ's example of loving our neighbour as ourselves.

The ultimate goal of the community was to follow Christ's example of loving our neighbour as ourselves. Really, he was just following the ideal which had been stated simply and purely in the Old Testament writings. Jesus' goal for unity between divinity and humanity was an ancient one, simply embodied in human flesh for thirty-three years in order to be firmly established.

Jesus affirmed that 'to love God' means to 'love your neighbour'. And the word *neighbour* encompasses all human beings, despite their differences and imperfections. But you ask, 'Who is my neighbour?' That question was famously posed by a lawyer who had backed himself into a corner by attempting to test Jesus, the self-appointed upstart rabbi from Galilee.[760] Their conversation started with the religious question: 'Rabbi, what must I do to inherit eternal life?' Jesus responded with another question: 'What is the law? What is written?' He knew that the lawyer knew exactly what to say, and on cue he replied: 'You shall love the Lord your God with all your heart, and with all your soul, and with all your strength, and with all your mind. And you shall love your neighbour as yourself.'

Jesus responds, in essence, 'So what is the problem? What do you not understand? Do this and you will live.' Now the lawyer is embarrassed, but rather than admit it he presses on. He asks (seeking to justify himself, as the text shrewdly comments), 'And just who is my neighbour?'

If the original question can be called the *religious question*, then perhaps this is the *ethical question*. But if the real motive is to justify himself, we could conclude that he is not looking for enlightenment so much as for a way to catch the teacher in a contradiction. Yet this time his question elicits a profound, albeit indirect, response from Jesus. His response takes the form of a parable, one that many of us have heard at one time or another and come to know as the Parable of the Good Samaritan.[761]

Notice that the lawyer is asking an adversarial question. 'Rabbi, just who is my neighbour so that I will always know that I am in strict adherence with the law?' His question is about definitions and, once again, it focuses not on what he is to *be*, but upon what he is to *do*: 'Who qualifies as "neighbour" according to the Torah? How do I limit the field to fit this definition? Who is in? Who is out? Whom can I exclude and still satisfy the letter of the law and my own conscience?' While Jesus' answer is focusing on the *neighbour*, the lawyer puts the emphasis on the definition of *who*.

I suspect that Jesus was fully aware that the second part of the commandment – the part that says, 'You shall love your neighbour as yourself' – is really not that difficult to grasp. However, Jesus takes some pains to respond, not because he believes this lawyer is asking a profound question, but because he recognises there is something profound just beneath the surface of it.

I think, if Jesus were asked the same question in today's culture, his answering story would have been framed to apply to our culture. If he were speaking to a Christian lawyer, this story might have been about the 'Good Muslim' or maybe the 'Good Prostitute'. If he were speaking to a secular lawyer, his story might have been about the 'Good Christian', the 'Good Farmer' or the 'Good Homeless Guy'.

George Aiken once said: 'If we were to wake up some morning and find that everyone was the same race, creed and colour, we would find some other cause for prejudice by noon.' For every category of person, there are others whom they generally despise, and Jesus wanted to show that social boundaries are not only unimportant but destructive. His point in telling the story of the Good Samaritan? To help this self-righteous Jewish lawyer realise that even those who are the outcasts of society – as the Samaritans were – can recognise a person in need and help even those who hate them.

When humans are freed from social convention, we can show great compassion, if given the opportunity. In the spring of 2009, a homeless man in Winnipeg, Manitoba, Canada, was honoured by the city's mayor for his bravery in jumping into the frigid Red River to save a drowning teenager. As hard times had overtaken Faron Hall, he had gone from teaching to can-collecting and called a park bench his home. But, when he saw another person in need, he knew he could help and he did, saving the boy's life. Mr Hall would probably have been ignored or even spurned by the average passer-by – maybe even by the very boy he rescued – but he knew what it meant to value another person, regardless of social convention.

Jesus is aware of the tendency of human nature to adhere selfishly to social customs and rules. He knows our tendency to hide behind numerous excuses and even religious knowledge, rather than make an effort to fulfil our duty to fellow human beings in need. The answer to the inquiry, 'Who is my neighbour?' is easy to grasp, but our natural self-centredness complicates things. It's easier to waste time and energy debating the obvious, while classifying each other in terms of our social status, ethnic roots, material possessions, personal achievements, gender or racial differences, instead of concentrating on simply loving our neighbours.

The type of love for our neighbour which Jesus had in mind goes beyond the barriers of prejudice, misconceptions and stereotypes. It goes beyond the reasons we label each other inferior or less important. By his own example, Christ showed that, for the purpose of achieving his dream of restoring cosmic unity,[762] he didn't hesitate to make *any* necessary effort to reach every individual who came into his life, even those people who were marginalised by their society. He mingled with prostitutes, sinners, lepers and even his own enemies. He broke traditional conventions and prejudices. He had nothing to do with the labels which bigotry placed on people.

To love God means to love your neighbour. And the word *neighbour* encompasses all human beings, no matter their differences or imperfections. There is no restriction! No exclusivity! Everybody is equally valuable in God's eyes and thus called to belong to his universal family.

Relationships in our world today are just as broken and distorted as they were when Jesus lived here on this planet. From the smallest, most intimate of relations – the family – to the largest relations of states and countries, we humans have a terrible capacity to shatter community through prejudice and injustice towards each other.

Isn't the idea of an authentic, all-inclusive and all-loving family of God both attractive and scandalous, even to the present world? Yet it is what we all long for. We long for community, connection and a sense of belonging to something bigger than ourselves.

Who wouldn't like to participate in such a fascinating and rich communal experience which gives an individual the ultimate sense of belonging and purpose?

re: consider

How is God calling you to love the humanity around you – your neighbours – in a way that may be new or unconventional to you?

REFERENCES

748. Acts 2:43, NIV.
749. The same intense *aphobos* reaction of fear and wonder was evoked when God acted miraculously in history and revealed his power and sovereignty by opening the sea, calming the storm, or controlling other natural elements.
750. 1 Corinthians 1:9, NIV.
751. 1 John 1:1-4, NIV.
752. Seeing that this new social phenomenon was initiated by the divine agency (Father, Son, and Holy Spirit) and that it contained the unseen spiritual dimension, it is evident that no single human word, concept, image, analogy, metaphor or other linguistic construct could successfully capture the totality and essence of this reality. Its nature simply transcended human capacities and intellectual categories. The New Testament writers still attempted to do the impossible task and their effort resulted in creating over 95 different profound metaphors and analogies with the intent of describing the various aspects of this complex divine-human communion. For a useful systematic overview of the various images used by the New Testament writers to describe the nature of church, see Minear, Paul S. *Images of the Church in the New Testament.* Westminster P, 1960.
753. John 15:12, NIV.
754. Acts 2:47, NIV.
755. John 1:12, NIV.
756. Finger, Reta Halteman. *Of Widows and Meals: Communal Meals in the Book of Acts.* Wm. B. Eerdmans Company, 2007.
757. Genesis 1:26, 27, NIV.
758. Revelation 21:3, NIV.
759. 1 John 1:4, NIV.
760. See Luke 10:25-37 for the full story.
761. David Robb provides an insightful discussion about the dialogue between Christ and lawyer. See: *www.allsoulsnyc.org/publications/sermons/drsermons/who-is-my-neighbor.html.*
762. The centrality of communion for human existence and its indispensability is clearly reinforced by Christ's intercessory prayer (John 17) towards the end of his earthly life. In this long and rich discourse in which Jesus asks his Father to make the disciples 'one' as they are one (John 17:11, 21, 22, NIV), his grand vision of the 'relational mode' of human existence (which was once the reality in the unfallen world) is clearly revealed. It is precisely that 'one-ness' which became the ultimate purpose of all divine efforts throughout history to save humanity.

41. HAPPY HOME

God, just as the trinity interacts as Father, Son and Holy Spirit, we also were created to reflect this part of your character. Teach me what it means to connect in a real, meaningful relationship with others.

re: tell

Two school friends waited together one morning for the school bus, book bags slung carelessly over their shoulders. Magda turned to Julia to ask, 'You're coming to the party tonight, right? It's going to be great!'

Julia looked annoyed, 'No, my parents heard about it – don't ask me where! Someone told them that the whole school is coming, and they heard about the beer. Mum says beer and boys don't mix.' She rolled her eyes at her mother's rule.

'My parents aren't nearly so strict. But then, they never have a clue what I'm doing either. Why do yours have all these rules?'

Julia stopped to think about it for a minute. 'I really don't know. Sometimes I hate it but, then, I know it keeps me out of trouble, and I do really love them. I guess it's just because they love me and they want me to be safe.' She looked down, pondering the insight of her own revelation.

They both stood in silence for few moments and then, wistfully, 'I wish mine loved me like that.' The words were almost whispered, and Julia almost missed them. The bus pulled up, belching exhaust and crunching on the pavement. Julia watched Magda clamber on to the bus and wondered why she'd never realised how lucky she was to have parents who cared.[763]

re: think

Have you ever been *really* alone? Did you ever get lost as a child and think you'd never find your parents again? Have you been in a strange place where you knew no one, or at a party with all your friends but you still felt alone? Have you been somewhere beautiful and wanted to share your sense of wonder, but there was no one to talk to and afterwards, no matter how hard you tried to describe it, words just seemed inadequate?

God knew that it was not good for us to be alone. Before anything in the world had gone wrong – even in a place that was perfect – humans needed each other. So God let Adam sleep and then he sculpted a woman from the man's bone and flesh, so that he wouldn't have to be alone.[764]

We were created from the same source and yet in some ways we spend our lives trying to work out how to achieve the oneness God originally planned for us. The same kind of oneness that the Father, Jesus and the Holy Spirit experience together.[765]

God invented marriage. One man and one woman, together, growing closer and closer over time. God said that a man and a woman need to leave their families of origin behind them and make a new life together and become 'one',[766] growing into a family of their own.[767]

God's ideal plan was for one man to marry one woman and for their children to grow up in a happy and loving family. For thousands of years people lived this way, interacting together closely in communities, where everyone was part of an extended and supportive family.

Raising children in a complete family is still the best plan. In the United Kingdom, the Family Matters Institute[768] estimates that family breakdown costs the UK Government £15 billion a year in benefits and services. That's about £11 a week for every taxpayer. And that doesn't include the cost to families paying for divorces, separate homes or child support. Besides that, there is an immeasurable emotional cost, including depression, increased illness, academic difficulties, increased risk of drug involvement and anti-social behaviour. The ideal is for children to have strong role models as they grow up.

When we live with other people, we have to consider their needs as well as ours. We learn to live with our individual differences and see them as assets, rather than problems. We have to work through conflicts and support each other through the painful and challenging aspects of our lives.

Living together in a family unit can help us grow and develop personally, enabling us to become better people. God gave us marriage and family and community because he wants the best for us. He wants us to experience what it means to live a life of love with him and with each other.[769]

'But,' you say, 'I want to have fun! I want to do my own thing. Life would be simpler if I didn't have to think about the needs of other people. This stuff isn't easy. I'd rather walk away from a relationship than have to experience pain or learn to forgive.'

Scott Haltzmann,[770] a psychiatrist and counsellor, wanted to discover the secret of happy relationships. He began a website, *www.secretsofmarriedmen.com,* and invited men and women to respond to his questions about what makes happy relationships. The collected wisdom formed the basis of his book *The Secrets of Happily Married Men.*

His secret to happy relationships was the ability to put the other person first, to listen to his or her experiences and ideas, to be there for him or her, to discover the things that made the other person happy, and then to do them. Not rocket science, but definitely some upside-down wisdom in today's 'me-first' culture. Prioritising our own desires isn't the pathway to happiness that we imagine, and our selfishness hurts and neglects those we claim to love.

> Living together in a family unit can help us grow and develop personally, enabling us to become better people.

Jesus knew this when he summed up the golden rules for life: 'Love the Lord your God with all your heart and with all your soul and with all your mind. And the second is like it: Love your neighbour as yourself.'[771]

What does 'love' mean to you?

'I love chocolate!'

'I love your jeans!'

But what does it mean to love another human being? What does it mean to *be* loved? If you knew someone loved you, what would that person do or say to express it?

The famous love chapter in the Bible[772] describes love, not as a feeling, but as the actions and choices we make in our everyday encounters. Love is patient, kind, polite and respectful, unselfish, forgiving, believes the best about others and is protective, loyal, persevering, hopeful and never-ending. That sounds almost impossible! How can anyone love like that all the time?

One secret to loving others? Be continually topped up with love yourself. Jesus knew this when he told us to love God before loving each other.[773] When we're passionate about God and aware of his generous and forgiving love, we're in a better position to love others.[774] Interestingly, the more we give love to others, the more it's returned to us.[775] But when we aren't receiving love from others, God's love is still there all the time, whenever we need it.[776]

God works with us to make a difference in our relationships.[777] We can look at our spouses through God's eyes and wonder how he would like us to show them what his love is all about. God helps us accept our children when they make mistakes rather than criticising them;[778] we can support friends struggling with challenges[779] and offer comfort when we see someone who is sad.[780]

Just as a house is built brick by brick, so a home, a marriage, a parent/child relationship, a friendship and a community grow through individual loving actions. Don't know where to start? Try doing one thing each day to show your love, whether you feel like it or not.

Life is messy. Relationships are complicated. But that's not the final word on getting along.

There's a story in the Bible[781] about a perfect wedding; perfect, that is, until they ran out of wine at the reception. The family was embarrassed, the wedding was going to be ruined, and nobody would forget the day the refreshments ran short! Jesus was a guest in the crowd; he overheard the panic and decided to help. He asked the waiters to fill some barrels with water, then dip in their jugs and serve it to the guests. The *water* came out as the best wine they'd ever tasted – Jesus had transformed plain water into something spectacular!

God still does amazing things for families. He takes the plain water that we give him – our relationships tainted with conflict, infidelity, painful memories and distorted priorities – and he transforms us. Just as the waiters, acting in faith, filled the water pots and then poured the jugs, sometimes we need to live our relationships as though the miracle of love had already occurred.

Think about the people who matter to you. Every relationship has room for growth, and every relationship can benefit from being transformed through God's love. You can give them all to God and be part of the action as he transforms you and your relationships through his love, one day at a time.

re: consider

How does God's advice for happy marriages and families differ from your past experience? What changes can you make in your daily life to develop stronger relationships?

REFERENCES

763. Story by Sarah K. Asaftei.
764. Genesis 2:21-24.
765. John 17:22-23.
766. Genesis 2:24.
767. Genesis 1:28.
768. 'The Cost of Family Breakdown'. Report available from: The Family Matters Institute, The Park, Moggerhanger, Bedford MK4 3RW. *www.familymatters.org.uk.*
769. 1 John 4:11, 12.
770. Haltzmann, Scott. *The Secrets of Happily Married Men.* Jossey-Bass, 2006.
771. Matthew 22:37-39, NIV.
772. 1 Corinthians 13:4-8.
773. Matthew 22:37.
774. Psalm 103:3-13.
775. Proverbs 11:25.
776. 1 John 4:7, 11, 12, 16, 19.
777. 1 John 4:12.
778. Romans 15:7.
779. Galatians 6:2.
780. 2 Corinthians 1:3, 4.
781. John 2:1-11.

42. GETTING OUT THERE

God, once more, I have a feeling that you're going to stretch me to the limit and take me outside my comfort zone, but I know you well enough now to understand that you always give me everything that I need in order to do what you ask of me. Please be here as I read and show me how I can help my neighbour.

re: tell

A little boy came home from school one day to discover his pet goldfish lying stiff and motionless on the surface of the fishbowl. He was devastated and began to cry. His father consoled him, saying, 'It's so sad when a pet dies, but here's what we'll do. We'll put the dead little fish in a matchbox, take it to the garden and invite your friends to join us for a funeral. Then afterwards I will take you and your friends and buy you all an ice cream.'

That cheered the little boy up. Then suddenly he noticed that the goldfish wasn't really dead, but had revived and was swimming merrily around the bowl. He gave a whoop of joy and clapped his hands with glee that his pet was alive.

A few minutes later, however, he remembered his father's promise of an ice cream. Now that the fish wasn't dead, the ice cream wasn't going to happen! He had mixed emotions – glad that his fish was alive, but sad that he would miss the treat. Finally one emotion dominated, and turning to his father he said, 'Let's kill it!'[782]

re: think

Isn't that the basic nature of human beings in society today? To some degree we're all smeared with self-centredness. Our constant reaction is, 'How will this affect *me*?' Our general thinking has shifted from being communal to taking care of self.

Community is the foundation of society. It is within the community that the ingredients for a cohesive and integrated society are put together. The desire to ensure people are accepted and feel a part of their community is a significant and important role.

How should Christians interact with the local community? Does being a Christian bring a greater level of responsibility as a result of our practical teachings? Shouldn't Christians lead out in building community cohesiveness? Isn't one of our basic principles to 'Love your neighbour as yourself?'[783]

Many charity organisations were originally founded on Christian philosophy: the Salvation Army, the Samaritans, the Red Cross. But just as many claim to be secular. Should the Christian's role be any different from an unbeliever's? Apart from the command to 'love our neighbour', what biblical mission inspires Christians in a greater way than a nonbeliever?

The Bible calls us to make a positive difference in the lives of others. The Ten Commandments imply that we are each responsible for the well-being of others, by avoiding situations that damage human relationships – like telling lies, stealing, cheating or killing other people. However, you could argue that these commands are considered morally important by everyone, regardless of faith. So is there anything else, biblically, that speaks to the Christian?

What about the life of Jesus? What examples did he show regarding a community-focused practical mission?

'The Spirit of the Lord is on me, because he has anointed me to preach good news to the poor. He has sent me to proclaim freedom for the prisoners and recovery of sight for the blind, to release the oppressed, . . .' (Luke 4:18-19, NIV).

Although originally penned by the prophet Isaiah, Jesus understood this passage to be a fulfilment of his personal mission.

We see this initially through his interaction with people. Jesus engaged with people from all social spectrums. Called 'Rabbi' or 'Teacher', he never refused to mingle with the outcasts, the disenfranchised and the unpopular. He spent time with women (a cultural taboo in his time), the sick, prostitutes, drunkards and people outside his ethnicity.

He brought hope through words of assurance and forgiveness. He sought to meet their basic human needs and then led them to spiritual lessons of restoration. Jesus spoke out against social injustice and challenged the hypocritical lifestyle of civic and religious leaders. Children loved him, and he affirmed their value and importance. He welcomed people outside the Jewish faith and foreigners from other cultures – all were equally embraced by his mission of community involvement.

'He went around doing good.'[784] He fed the hungry, cheered the sad, healed the sick and hurting. Jesus not only displayed acts of practical involvement, he sought to teach others to do the same.

> Jesus spoke out against social injustice and challenged the hypocritical lifestyle of civic and religious leaders.

Jesus also challenged his followers to become the 'salt of the earth.'[785] He was talking about being the kind of Christians who strive to make a positive difference in the community where they live.

Pete Storz writes in his article *Liberal Arts Christians*:

'Christians (individually and corporately) need to have a critical understanding of the ideas and attitudes of their society's culture and have the knowledge base to give intelligent Christian responses to its issues and challenges. Christians need to be willing, as well as prepared, to take on social issues and philosophical challenges in addition to (actually part of) their normal lives (families, churches, careers, hobbies).'[786]

Christian faith challenges us to use our social gifts for a greater purpose. Isolating ourselves from our community denies the very essence of our faith, but Christian disciples naturally respond to the need of others by giving of themselves. This is a message of influence and self-sacrifice, of doing to others what you would have others do to you. Ultimately, it is a message of love. Love in action.

And what about the non-Christians who subscribe to similar teachings and who genuinely express impartial love? Those who are wonderful people but choose not to be associated with the Christian faith? The distinguishing factor between Christian service to others and that of unbelievers is the internal motivation.

The Christian's motivation for his or her responsibility in society springs from intrinsic spiritual conviction, propelled by an understanding of God's desire in his or her life.

Just as Jesus' mission was to do 'the will of my father',[787] so a follower of Christ desires to live a life that matches up to the mission of God. This Christian life is borne out of a love for God that expresses itself naturally to others.[788]

This means that self-exaltation should not be present in the Christian's role in society. To be of godly service is ultimately to redirect any accolade or praise or honour back to the motivating influence – God.

'Do nothing out of selfish ambition or vain conceit, but in humility consider others better than yourselves. Each of you should look not only to your own interests, but also to the interests of others.'[789]

As disciples of Jesus, we ultimately desire to exhibit his character in our lives. Our primary aim becomes the reflection of his nature. Jesus did the same for his father, saying, 'Anyone who has seen me has seen the Father.'[790]

Jesus asks us to share his life with others, as we live out our daily routine. 'In the same way, let your light shine before men, that they may see your good deeds and praise your Father in heaven.'[791]

This is the significant difference between believers and unbelievers. This desire to reflect Jesus ought to be the greatest motivating force reminding us of our responsibility within society.

Early one chilly winter morning in London during the Second World War a soldier was making his way to his barracks when he spotted a boy with his nose pressed against the window of a baker's shop.

Inside, the baker was kneading dough for a fresh supply of dough-nuts, and the hungry boy stared in silence watching every move. The soldier walked over to the shop and stood by the little boy's side. Through the steamed up window they could see the mouth-watering items being pulled from the oven and they watched as the baker put them in a glass-enclosed counter.

The soldier's heart went out to the little boy. He said, 'Son, would you like some of those doughnuts?' The startled boy said, 'Yes, I would.'

The soldier stepped inside and bought a few of the doughnuts and walked back to the lad. He smiled as he held out the bag and simply said, 'They're yours.'

The soldier hadn't gone far when he felt a tug at his coat. He looked down and heard the child ask quietly, 'Mister, are you Jesus?'

We are never more like Jesus than when we offer ourselves in serv-ice to others.

re: consider

How do your motives affect your acts of service? Is there any difference since you started studying the Scriptures?

REFERENCES
782. Story provided by author.
783. Mark 12:31, NIV.
784. Acts 10:38, NIV.
785. Matthew 5:13, NIV.
786. *http://home.earthlink.net/~bkwormtoo/id20.html*
787. Matthew 7:21, NIV.
788. John 13:34.
789. Philippians 2:3-4, NIV.
790. John 14:9, NIV.
791. Matthew 5:16, NIV.